Early Praise for *Network Programming in Elixir and Erlang*

Andrea does a great job of covering network programming techniques that I have been longing to learn more about in Elixir. The book is well-organized, engaging, and provides real-world examples that progressively build upon each other.

➤ **Carlos Souza**
Idopter Labs Cofounder

I didn't think I would enjoy a book on network programming this much. While I knew some of the content, it was good to get a refresher, and I learned a lot. Walking through Andrea's examples on connection pooling left me confident that I could implement my own solution faster than if I had tried to learn it any other way.

➤ **Jeffrey Matthias**
Co-author of *Testing Elixir*, Mechanical Orchard

Finally, a deep dive into both high-level and low-level abstractions, leveraging libraries in both the Elixir and Erlang ecosystems! As a passionate young Elixir developer, I found myself truly enjoying the journey through the OSI model, all seen through the lens of the languages I hold dear. This book beautifully bridges the gap between foundational networking concepts and practical implementation, leaving me with that satisfying "aha!" moment by the end.

➤ **Savannah Manning**
Software Engineer, Adobe (Frame.io)

Elixir/Erlang is the killer platform for building networked systems, and this is the killer book for learning the fundamentals of how to build them on the BEAM. After reading it, you will find it much easier to look under the hood and debug libraries such as Finch, Bandit, Postgrex, and many more. Also, who knew writing a simple DNS server from scratch and hitting it with dig could be this much fun?!

➤ **Wojtek Mach**
  Developer, Dashbit

Network Programming in Elixir and Erlang

Write High-Performance, Scalable, and Reliable Apps with TCP and UDP

Andrea Leopardi

The Pragmatic Bookshelf

Dallas, Texas

See our complete catalog of hands-on, practical,
and Pragmatic content for software developers:
https://pragprog.com

Sales, volume licensing, and support:
support@pragprog.com

Derivative works, AI training and testing,
international translations, and other rights:
rights@pragprog.com

The team that produced this book includes:

Publisher:	Dave Thomas
COO:	Janet Furlow
Executive Editor:	Susannah Davidson
Series Editor:	Sophie DeBenedetto
Development Editor:	Jacquelyn Carter
Copy Editor:	Sean Tommasi
Indexing:	Potomac Indexing, LLC
Layout:	Gilson Graphics

ISBN-13: 979-8-88865-105-6
Book version: P1.0—August 2025

Contents

Acknowledgments ix

Introduction xi

1. **What Is Network Programming Anyway?** 1
   Elixir and Erlang: The Perfect Fit   2
   Which One, Though: Elixir or Erlang?   4
   Where Do We Go Next?   5

Part I — TCP

2. **TCP: Exploring the Basics** 9
   TCP 101   9
   Building a TCP Echo Server   15
   Testing with TCP   25
   Becoming Socket Pros with Modes and Packet Parsing   28
   Wrapping Up   31

3. **Designing a Chat Protocol and Its TCP Server** 33
   Designing a Simple Chat Protocol   34
   Writing Code for the Chat Protocol   39
   Moving to the Server Side   46
   Chatting with Clients   55
   Wrapping Up   58

4. **Scaling TCP on the Server Side** 59
   Increasing Scalability with Multiple Acceptors   59
   Rewriting the Server with Thousand Island   66
   Wrapping Up   70

5. **Building TCP Clients** 73
   The Redis Protocol   74
   Building Our First Client   78
   Queuing Requests   85
   Wrapping Up   91

6. **Scaling and Optimizing TCP Clients** 93
   Pooling TCP Client Sockets   93
   Building State-Machine-Like TCP Clients   100
   Pooling Connections Through Registry   107
   Wrapping Up   110

7. **Securing Protocols: TLS** 113
   Understanding How TLS Works   114
   The ssl Application   116
   Securing Our Chat System   118
   Wrapping Up   123

Part II — UDP

8. **Same Layer, Different Protocol: Introducing UDP** . . . 127
   The Basics of the Protocol   128
   Building a Metrics Ingestion Daemon   132
   Wrapping Up   143

9. **Adding Guarantees to UDP** 145
   Ordering, Splitting, and Dropping Packets   145
   Adding Guarantees   149
   Wrapping Up   153

10. **UDP in the Wild: DNS** **155**
    Understanding How DNS Works 156
    Writing a Simple DNS Client 162
    inet_res 166
    Writing a DNS Server Is So Easy 168
    Wrapping Up 171

Part III — HTTP

11. **Talking the Internet Protocol: HTTP/1.1** **175**
    HTTP/1.1 Protocol Basics 176
    Serving JSON with Plug and Bandit 181
    Connecting to Servers with Mint 189
    Higher-Level Client Libraries: Finch and Req 194
    Wrapping Up 196

12. **HTTP/2 and the Future** **197**
    HTTP/2: Why It Was Needed and What Changed 198
    Using HTTP/2 with Plug and Mint 202
    Evolving in Parallel with QUIC and HTTP/3 202
    Wrapping Up 206

13. **Communicating in Real Time with WebSockets** **207**
    The WebSocket Protocol 207
    Making a Silly Real-Time Game 211
    Wrapping Up 219

Part IV — Appendixes

A1. **The OSI Model** **223**
A2. **TCP Protocol Details** **225**
    TCP Binary Format 225
    Connection States 226

A3. **UDP Broadcast and Multicast** **229**
    Broadcast 229
    Multicast 229

A4. **DNS Protocol Details** 231
        DNS Message Header   231
        DNS Message Body   233

A5. **Controlling Other Machines with SSH** 235
        Using SSH as Clients   236
        SSH Server   237

        Bibliography 239
        Index 241

Acknowledgments

My deepest gratitude to all reviewers who spent precious time helping me and reading rough copies of this book. Thank you to Jeffrey Matthias, Savannah Manning, Wojtek Mach, Jean Klingler, Carlos Souza, Simone Carletti, Mitchell Hanberg, Stefan Turalski, and Samuel Mullen.

This is the second chance I get to work with this book's development editor, Jackie Carter. Double thank you for your patience and expertise.

Thank you to Sophie DeBenedetto and Bruce Tate, who—knowingly or unknowingly—made this book happen.

A unique shout-out goes to Protohackers.[1] Solving its fun challenges is ultimately what led me to write this book. Also, thank you to all the people involved in all the software, tools, and libraries used in this book.

Thank you Gianluigi, Lia, and Alice for building and giving me a home to go to and write half of this stuff—and for being my other family, which is kind of nice too I guess.

Thank you to the light of my life—my wife, Kristina. This is the second time you've had to put up with me writing a book. I'm getting the hang of it, sunshine. This time we had help though: thank you, Asia (our firstborn dog).

---

1.   https://protohackers.com/

Introduction

Elixir and Erlang, and their shared ecosystems, are a fantastic choice for writing network code. After all, Erlang was invented to solve a specific network problem: routing and handling telephone calls. Even though networks have evolved since then, the underlying problems have remained the same. Real-time web applications have a lot in common with telephone calls—you have clients in different places that should ideally stay connected with each other and exchange data efficiently and reliably.

Erlang's standard library includes all the fundamental tools you need to work with network protocols and to build network applications. You'll learn about ecosystem libraries as well as the design patterns and best practices to use when writing this kind of software on the BEAM. Elixir's and Erlang's ecosystems also have plenty of third-party libraries that abstract away the most common network patterns and use cases (such as HTTP servers and clients).

I've been working in Elixir for more than ten years, mostly as part of its core team. I've never seen a platform this good at working with networks. Part of it, no doubt, is its telecoms heritage. But another part of it *has* to be the concurrency primitives and process-oriented design of the BEAM. With Elixir and Erlang, you're forced to think about the same problems you deal with when working with systems distributed across networks. You send data asynchronously to other processes, implement acknowledgments, and monitor other processes to detect failures. If all this sounds like networks, it's because it is: it involves exchanging data across nodes, request/response cycles, handling disconnections, and so on.

Hopefully, your journey through this book will make these similarities so obvious that you'll never stop seeing them. Let me tell a quick story about the origins of this project. I was learning another language at the time and tried to expand my knowledge of it by working on some networking challenges just for fun. None of the language (and ecosystem) abstractions matched networks as well as the BEAM did. This made me appreciate Elixir and Erlang like never before. I want to share this feeling with as many folks as possible.

Is This Book for You?

This book is mainly aimed at developers with Elixir and Erlang experience but without much experience in networks. It assumes a basic understanding of the syntax of these languages as well as of core concepts such as functions, processes, and message passing. You'll also need some understanding of OTP and its abstractions—such as GenServers and supervisors. But the book doesn't assume any network knowledge. Instead, it'll walk you through the basic principles of networks and network protocols from the ground up.

This book might also be a good fit for you if you are knowledgeable in networks but have no experience with Elixir or Erlang. You'll get a fantastic tool under your belt for working with networks. You might have to read up on Elixir- and Erlang-specific concepts here and there, but the book will show you how well these languages fit this domain.

About This Book

This book is split up into three parts, each focusing on one of three important network protocols: TCP, UDP, and HTTP.

Let's take a more detailed look at the plan.

We start with an introduction to networks in Chapter 1, What Is Network Programming Anyway?, on page 1. Learning how to use the tools that Elixir and Erlang provide requires some understanding of how networks work and the details of the protocols involved.

Part I: TCP

The first part of the book is dedicated to TCP, the most widely used network protocol. Chapter 2, TCP: Exploring the Basics, on page 9, introduces the protocol itself. The following two chapters, Chapter 3, Designing a Chat Protocol and Its TCP Server, on page 33, and Chapter 4, Scaling TCP on the Server Side, on page 59, focus on the server-side aspect of working with TCP. Then, Chapter 5, Building TCP Clients, on page 73, and Chapter 6, Scaling and Optimizing TCP Clients, on page 93, switch to the client side. The last chapter in this part, Chapter 7, Securing Protocols: TLS, on page 113, is about securing network traffic over TCP by using TLS.

Part II: UDP

In this second part, we explore UDP, a protocol that is quite different from TCP but in widespread use nonetheless. You'll start by learning the protocol basics in Chapter 8, Same Layer, Different Protocol:, on page 127. Then, you'll learn about techniques to increase the reliability of UDP with fine-grained control (Chapter 9, Adding Guarantees to UDP, on page 145). The last chapter in this part, Chapter 10, UDP in the Wild: DNS, on page 155, is about DNS, the "Internet phone book" and a protocol mostly used on top of UDP.

Part III: HTTP

In the last part of the book, we focus on HTTP, which is a protocol you'll most likely use directly at some point in your career (if not for most of it). In the first chapter, Chapter 11, Talking the Internet Protocol: HTTP/1.1, on page 175, we explore HTTP/1.1 to build a foundational understanding of HTTP. Then, we explore HTTP/2—and even some HTTP/3!—in Chapter 12, HTTP/2 and the Future, on page 197. Finally, we look at a protocol built on top of HTTP that powers many real-time interactions on the web: WebSockets (Chapter 13, Communicating in Real Time with WebSockets, on page 207).

About the Code

The code in this book is mostly structured so that you can follow along and type it out yourself if that's your thing. But we'll sometimes just refer you to code that you can find in the online resources to avoid interrupting the flow too much.

All the example code is in Elixir, even though the book mentions Erlang in its title. We talk more about this in Which One, Though: Elixir or Erlang?, on page 4. The concepts discussed in this book are not specific to either language, and the two languages share so much of their DNA that we believe a "translation guide" is enough for everyone to enjoy the content.

Online Resources

The apps and example code in this book can be found at the Pragmatic Programmers website for this book.[1] You'll also find the errata submission form, where you can report problems with the text or make suggestions for future versions.

When you're ready, turn the page and we'll get started.

---

1. https://pragprog.com/titles/alnpee/

## CHAPTER 1

What Is Network Programming Anyway?

Nowadays, networks are a fundamental component of computer systems, software engineering, and society at large. Many types of applications and use cases require some sort of network connectivity: from enormous search engines to smart appliances, from real-time connected social networks to tiny embedded devices. But most folks in the industry these days don't normally have to work on the lower levels of the network stack. It's somewhat rare to have to work with protocols such as TCP or UDP, because a lot of the underlying complexity is hidden from view by abstractions, libraries, and frameworks.

Even so, knowing how to "go down" and work with networks and network protocols is a skill that will improve the tool set of every engineer out there. More often than not, working with these things is not that hard, and Elixir and Erlang only make it easier and more natural.

But what *is* network programming? It's hard to give a formal definition that most folks would agree with, since it's such a wide area of programming and of computer systems in general. Informally, network programming is an umbrella term for writing software that operates across networks. Most often, this means software that communicates with other software, potentially on different machines, through a network. Examples vary widely here.

On one end of the spectrum, you have software running on a machine communicating with other software running on that same machine. As it turns out, that's often done via network protocols, even if the software executes in a single runtime. Docker on macOS is a prime example of this. On the opposite end of the spectrum, you have software on planet Earth communicating with satellites in orbit. You could argue that every time two programs talk to each other, they're doing so through a network of some sort. We're getting a bit philosophical here.

What About Distributed Systems?

While it's an important feature of the BEAM, this book won't cover the *distribution* aspect of the BEAM. In the real world, networks are made of multiple computers, and often the same application runs on many nodes to increase reliability and scalability. Erlang and the BEAM provide fantastic tools to work with these *distributed* applications.

Distribution in Erlang is fundamentally based on networking, since Erlang nodes in a cluster generally communicate with each other via TCP. But the distribution aspect is orthogonal to networking itself. In fact, distributing a system has its own class of problems. Some of those problems are shared with networking, since networks are distributed systems after all. But many of those problems are specific to how distributed systems handle things such as partitions in clusters, data integrity, system availability, and more.

If you want to learn more about distributed Erlang, we recommend Francesco Cesarini's *Designing for Scalability with Erlang/OTP [CV16]*.

In this book, our focus will be on writing applications that use different network protocols to have computers communicate with each other one way or another. You've probably already worked on something that falls in this category. Maybe you wrote a web application or an HTTP API client for a service you use. We'll talk a lot about the specific protocols themselves, since only a handful of them account for most of the traffic on the Internet.

Next, let's see why Elixir and Erlang are such a good fit for this domain.

Elixir and Erlang: The Perfect Fit

Erlang and the BEAM are a fantastic choice for developing applications that communicate over a network. Ericsson developed Erlang in the mid-1990s to power telephone switches. Since then, its presence in the telecommunication field has been constant, so much so that even many of today's mobile networks (4G, 5G, LTE) have a significant Erlang presence in their infrastructure. Elixir came to the scene much later than Erlang. But given that it's built directly on top of Erlang and can seamlessly access Erlang's standard library, it's just as much of a natural choice.

Because of its roots, Erlang provides great tools for network programming as well as many language primitives that make writing network applications a breeze. Erlang's actor model, lightweight processes, and message passing are a perfect fit for network applications, which are often made of separate, independent clients and servers (processes) passing information around (messages) in an asynchronous, reactive way. The following image gives you a rough visual idea of how networks match with systems running the BEAM.

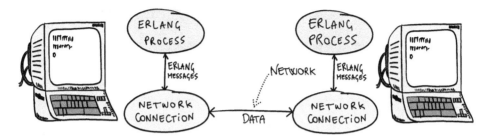

Using processes to model clients and servers is a natural approach. In most languages and ecosystems, processes (and threads) are not cheap to create and run. This usually means processes and threads have to share resources and handle multiple connections, which can make programs built this way hard to reason about. On the BEAM, however, processes are as cheap as it gets, so much so that most Elixir or Erlang network applications allocate one process for each network connection. These processes have isolated memory and isolated failure semantics. If a process crashes, it only brings down the connection that *it* is managing, without affecting other connections. That's rarely the case in other ecosystems: if a thread crashes, *all* the connections it's responsible for usually get lost. Isolated memory makes garbage collection fast and distributed across processes, so that network clients never see a big garbage collection sweep.

But the reasons that Elixir and Erlang are such a perfect fit don't end here. Because of the way processes and message passing work, you naturally end up writing code that resembles network code. If you work with Elixir or Erlang, you are used to these independent actors sending each other messages, having to check for crashes, acknowledging requests, and reacting to incoming messages. These are all patterns that perfectly mirror the ones you'll find yourself needing when working with network code. Take a look at this table, which gives you a one-to-one comparison between things that happen on the BEAM and things that happen in networks:

Elixir/Erlang	Network
A process	One side of a connection—server or client
Sending a message from one process to another	Sending a packet from one side of a connection to another

Elixir/Erlang	Network
Receiving an acknowledgment that a message has been processed	Receiving an acknowledgment that a packet has been processed
Monitoring a process to know if it exits	Monitoring a socket to know if the connection gets interrupted
Each process has its own memory	Connections often run on different machines, so by definition memory can't be shared

Which One, Though: Elixir or Erlang?

So, if these languages have mostly equivalent semantics and capabilities, which one should you pick?

Historically, even after folks started using Elixir, it seems like Erlang has been the most common choice for lower-level network applications, such as applications built directly on top of protocols like TCP or UDP. Elixir has been more present in the higher-level application space, such as the web using the Phoenix framework. Still, the two are mostly interchangeable when working with networks.

Elixir made the choice to avoid wrapping most of Erlang's standard library, which includes network-related modules and applications. This has led to the two languages even using the same APIs to work with network protocols. When it comes to higher-level libraries, such as HTTP servers and clients, both Elixir and Erlang have thriving ecosystems, which means neither language is a clear winner over the other.

To get an idea of how similar the languages are, take a look at this snippet of Elixir code:

```elixir
defmodule MyModule do
  def monitor_process(pid) do
    Process.monitor(pid, tag: :my_monitor)
  end
end
```

In Erlang, it would look something like this:

```erlang
-module(my_module).

monitor_process(Pid) ->
  erlang:monitor(Pid, [{tag, my_monitor}])
```

While the syntax is not exactly the same, the *semantics* are identical: each snippet defines a module with a function in it.

Why Are All the Code Samples in This Book in Elixir?

The main reason is that I am most fluent in Elixir. I'm also deeply convinced that Elixir and Erlang are interchangeable when it comes to syntax and data structures. Elixir provides a handful of additional features compared to Erlang, such as macros and protocols, but they're seldom seen in code that works with networks. Furthermore, picking one of the two languages for the samples makes for content that flows a bit better compared to having each code sample shown in both.

Even though its sample code is in Elixir, this book is targeted at Erlang developers as much as those working in Elixir. If you're an Erlang programmer who is not familiar with Elixir, and you want to learn just enough of the syntax to follow along, look no further than the crash course on the Elixir website.[1] This short guide does a great job of introducing syntax differences between the languages and should be enough for you to understand the examples here.

Where Do We Go Next?

This chapter was a broad-strokes introduction to the topic of network programming and how Elixir and Erlang fit into this landscape. We talked about why Elixir and Erlang are such a good choice when working with network applications, and we compared the two languages to help you decide which one to pick.

We'll now move on to a comprehensive part about TCP, the most commonly used protocol on the Internet. The next chapter will introduce the protocol with its semantics and will get you warmed up to this world. The rest of the part will dig deeper into TCP and the techniques and patterns you'll want to use when working with it.

See you in the next chapter.

---

1. https://elixir-lang.org/crash-course.html

Part I

TCP

The most widely used network protocol on the Internet is TCP. You'll learn about the fundamentals of the protocol, how to build clients and servers, and how to make them scalable and resilient. You'll also learn about how to make communication over TCP secure thanks to TLS.

## CHAPTER 2

TCP: Exploring the Basics

TCP is the most commonly used network protocol around. TCP stands for *Transmission Control Protocol*, so beware: it's not the "TCP protocol"—that would be redundant!

TCP powers a lot of the Internet. Browsers talk to servers over HTTP, which is built on top of TCP. Most databases and queue systems also use TCP to communicate with clients. It's easy to work with, and it's the foundation you need to know to get started with network applications. Throughout this chapter, you'll create a TCP client that connects to an existing TCP server, then build a simple TCP server yourself. In the process, we'll get an idea of how more complex TCP servers work under the hood.

Let's start things off with a quick overview of this network protocol.

TCP 101

Unless you're working in less mainstream corners of the Elixir world, it's likely that TCP is what you'll directly use the most. TCP is the most ubiquitous transport layer protocol for network applications. In this section, we'll write a simple TCP client to connect to an existing TCP server to cover the basics of TCP. Let's start with its client-server architecture.

Clients and Servers

It might be a generalization, but you'll find that most interactions on networks can be modeled as a *server* and a *client* talking to each other. This distinction is important. A server is a computer program that uses a protocol to *listen* on some sort of network interface. The protocol is generally a transport layer protocol underneath (TCP or UDP), but the interface provided by the server can be one that uses an application layer protocol (such as HTTP).

This is definitely true for TCP. In TCP, a server has to actively listen for incoming connections on a specific address and port combination. A TCP client can then establish a connection to that server to exchange data with it. The following figure is a rough representation of a server talking with multiple clients.

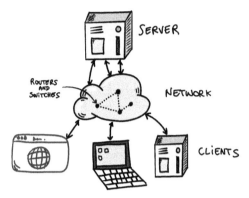

When a client connects to a server, a *connection* is opened on each side. This connection is persistent and remains open until one of the two sides terminates it. This is possible because TCP is a *stateful* protocol. Clients and servers have to store some state in the connection. TCP uses this state to keep track of packet order and deal with duplicated packets. Next up, sockets.

Sockets

TCP connections are always represented by an operating-system-level abstraction: the *socket*. The term *socket* dates back to RFC 147[1] in 1971, so we're talking about pretty old stuff here. Sockets are the mechanism that the OS provides to give programs access to the network.

You can imagine a network socket as an actual wall-mounted telephone socket. You plug in your application and send and receive phone calls (data). The phone lines, or the network in our case, transport the data to another socket mounted on another wall, where another phone (a server) is listening for calls (connections).

1.　https://datatracker.ietf.org/doc/html/rfc147

You'll see the name *socket* pretty much everywhere when dealing with network-related code. Most libraries and language bindings that provide interfaces for working with network protocols use the same terminology. Elixir and Erlang are no exception.

A language's standard libraries use the OS socket APIs under the hood. At the OS level, a socket is a *data structure* that contains a bunch of data related to the connection. It holds information about the source and destination of the traffic, the buffered in-flight data, and the protocol being used. On that note, sockets are not specific to TCP. They're independent of the network type and the protocol. If you want to learn more about sockets at the OS level, Rutgers University provides a great introduction to socket programming.[2]

In Elixir and Erlang, the socket abstraction is represented by a *port*. A port is an Erlang primitive data type used to communicate with external programs—not just network sockets. Ports share many traits with processes, such as passing data around through messages. Furthermore, ports are linked to the process that opens them. This is a desirable behavior for network applications: you don't want your application to leave open sockets behind, and in this case just terminating your application (and all its processes) is enough to ensure all sockets get closed as well. If you want to read more about ports, the Erlang documentation[3] is a great resource.

It might be a little confusing, but an Erlang port has nothing to do with a network port, which is an entirely different concept. We'll look at that next as we briefly touch on how TCP routes traffic.

IPs and Ports

TCP is also known as TCP/IP. IP stands for *Internet Protocol*. It's the most common network protocol (layer 3 of the OSI model; see Appendix 1, The OSI Model, on page 223). Its job is to route packets from sources to destinations. The way it does that is by annotating packets with two pieces of information: an *address* and a *port*.

Addresses, also known as *IP addresses*, identify hosts on the network. They look like four-element a.b.c.d strings, where each letter represents an integer from 0 to 255—for example, 140.82.121.3.

In network-speak, ports are a way to route packets to different programs within the same host. They range from 1 to 65535 (the possible values of 16

---

2. https://people.cs.rutgers.edu/~pxk/rutgers/notes/sockets/
3. https://www.erlang.org/doc/system/c_port.html

bits). For example, it's standard to use port 443 to listen for HTTPS traffic and port 22 for SSH traffic. These ports have nothing to do with the Erlang data type—they just (sadly) share the same name.

You'll sometimes see address-port combinations represented with a colon separating them, as in 140.82.121.3:443.

Now, enough talk—let's see some code.

Writing a TCP Client with the gen_tcp Module

Writing a TCP server is slightly harder than writing a TCP client, so let's look at clients first. Lucky for us, there are literally millions of TCP servers all around that we can connect to. Let's start by writing a little program that opens a TCP socket by connecting to a TCP server listening at tcpbin.com on port 4242. This little service built by Harry Bagdi provides a simple TCP server that echoes back lines of data that we send to it. It's perfect for starting out. You can find more details on the website.[4]

In this chapter (and most of this book), we'll use modules that are part of Erlang's standard distribution. When it comes to TCP, Erlang ships with the gen_tcp module.[5] gen_tcp provides a complete API for working with TCP, from creating client and server sockets to sending data and receiving data. To open a new connection, the function you want is :gen_tcp.connect/4.[6] Open an Elixir interactive shell by typing iex in your terminal, and then type the following:

```
iex> {:ok, socket} =
...>    :gen_tcp.connect(~c"tcpbin.com", 4242, [:binary], 5000)
{:ok, #Port<0.6>}
```

The first argument is an Erlang string with the address to connect to. It could also be a raw IP address, but we'll get to that a bit later. The second argument is the port that the server is listening on. We're using 4242 here because that's what tcpbin.com uses. The third argument is a list of options, and the fourth argument is a connection timeout in milliseconds. Milliseconds are the "lingua franca" for timeouts on the BEAM—see things such as timeout:minutes/1[7] or Kernel.to_timeout/1.[8] The :binary option is important: if we don't pass it, all data sent and received through the socket will be in the form of charlists

---

4. https://tcpbin.com
5. https://www.erlang.org/doc/man/gen_tcp.html
6. https://www.erlang.org/doc/man/gen_tcp.html#connect-port4
7. https://www.erlang.org/doc/apps/stdlib/timer.html#seconds/1
8. https://hexdocs.pm/elixir/Kernel.html#to_timeout/1

rather than binaries. We generally don't want that, since binaries are more efficient and usually easier to work with.

> ## Erlang Strings (or Charlists) vs. Binaries
>
> Ah, Erlang strings—a remnant of darker times. Jokes aside, an Erlang string is a data structure used to represent a list of characters. It's literally a list of integers, where each integer is between 0 and 255 and represents the value of an 8-bit byte. I'm calling them Erlang strings here because they were mostly used in the early days of Erlang. Erlang uses the "double quotes" syntax for strings. Nowadays, Erlang strings are often used in APIs to avoid introducing backward-incompatible changes to existing code. Erlang strings are being mostly replaced with *binaries*. Binaries are blobs of bytes. In Erlang, you can create binaries with the <<>> syntax, as in <<13, 23, 0>>. Binaries are generally preferred in modern Elixir and Erlang code since they're usually more efficient than Erlang strings. They're stored contiguously in memory, you can retrieve their size in constant time, and you can index them in constant time as well.
>
> Elixir took a slightly different syntactic approach for these data structures. In order to promote the use of binaries over Erlang strings, Elixir uses the "double quote" syntax to represent binaries. You can still create Erlang strings by using 'single quotes' or the ~c sigil (~c"localhost"), but this can sometimes lead to confusion.
>
> In this book, we'll only use Erlang strings when we need to interface with older Erlang APIs. To be fair, though, that's most of the network-related APIs!

The return value is an {:ok, socket} tuple. socket is a data structure that wraps the OS-level socket we talked about earlier. This returned socket identifies our client connection, and we can use it to exchange data with the server. Elixir prints the socket as #Port<...> because a socket is an Erlang port.[9] We'll talk more about ports later in the book. The other possible return value of :gen_tcp.connect/4 is {:error, reason} in the case that something goes wrong. Returning {:ok, value} or {:error, reason} is a common pattern in Elixir and Erlang when dealing with functions that can fail. In the case of :gen_tcp.connect/4 and most other :gen_tcp functions, reason is a representation of a POSIX error code, such as ECONNREFUSED (represented as :econnrefused). The Erlang documentation has a whole section[10] on POSIX error codes that you can use for reference.

Well, time to send some data. To do that, we can use .send/2:

```
iex> :gen_tcp.send(socket, "Hello, world!\n")
:ok
```

---

9. https://www.erlang.org/doc/tutorial/c_port.html
10. https://www.erlang.org/doc/man/inet.html#error_codes

The data is a binary and ends with a newline character (\n). Okay, where's our response? Shouldn't we get "Hello, world!\n" echoed back somehow? It turns out that *sending* data is more straightforward than *receiving* data. Let's rip the Band-Aid off sooner rather than later and explore socket modes.

Active and Passive Modes for Sockets

The response from the server didn't show up in our previous IEx session, because it was delivered to the current process as a message. We can verify that with the flush/0 IEx helper,[11] which we can use to print out all the messages that we received in our IEx session:

```
iex> flush()
{:tcp, #Port<0.6>, "Hello, world!\n"}
```

You could also use Process.info(self(), :messages)[12] to inspect the messages without removing them from the mailbox.

:gen_tcp sockets can generally be in one of two modes: *active mode* or *passive mode*. By default, they start in active mode. In this mode, :gen_tcp delivers all the data that the socket receives—as well as some socket-related information—as *messages* to the process that controls the socket. For our purposes right now, that's the process that initially created the socket—that is, the IEx session. This way, the :gen_tcp API and the interaction with the socket mimic the way that message passing works on the BEAM. Sending data with :gen_tcp.send/2 is asynchronous and non-blocking, as when sending messages with send/2[13] (or ! in Erlang). Receiving data is the same as receiving any other message.

The :gen_tcp API defines three possible messages:

- {:tcp, socket, data}: This message represents data received through the socket. socket is the one that received the data, which is important if you've opened multiple sockets and need to know which one the data came from.

- {:tcp_closed, socket}: This message signals that the other end (the TCP server, in this case) *closed* the given socket.

- {:tcp_error, socket, reason}: This message means that there was an error with the socket. reason is a POSIX reason, similar to the ones that :gen_tcp.connect/4 might return.

---

11. https://hexdocs.pm/iex/IEx.Helpers.html#flush/0

12. https://hexdocs.pm/elixir/Process.html#info/2

13. https://hexdocs.pm/elixir/Kernel.html#send/2

The other possible mode that a socket can be in is *passive mode.* To actively retrieve data that a socket might have received in passive mode, you have to use the :gen_tcp.recv/3 function.[14] Let's try it out by starting a socket and setting the :active option to false:

```
iex> {:ok, socket} =
...>    :gen_tcp.connect(
...>      ~c"tcpbin.com",
...>      4242,
...>      [:binary, active: false],
...>      5000
...>    )
iex> :gen_tcp.send(socket, "Hello from a passive socket\n")
:ok
iex> :gen_tcp.recv(socket, 0, 5000)
{:ok, "Hello from a passive socket\n"}
```

:gen_tcp.recv/3 takes a socket as its first argument. The second argument is the number of bytes that we want to read from the socket. 0 is a special (and commonly used) value that tells the socket to return all available data. The third argument is a timeout (in milliseconds), after which the function returns {:error, :timeout} if it doesn't receive any data.

> ## Which Is Better: Active or Passive?
>
> These two modes have different properties intended for different use cases. For example, active sockets are generally preferred when you want to avoid blocking the receiving process, such as an OTP process like a GenServer. Passive mode, however, can be more efficient and gives you finer control over how much data is received. We'll see use cases for both throughout the book.

Well, we have a working TCP client. Pretty easy, wasn't it? There's more to learn about the :gen_tcp API and about writing efficient and safe clients, but this is a great start. Now, to get a complete view of the basics of TCP, we need to write a TCP server. We'll start by building a clone of the TCP echo server we've been talking to until now.

Building a TCP Echo Server

Our echo server will listen for TCP client connections and will be able to keep multiple connections open at the same time. When a client sends a line of data (characters ending in a newline \n), our server will send that line of data back. That's all.

---

14. https://www.erlang.org/doc/man/gen_tcp.html#recv-3

First things first—let's create a new Mix project for our server:

```
> mix new tcp_echo_server --sup --module TCPEchoServer
* creating README.md
* creating .formatter.exs
* creating .gitignore
* creating mix.exs
* creating lib
* creating lib/tcp_echo_server.ex
* creating lib/tcp_echo_server/application.ex
* creating test
* creating test/test_helper.exs
* creating test/tcp_echo_server_test.exs

Your Mix project was created successfully.
You can use "mix" to compile it, test it, and more:

    cd tcp_echo_server
    mix test

Run "mix help" for more commands.
```

Make sure to pass the --sup flag so that Mix scaffolds a supervision tree for our application and hooks it up to start when the application starts. The --module argument just makes sure that the "TCP" acronym doesn't get converted to Tcp in code.

To make sure you wired everything correctly, let's ensure that you can run tests and that they pass:

```
> mix test
Compiling 2 files (.ex)
Generated tcp_echo_server app
..
Finished in 0.01 seconds (0.00s async, 0.01s sync)
1 doctest, 1 test, 0 failures

Randomized with seed 404120
```

Fantastic.

TCP Servers: How Do They Work?

While TCP clients *initiate* connections and have to specify the address and port of a TCP server, TCP servers have to *listen* for incoming connections on a given address and port combination. This is also called *binding* on the address and port.

To listen for TCP connections in Elixir and Erlang, we can use the :gen_tcp.listen/2 function.[15] It takes a port to bind to and a list of options. It looks like this:

```
iex> {:ok, listen_socket} =
...>   :gen_tcp.listen(4000, [:binary, active: true])
{:ok, #Port<0.5>}
```

This code binds on port 4000. The return value of :gen_tcp.listen/2 is similar to that of :gen_tcp.connect/4: it's a tuple with the atom :ok and a *listen socket*, if everything goes well, or {:error, reason} if there's an error. A listen socket is sort of a special TCP socket whose job is to listen for connections and then set up TCP sockets for each new connection. The options that we passed as the second argument to :gen_tcp.listen/2 are applied to all new sockets set up through this listen socket. Now that our listen socket is listening, we can accept new connections using the :gen_tcp.accept/2 function.[16]

```
iex(2)> {:ok, socket} = :gen_tcp.accept(listen_socket, 10_000)
```

:gen_tcp.accept/2 takes the listen socket and a timeout. It blocks until a client connects, and when one does, it returns {:ok, socket}, where socket is the socket for the new connection. The returned socket is the same as the client socket we dealt with earlier in the chapter. You can receive and send data through it in the exact same way. If you run this code, it'll probably return {:error, :timeout} unless you connect a TCP client to the server within the ten-second timeout. In order to have the :gen_tcp.accept/2 call return a socket, let's write some structured code and accompanying tests

Accepting TCP Connections in a Process

Let's start with a process that we'll place under our application's supervision tree. This process will do the following:

1. Call :gen_tcp.listen/2 to set up a listen socket
2. Call :gen_tcp.accept/2 to accept a new connection
3. Spawn a new process to handle the new connection
4. Go back to the :gen_tcp.accept/2 call to accept new connections

In the figure shown on page 18 you can see a visual representation of this accept loop.

We'll use a GenServer for the listening process. In Elixir, you might also use a task,[17] since we won't use most features of GenServers. But tasks are not

---

15. https://erlang.org/doc/man/gen_tcp.html#listen-2

16. https://erlang.org/doc/man/gen_tcp.html#accept-2

17. https://hexdocs.pm/elixir/Task.html

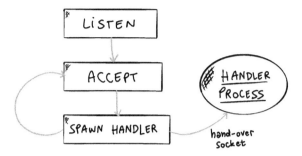

available in Erlang, so we might as well pick an abstraction that is included in both languages. Create the file lib/tcp_echo_server/acceptor.ex.

tcp_echo_server/lib/tcp_echo_server/acceptor.ex

```elixir
defmodule TCPEchoServer.Acceptor do
  use GenServer

  require Logger

  @spec start_link(keyword()) :: GenServer.on_start()
  def start_link(options) do
    GenServer.start_link(__MODULE__, options)
  end

  @impl true
  def init(options) do
    port = Keyword.fetch!(options, :port)

    listen_options = [
      :binary,
      active: true,
      exit_on_close: false,
      reuseaddr: true,
      backlog: 25
    ]

    case :gen_tcp.listen(port, listen_options) do
      {:ok, listen_socket} ->
        Logger.info("Started TCP server on port #{port}")
        send(self(), :accept)
        {:ok, listen_socket}

      {:error, reason} ->
        {:stop, reason}
    end
  end

  @impl true
  def handle_info(:accept, listen_socket) do
    case :gen_tcp.accept(listen_socket, 2_000) do
      {:ok, socket} ->
        {:ok, pid} = TCPEchoServer.Connection.start_link(socket)
```

The annotation markers in the left margin are: ① use GenServer; ② listen_options = [; ③ case :gen_tcp.listen; ④ send(self(), :accept); ⑤ {:ok, listen_socket}; ⑥ def handle_info(:accept, listen_socket) do; ⑦ case :gen_tcp.accept; ⑧ {:ok, pid} = TCPEchoServer.Connection.start_link(socket)

```
⑨          :ok = :gen_tcp.controlling_process(socket, pid)
⑩          send(self(), :accept)
           {:noreply, listen_socket}

⑪        {:error, :timeout} ->
           send(self(), :accept)
           {:noreply, listen_socket}

⑫        {:error, reason} ->
           {:stop, reason, listen_socket}
     end
   end
end
```

That's a lot of code. Let's take a look at it step by step.

❶ We call use GenServer to define a GenServer, then define a standard start_link/1 function.

❷ We know what the :binary and active: true options do from Active and Passive Modes for Sockets, on page 14. We also use the :exit_on_close option here so that the socket isn't linked to the process that creates it. Setting this option to false is useful to avoid closing the socket if the client shuts down its side. Next, with the :reuseaddr option, we can run and shut down the server multiple times without having to worry about unavailable ports. Last but not least, we use the :backlog option, which controls how many clients can be queued waiting to be accepted by the server. We'll talk more about this option in Moving to the Server Side, on page 46.

❸ When initializing the GenServer (inside the init/1 callback), we use the :gen_tcp.listen/2 function we talked about earlier. We are passing along the port from the options argument that was passed to TCPEchoServer.Acceptor.start_link/1. Calling :gen_tcp.listen/2 when initializing the GenServer makes sense, since we want to make sure that our process is already listening once start_link/1 returns. We're also using a case here to match on the return value of :gen_tcp.listen/2. If it returns an error, we stop our GenServer directly.

❹ We consider initialization complete once the call to :gen_tcp.listen/2 returns. As we saw earlier, we still need to call :gen_tcp.accept/2 to accept new connections, but we want to do that outside of the initialization—otherwise, our GenServer would not finish initializing until a client attempted to connect (and a GenServer that doesn't initialize would stop its supervisor from starting and cause other issues). To accept connections after initializing, we use the good old trick of sending a message to self(). Doing this allows initialization to complete and *accepting* to happen asynchronously after that. Remember, messages sent to self() within the init/1 callback get queued in the GenServer's mailbox and are only processed after init/1 returns.

❺ The state of this GenServer is the TCP listen socket itself, since for now we don't need anything else.

❻ We define a handle_info/2 callback to handle the :accept message that we send to self().

❼ Here, we finally call :gen_tcp.accept/2 to get a new listen socket. We keep the timeout pretty short, at two seconds, and we'll see why soon.

❽ Once we have a new TCP socket that represents the connection to a new client, we want to spawn a new process to handle it. We haven't defined TCPEchoServer.Connection yet, but we'll do it soon.

❾ We created a new socket, but before handing it over to the connection process, we need to change the socket's *controlling process*. We'll talk more about the controlling process in Understanding the Controlling Process of a Socket, on page 21.

❿ After spawning a new connection handler, we send :accept to self() again to keep accepting new connections.

⓫ If :gen_tcp.accept/2 returns {:error, :timeout}, we send :accept to self() again and go back to accepting. This is why we can keep a short timeout: if accepting times out, we go back to accepting again right away. We do this instead of passing a long timeout to :gen_tcp.accept/2 because it's generally a bad idea for GenServers to block for long periods of time. They should be able to handle system messages, for example.

⓬ Finally, if :gen_tcp.accept/2 returns any other error, we stop the GenServer.

In order to start our newly defined GenServer, let's add it to the list of children in lib/tcp_echo_server/application.ex.

```
tcp_echo_server/lib/tcp_echo_server/application.ex
@impl true
def start(_type, _args) do
  children = [
    {TCPEchoServer.Acceptor, port: 4000}
  ]

  # See https://hexdocs.pm/elixir/Supervisor.html
  # for other strategies and supported options
  opts = [strategy: :one_for_one, name: TCPEchoServer.Supervisor]
  Supervisor.start_link(children, opts)
end
```

Let's try to run our application as a sanity check.

```
> mix run --no-halt
Compiling 3 files (.ex)
warning: TCPEchoServer.Connection.start_link/1 is undefined
          (module TCPEchoServer.Connection is not available or
           is yet to be defined)
  lib/tcp_echo_server/acceptor.ex:30: TCPEchoServer.Acceptor.handle_info/2

Generated tcp_echo_server app

10:17:00.712 [info] Started TCP server on port 4000
```

We get a warning about TCPEchoServer.Connection not being defined, which we expect. After that, however, we can see the log that we emit in the init/1 callback of our acceptor GenServer. No errors in sight. Success! Let's take a quick detour to talk about the controlling process of a socket before we move on to handling connections.

Understanding the Controlling Process of a Socket

Every :gen_tcp socket has a controlling process. This is a BEAM process that is responsible for the socket itself. The controlling process of a socket starts by creating the socket (via :gen_tcp.connect/4 or :gen_tcp.accept/2). The socket is linked to its controlling process, which means that if the controlling process exits, then the BEAM automatically shuts the socket down and cleans things up. This is a useful behavior, because it avoids potential memory leaks and doesn't require you to do anything to keep things tidy.

The controlling process of a socket is also the only process that can *receive* data from the socket when the socket is in *active mode*. (We discussed active and passive modes in Active and Passive Modes for Sockets, on page 14.) While any process can call :gen_tcp.send/2 to send data through an open socket, only the controlling process receives the {:tcp, socket, data} messages. This is a sensible choice, since :gen_tcp has to know which process to send these messages to. If the socket is in *passive mode*, however, any process can call :gen_tcp.recv/3. But there is an important constraint here: only one process can be receiving data from the socket at any given time. If a process calls :gen_tcp.recv/3 on a socket, it will receive data from the socket. Until the call returns, however, any other process that calls :gen_tcp.recv/3 will get the return value {:error, :ealready}. If you think about it, this makes sense: if :gen_tcp allowed multiple processes to call :gen_tcp.recv/3 concurrently on the same socket, it wouldn't know which process to return the received data to.

The good news is that :gen_tcp provides a function to change the controlling process of a socket, aptly named :gen_tcp.controlling_process/2.[18] It takes a :gen_tcp socket and the PID of the new controlling process. Only a socket's controlling process can transfer the socket to another process by calling controlling_process/2, which is exactly what we did in the acceptor code on page 18.

```
iex> :gen_tcp.controlling_process(socket, new_controlling_pid)
```

Now, if you've been burned in the past by stray BEAM messages or message-related race conditions, you might be wondering about sockets in active mode. What if some TCP messages arrive at the controlling process between calling controlling_process/2 and when the transfer happens? Wouldn't you have leftover TCP messages in the old controlling process and missing messages in the new one? Well, the Erlang team thought of that. From the documentation for :gen_tcp.controlling_process/2:

> If the socket is set in active mode, this function will transfer any messages in the mailbox of the caller to the new controlling process.

The pattern we used in TCPEchoServer.Acceptor is common when working with TCP servers in Elixir and Erlang. An acceptor process calls :gen_tcp.accept/2, spawns a process to handle the new client, and changes the controlling process of the accepted socket to the newly spawned process.

We've talked about the acceptor code enough, so let's move on to code that handles single client connections.

Handling TCP Clients

We'll start with a TCPEchoServer.Connection module. Each connection will be handled by a separate process, and we'll once again use GenServer for these processes. Let's define the TCPEchoServer.Connection module in lib/tcp_echo_server/connection.ex. The start_link/1 function matches what we used in TCPEchoServer.Acceptor.

```
tcp_echo_server/lib/tcp_echo_server/connection.ex
@spec start_link(:gen_tcp.socket()) :: GenServer.on_start()
def start_link(socket) do
  GenServer.start_link(__MODULE__, socket)
end
```

The following code defines an init/1 callback, which doesn't need to do anything other than store the socket in the state. Let's also define a struct with defstruct[19]

---

18. https://www.erlang.org/doc/man/gen_tcp.html#controlling_process-2
19. https://hexdocs.pm/elixir/Kernel.html#defstruct/1

to represent the state of our GenServer. This struct also has a :buffer field that defaults to the empty binary <<>>, but we'll go over that in a second.

tcp_echo_server/lib/tcp_echo_server/connection.ex

```elixir
defstruct [:socket, buffer: <<>>]

@impl true
def init(socket) do
  state = %__MODULE__{socket: socket}
  {:ok, state}
end
```

Structs as State

 When working with OTP behaviors such as GenServer or gen_statem *in Elixir*, I almost always use a struct for the state of the module. I use defstruct/2 in the module itself so that the struct is usable as %__MODULE__{...} throughout the module's code. Structs in Elixir provide useful compile-time guarantees on field names. For example, if I were to misspell a field name or use a field that is not defined in the struct, the Elixir compiler would throw an error. I also like to use structs because they let me always match on at least %__MODULE__{} in any behavior callback, ensuring that all callbacks return a state with the correct shape.

Structs are not available in Erlang, but a common way to achieve similar results has historically been to use Erlang records. While this works, it seems the community is increasingly using *maps* as the state of these callback modules. Maps don't provide the same compile-time guarantees as Elixir structs, but I think they're usually the right choice in Erlang since they perform well and allow precise pattern matching.

:gen_tcp delivers data to our process the same way it does for TCP clients—with :tcp, :tcp_closed, and :tcp_error messages. So, let's define a few clauses of the handle_info/1 callback to handle those.

tcp_echo_server/lib/tcp_echo_server/connection.ex

```elixir
Line 1  @impl true
   -    def handle_info(message, state)
   -
   -    # The "socket" variable must be the same in this pattern match!
   5    def handle_info(
   -          {:tcp, socket, data},
   -          %__MODULE__{socket: socket} = state
   -        ) do
   -      state = update_in(state.buffer, &(&1 <> data))
  10      state = handle_new_data(state)
```

```
        {:noreply, state}
      end

      def handle_info(
15        {:tcp_closed, socket},
          %__MODULE__{socket: socket} = state
        ) do
        {:stop, :normal, state}
      end
20
      def handle_info(
          {:tcp_error, socket, reason},
          %__MODULE__{socket: socket} = state
        ) do
25      Logger.error("TCP connection error: #{inspect(reason)}")
        {:stop, :normal, state}
      end
```

The clauses for :tcp_closed (line 15) and :tcp_error (line 22) only stop the GenServer, which represents a connection to an ephemeral client. If the connection closes or drops, our process can't (and probably *shouldn't*) reconnect to the client, so shutting down with a :normal reason is the way to go. When handling new data on line 5, we append it to the state's buffer and then call the handle_new_data/1 helper function with the updated state. Create a new handle_new_data/1 private function and fill it in.

tcp_echo_server/lib/tcp_echo_server/connection.ex
```
Line 1  defp handle_new_data(state) do
        case String.split(state.buffer, "\n", parts: 2) do
          [line, rest] ->
            :ok = :gen_tcp.send(state.socket, line <> "\n")
5           state = put_in(state.buffer, rest)
            handle_new_data(state)

          _other ->
            state
10        end
      end
```

In the handle_new_data/1 function, we start by splitting the state's buffer on the next newline character (\n) on line 2. We pass parts: 2 to String.split/3 so that even if more than one newline character is present, we still split only on the *first* newline character. If String.split/3 returns a list with two elements (line 3), it means that there was at least one newline character, so we have at least a complete line. In this case, we use :gen_tcp.send/2 to "echo" the line back to the client (line 4). We then update the state's buffer and recursively call handle_new_data/1 again (lines 5 and 6) in case there are other lines available. The base case for the recursion is when no newline character is present—we return the state (line 9) and we're done.

Elixir's Access to Update the State

I've used the update_in/2[20] macro in the code for TCPEchoServer.Connection. update_in/2 is part of a set of accessors (such as get_in and put_in) that Elixir provides. These functions and macros provide a way to access and update nested data. They're generally based on the Access behavior,[21] but work on struct fields.

I tend to use these *a lot* when working with the states of OTP processes, such as the state of our GenServer. They let me write concise code to update or override deeply nested parts of the state and get the updated state back. If you're not familiar with these functions, I highly recommend taking a look at the documentation. You'll see me use them again and again in this book.

Buffering is a common technique in network programs, because application-level programs (such as our GenServer) don't know how TCP packets are split and delivered through the underlying TCP layer. For example, a client might send the string "hello\n" and then the string "world\n" with two separate TCP send calls, but the OS might buffer the data and send a single TCP packet containing the string "hello\nworld\n". Or it might decide to send data every 8 bytes, resulting in two TCP packets: one containing "hello\nwo" and one "rld\n". Buffering addresses all these problems by reconstructing the data at the application layer according to the agreed-upon protocol. In this case, the protocol specifies that each logical packet is a line.

Our TCP echo server is complete. We have an acceptor process that listens on a port and accepts new TCP connections. Once clients connect, the acceptor spawns a process for each client. Next, let's do some testing before taking a look at a few shortcomings of this approach.

Testing with TCP

When prototyping, it's common to do interactive manual testing early on—sometimes even before writing any automated tests. Luckily, most operating systems ship with great tools for working with network programs. In our case, we'll use netcat[22] (often used as nc), a widely known tool from the

---

20. https://hexdocs.pm/elixir/Kernel.html#update_in/2

21. https://hexdocs.pm/elixir/Access.html

22. https://en.wikipedia.org/wiki/Netcat

1990s that should be available on most Unix-based and Windows systems. It's a little program that lets you read from and write to TCP (or UDP) connections. First things first, let's start our shiny new echo server.

```
> mix run --no-halt
19:01:05.073 [info] Started TCP server on port 4000
```

Our server is listening for connections on the address localhost and port 4000. Now we're ready to test this out with netcat. The easiest way to do that is to write lines of text to standard output and then pipe it through netcat.

```
> echo "Hello world" | nc localhost 4000
Hello world
```

This example works because echo adds a newline to the string it echoes by default. If we try to send multiple lines, it still works.

```
> echo -en "Hello\nworld\n" | nc localhost 4000
Hello
world
```

Our rudimentary manual testing indicates that our server is working correctly. Let's also write some automated tests. As we know by now, Erlang's :gen_tcp supports creating both sides of a TCP connection: the client and the server. To be fair, this is what most TCP bindings for other languages do as well. The nice thing is that it makes testing easier. If we want to test a server, as in this case, we can use :gen_tcp again to write clients for our server.

We'll start with a simple test for a single TCP client that connects to our server (at localhost:4000) and sends one line of text. Then, we can assert that our server echoes that line back. Create the file test/tcp_echo_server/integration_test.exs.

```
tcp_echo_server/test/tcp_echo_server/integration_test.exs
test "sends back the received data" do
  {:ok, socket} =
    :gen_tcp.connect(~c"localhost", 4000, [:binary, active: false])

  assert :ok = :gen_tcp.send(socket, "Hello world\n")

  assert {:ok, data} = :gen_tcp.recv(socket, 0, 500)
  assert data == "Hello world\n"
end
```

We used the client socket in passive mode in this test to make it easy to receive all available data with :gen_tcp.recv/3. Next, we can add a similar test for *fragmented* data—that is, data with no newline characters in it or with more than one.

tcp_echo_server/test/tcp_echo_server/integration_test.exs

```
test "handles fragmented data" do
  {:ok, socket} =
    :gen_tcp.connect(~c"localhost", 4000, [:binary, active: false])

  assert :ok = :gen_tcp.send(socket, "Hello")
  assert :ok = :gen_tcp.send(socket, " world\nand one more\n")

  assert {:ok, data} = :gen_tcp.recv(socket, 0, 500)
  assert data == "Hello world\nand one more\n"
end
```

Flaky Test

This test might fail here and there. Oops! That's because our echo server calls :gen_tcp.send/2 on each line it breaks down from the incoming data. But we can't have too much control over how the operating system's TCP stack decides to buffer those multiple send calls. Usually, being small strings, they're buffered into a single TCP packet returned from a single recv/3 call. Sometimes, though, there will be two packets (one per send/2), which results in the recv/3 call returning just "hello\n". You could make this test deterministic by checking the result of the first recv/3 and calling recv/3 once more if necessary. This is left as an exercise to the reader.

Kids, the lesson here is this: you never know how the other end of a connection is going to behave.

The last test we'll add makes sure our server can handle multiple clients simultaneously.

tcp_echo_server/test/tcp_echo_server/integration_test.exs

```
Line 1  test "handles multiple clients simultaneously" do
   -      tasks =
   -        for _ <- 1..5 do
   -          Task.async(fn ->
   5            {:ok, socket} =
   -              :gen_tcp.connect(~c"localhost", 4000, [:binary, active: false])

   -            assert :ok = :gen_tcp.send(socket, "Hello world\n")

  10            assert {:ok, data} = :gen_tcp.recv(socket, 0, 500)
   -            assert data == "Hello world\n"
   -          end)
   -        end

  15      Task.await_many(tasks)
   -    end
```

To simulate multiple clients, we used Elixir tasks. We spawned a bunch of tasks with Task.async/1 (line 4), each setting up a socket, sending data, and receiving the echoed data back. Then, we used Task.await_many/1 (line 15) to wait until all the tasks in the list finish. There's nothing left to do but *run* the tests.

```
> mix test
19:41:08.005 [info] Started TCP server on port 4000
.....
Finished in 0.03 seconds (0.03s async, 0.00s sync)
1 doctest, 4 tests, 0 failures

Randomized with seed 13966
```

Success! For the last part of this chapter, let's take a closer look at two :gen_tcp options that have a lot to offer: :active and :packet.

Becoming Socket Pros with Modes and Packet Parsing

Erlang's :gen_tcp module provides many options you can use when starting sockets. We won't use most of them in this book, but we'll use :active and :packet in the next chapters. We've already seen active: true (active mode) and active: false (passive mode), but it turns out that we can pass other values to change the behavior of the socket. The :packet option, instead, lets you off-load some parsing or packing of the data to :gen_tcp.

Being More Precise with Active Sockets

The :active option controls how :gen_tcp delivers data to a socket. As you learned, active: true means the data is delivered as process messages, while active: false means you need to manually receive data. As a matter of fact, :active can take not only a boolean value but also the atom :once or an integer n. When :active is :once, the socket is in active mode until it sends a message to the controlling process (for example, if the socket receives TCP data). Once the socket sends the message, it automatically goes back into passive mode. You have to manually set it back if you need to return to active mode.

Active once sockets tend to be common in practice, because they're often the perfect compromise between active and passive modes. If your socket is in passive mode, you'll have to call :gen_tcp.recv/3 every time you want to fetch new data and be able to copy it to the controlling process. Not ideal if the other peer can send data at any time, since you'd be blocking the process calling recv/3. This can be the opposite of a *reactive* model, since you have to either fetch often or risk data delays. Active mode solves the reactivity issue, but it opens the socket's controlling process to a sort of *denial-of-service attack.* If a client sends data frequently and your TCP receive buffer is small, the controlling process might end up receiving a lot of messages. This can be a problem if the controlling process can't keep up with them. In such a case, the message queue of the controlling process would fill up and potentially cause a memory leak. By using active: :once, you can avoid having to constantly call recv/3, and at the same time you'll have to explicitly reactivate the socket to eliminate the message-queuing situation.

Setting the socket back to active: :once every time the controlling process receives a message is a common approach in the real world. It usually looks something like the code sketched out here.

```elixir
defmodule Connection do
  «usual GenServer code»

  def handle_info({:tcp, socket, data}, %{socket: socket} = state) do
    :ok = :inet.setopts(socket, active: :once)
    handle_data(data)
    {:noreply, state}
  end
end
```

The function you need to use to change a socket's mode is not in the :gen_tcp module but in :inet.setopts/2.[23] This is because :gen_tcp is not the only module that provides a socket-based API in Erlang. For example, we'll work with sockets using the :ssl module as well. :inet supports sockets from all of these modules, so some common functions (such as setopts/2) live in there.

Changing Socket Options

 Pay special attention to :inet.setopts/2. We'll use it often in this book, since it works on TCP sockets (client and server) *and* UDP sockets.

:active can also take one other value: an integer n. This mode is similar to active: :once, but the socket will deliver n messages before going back to passive mode. When it *does* go back to passive mode, it delivers one more {:tcp_passive, socket} message to the controlling process. This message allows the controlling process to know when it has to set the socket back to active mode. active: n is slightly more complex than that. In fact, n can even be a negative number. The socket keeps a count of messages it can deliver, and setting active: n with a negative n *subtracts* from that count. active: n seems to be used less often than the alternatives, but it can be a nifty tool to deal with flow control. For example,

---

23. https://www.erlang.org/doc/man/inet.html#setopts-2

the controlling process might regulate and update the number n of allowed messages based on message size, how "busy" it is, and other such factors.

To put active: :once into practice, let's modify our TCP echo server from the previous section. Instead of passing active: true when starting the TCP listen socket in code/tcp_echo_server/lib/tcp_echo_server/acceptor.ex, we'll use active: :once:

```
-listen_options = [:binary, active: true, exit_on_close: false]
+listen_options = [:binary, active: :once, exit_on_close: false]
```

We then need to set the socket back to active: :once every time we get a {:tcp, socket, data} message in code/tcp_echo_server/lib/tcp_echo_server/connection.ex.

```
  def handle_info(
        {:tcp, socket, data},
        %__MODULE__{socket: socket} = state
      ) do
+    :ok = :inet.setopts(socket, active: :once)
    state = update_in(state.buffer, &(&1 <> data))
    state = handle_new_data(state)
    {:noreply, state}
  end
```

active: :once is especially powerful when paired with the :packet option, which we'll look at next.

Off-Loading Some Parsing with the Packet Option

In the code we've written so far, we parsed and packed our own data, but we've only received *all available data*. :gen_tcp offers a powerful alternative with the :packet option. :packet can be many different values. We won't explore all of them here, but you can refer to the documentation for :inet.setopts/2[24] for a comprehensive list.

If not specified, the default value for the :packet option is :raw, which means that :gen_tcp (or rather :inet) won't do anything to incoming or outgoing data. Let's start with another possible value: :line. This value only affects the received data. If you set it, the socket will only deliver complete lines—that is, sequences of bytes that end with the byte 10, which represents a newline (\n) in ASCII. In active mode, lines are delivered as {:tcp, socket, line} messages. In passive mode, :gen_tcp.recv(socket, 0, timeout) returns {:ok, line} if successful. You'll still have to add a newline character manually to data you send through the socket, but you won't have the headache of splitting and buffering incoming data.

---

24. https://www.erlang.org/doc/man/inet.html#setopts-2

If we were to use packet: :line in our TCPEchoServer.Acceptor, we could simplify TCPEchoServer.Connection significantly by not buffering data and just sending back every line received through a {:tcp, socket, data} message. The relevant handle_info/2 clause would look like this:

```
def handle_info(
      {:tcp, socket, line},
      %__MODULE__{socket: socket} = state
    ) do
  :ok = :gen_tcp.send(state.socket, line)
  {:noreply, state}
end
```

Another powerful value for :packet is one of the integers 1, 2, and 4. In this case, the value represents a number of bytes to use as the header for received and sent data. This header encodes the number of bytes expected to follow. For example, if :packet equals 2 and you send the data "hello", :gen_tcp will in fact send the data <<0, 5, "hello">> through the socket—that is, two bytes encoding the number 5 (the number of bytes in the string "hello") and then the string itself. When :packet is set to one of the supported integer values, :gen_tcp applies the corresponding header logic to incoming data and strips the header when delivering the data to the controlling process. This :packet mode is especially useful for binary protocols that specify packet length. In those cases, it feels like cheating: your code just sends and receives data without thinking about encoding, because :gen_tcp takes care of it for you.

Wrapping Up

You've made it through the introduction to the first protocol. Great job! You're one step closer to unlocking your full network programming potential. We got a good look at TCP, one of the most widely used transport layer protocols, and we reviewed some important networking concepts, such as sockets, addresses, and ports. You also became familiar with using TCP in Elixir and Erlang through the :gen_tcp standard-library module, writing both a TCP client and a TCP server.

In the next chapter, we'll step up our TCP game by going over best practices and design patterns for building scalable and reliable TCP clients and servers on the BEAM.

## CHAPTER 3

Designing a Chat Protocol and Its TCP Server

In the previous chapter, you got an overview of TCP as a protocol and of :gen_tcp, Erlang's built-in module for working with TCP clients and servers. You now know how to write a basic TCP client and a basic TCP server. In this chapter, we'll face the challenges that come with writing a TCP-based application. You'll learn how to design a serialization protocol, and we'll put together our first proper TCP server.

We'll build a simple text-based chat system on top of TCP, working on both the server interface (in this chapter) and the client interface (in the next chapter, Chapter 4, Scaling TCP on the Server Side, on page 59). Our chat system will support

- A single global chat room where users connected to the server hang out.
- Broadcast messages, which a user sends to all other users in the chat room.

We're keeping it simple on purpose so that we can focus on the network challenges without getting lost in implementing a complex system. Before we dive in, here's how our chat is going to look from the perspective of clients:

```
● ● ●   \X2
→ mix chat_client
Enter your username: Andrea
Andrea#
Eric> Hi friends!

Hey Eric 🦝
Andrea# []
```

```
|☰ Shell
→ mix chat_client
Enter your username: Eric
Eric#  Hi friends!
Eric#
Andrea> Hey Eric 🦝

|
```

It's not a fancy UI, but most of our effort will go toward the server side, so a terminal window will have to do.

Let's start with an overview of the protocol we'll use in our chat system.

Designing a Simple Chat Protocol

Having a well-defined protocol is a must in network systems, and you'll stumble upon a lot of these specifications when working with existing networking code. If you're curious, there are a few official protocol specifications you can check out to get an idea of what a real-world, detailed protocol spec looks like:

- The Redis Serialization Protocol (RESP) specification[1]
- The spec for the HPACK header serialization protocol used in HTTP/2[2]
- The header format of TCP itself (section 3 of the original spec from 1981)[3]

In this section, we'll define our simple chat protocol and talk a bit more about protocols in general. One of the most important protocol distinctions we can make is between binary and textual protocols, so let's kick off with that.

Binary Protocols and Textual Protocols

A *binary protocol* is generally characterized by encoding information in bytes or bits, without worrying about whether messages in the protocol can be read as text by humans. For example, a protocol that uses the first byte of a message to signal the length of the rest of the message is a binary protocol. Many of that byte's possible values, such as 0, don't represent valid characters in most encodings. Real-world examples of binary protocols are HTTP/2, the protocol used by the Cassandra database,[4] the Protobuf serialization format,[5] and the underlying data serialization format used by TCP itself (which we talk about in Appendix 2, TCP Protocol Details, on page 225).

Textual protocols are protocols meant to be readable by machines and humans alike. Bytes of information are interpreted through a specified encoding, most commonly ASCII.[6] One of the most famous examples of this kind of protocol is JSON.[7] JSON is a data serialization format derived from the syntax of JavaScript objects. Here's an example of a JSON object:

---

1.   https://redis.io/docs/reference/protocol-spec/
2.   https://http2.github.io/compression-spec/compression-spec.html
3.   https://www.ietf.org/rfc/rfc793.txt
4.   https://cassandra.apache.org/_/index.html
5.   https://protobuf.dev
6.   https://en.wikipedia.org/wiki/ASCII
7.   https://www.json.org/json-en.html

```
{
  "type": "user_message",
  "contents": "Hello! My name is \"Bernaco\""
}
```

You can read this example because JSON objects are readable by humans. They also have elements such as braces ({}) and quotes (") that allow machines to correctly parse the data they encode. In this example, we can see how this requirement sometimes means having to escape characters (\") so that the data can be parsed. Another well-known example of a textual protocol is HTTP/1.1.

Which kind of protocol should you choose—textual or binary? As always, the best answer to this sort of question is, "It depends." Two of the main factors to consider are performance and size.

Well-designed binary protocols are inevitably more space-efficient when serializing data, since they can use a granularity of a single bit to encode information. This is common in real-world protocols such as HTTP/2 and DNS. In general, serialization and deserialization programs are also faster and more memory-efficient when dealing with binary data, since it's easier to include information such as the size of data in the protocol. The downside of binary protocols is that they're mostly unintelligible to humans. For example, if you happen to intercept an HTTP/2 request and you don't have software to help you make sense of it, chances are you'll just see a bunch of bytes that look like gibberish.

Textual protocols, by contrast, are easy for humans to read and easy to write by hand. We're willing to bet that many readers have written at least one JSON object by hand in their careers. But this readability comes at the expense of speed and space. For example, in JSON you have to escape some characters (adding to the size of the data) and parse whole objects to know where they end.

Endianness in Binary Protocols

Endianness[a] is the order in which bytes are interpreted. For example, when the binary <<0, 1>> is interpreted from right to left (with the least significant byte on the right), these bytes encode the number 256 in base ten. This is called *big endianness*. If interpreted from left to right, however, these bytes represent the number 1 (*little endianness*).

When working with binary protocols, the specification should clearly define the endianness used in the protocol. Textual protocols generally don't have to clarify this.

a. https://en.wikipedia.org/wiki/Endianness

Now, let's figure out which type of protocol is right for our chat. A possible choice is JSON itself. In that case, we wouldn't need to come up with the serialization layer itself but only the semantics of the protocol (such as which kinds of messages to support). But by using a binary protocol, you'll have a chance to learn more about how real networks are often designed. So, let's try to come up with a binary protocol that makes sense.

Specifying Our Chat Binary Protocol

When designing a protocol, start with its requirements. Messages in our binary protocol need to encode different information based on their *type*. For example, broadcasted messages have to carry information about the contents of the message, while handshake messages only have to carry the username. This already suggests that we need to attach a type to each message. We know we won't have too many kinds of messages, so we'll use a single byte to encode the message type. A byte can encode 255 different values, which will be plenty.

> ### Representing Bytes
>
> Let's talk about how to generally represent bytes. We could represent a byte with the value of its bits, in decimal base, or in hexadecimal base. The binary base tends to be hard to read for humans due to the long sequences of digits. The decimal base works, but it leads to some nasty cases: for example, the biggest single byte has value 255, which means that we cannot use all three digits up to 999.
>
> The most common representation of single bytes seems to be in *hex notation*, denoted as two digits in hexadecimal base. This works great because two hexadecimal digits can represent 8 bits (a byte). If you want to see for yourself, you can verify that 16^2 (sixteen possible values with two digits) is the same as 2^8 (two possible values with eight digits). For example, you can represent the byte 10110111 (in base two) with the hexadecimal value b7. It's common to prefix the hexadecimal value with 0x, which we'll do throughout the book. So, we would write out the byte in the previous example as 0xb7.

We'll then need to encode strings of text. A common way to do that in binary protocols is to use a few bytes to encode the length of the string, followed by the contents of the string itself. Let's go with 2 bytes to encode the length for our case. It's more than enough, since it lets us encode strings of up to 65536 bytes. We also need to specify the encoding of the string's contents—otherwise, the bytes won't mean anything. We'll go with UTF-8,[8] the most common

---

8.   https://en.wikipedia.org/wiki/UTF-8

encoding standard and one that Elixir supports well. To get an idea of how we'd encode a string, "hello" would be encoded as in the following image:

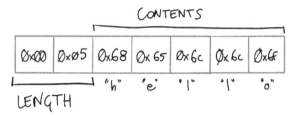

This encoding also works well for strings with Unicode code points that span more than one byte. For example, the character ∞ takes a whopping *3 bytes* to be represented (as 0xe2 0x88 0x9e), as you can see in the following image:

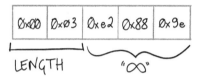

In binary protocols, some messages are unidirectional (client-to-server or server-to-client), while others are bidirectional, meaning that they can be sent and interpreted by both clients and servers. We'll have one of each.

Getting the Byte Size and Hex Representation of a Binary

You can use the Kernel.byte_size/1 function in Elixir or erlang:byte_size/1 function in Erlang to get the number of bytes inside a binary, regardless of how the binary is supposed to be interpreted. This is useful when working with Unicode strings, which is how Elixir represents strings by default. For example, in Elixir, byte_size("∞") returns 3. In Erlang, it would be byte_size(<<"∞"/utf8>>).

Now, say you have a binary and want to get its byte-by-byte hex representation. In Elixir, you can use the base: :hex option when inspecting the binary. For example, inspect("∞", base: :hex) will return the string "<<0xE2, 0x88, 0x9E>>". This is only available in Elixir. In Erlang, you'll have to write some custom code. You can find ideas on how to do that on the Internet.[9]

Now that we have the building blocks for our binary protocols, let's go ahead and define each type of message that clients can send to servers. We'll start with the *register message*. This is a unidirectional message that clients *must* send as the first message after establishing a connection. When the server

---

9. https://stackoverflow.com/questions/3768197/erlang-ioformatting-a-binary-to-hex

receives this type of message, it must identify the connection through the specified username. Usernames must be unique across connected clients. The type byte for this message has value 0x01. Following that, we have a single string containing the username. Here's a visual representation.

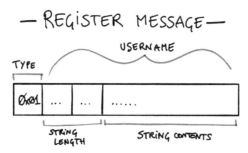

Next up are *broadcast messages*. These are bidirectional messages. Their type byte has value 0x02, followed by a string representing the *from* username of the message, and then one more string with the contents of the message itself. When a client sends a broadcast message to the server, from_username must be an empty string—the connection already stores the client's username, so including it would be redundant. When the server sends a broadcast message to clients, from_username will be the username of the sender of the broadcast message or, if the broadcast message comes from the server itself, an empty string. Keeping the from_username field empty sometimes lets us reuse it as a bidirectional message type instead of creating two separate types. The visual representation of the message looks like this:

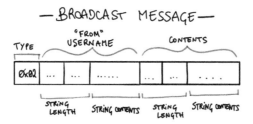

We got our messages down. The image shown on page 39 shows you a visual representation of an example session, in which a client connects, registers, and then broadcasts a message.

Okay, we have designed our first protocol. We started by looking at the difference between textual and binary protocols. We then came up with a binary protocol for our chat server. Our binary protocol is simple, but that's a good thing! It means it will be easy to reason about and implement. Let's move on to writing code for our protocol.

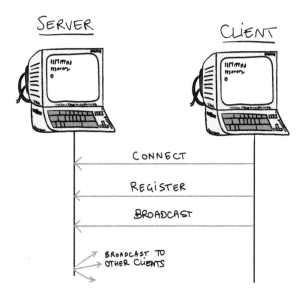

Writing Code for the Chat Protocol

It's almost always a good idea to keep the protocol code separate from the networking code when possible. Protocol code is often stateless and free of side effects, which makes it a good candidate for isolation and easy unit testing. We'll do this by keeping the protocol code inside a separate module, Chat.Protocol. Our protocol code will provide two functions:

- decode_message/1 will take a binary and decode it into a message struct according to our chat protocol
- encode_message/1 will take a message struct and encode it into a binary

Let's set up a project before diving in. Hop into a shell and run the following command:

```
> mix new chat --sup
* creating README.md
* creating .formatter.exs
* creating .gitignore
* creating mix.exs
* creating lib
* creating lib/chat.ex
* creating lib/chat/application.ex
* creating test
* creating test/test_helper.exs
* creating test/chat_test.exs

Your Mix project was created successfully.
```

```
You can use "mix" to compile it, test it, and more:

    cd chat
    mix test

Run "mix help" for more commands.
```

We created a new app called chat and passed the --sup flag to scaffold a supervision tree just as we did in the previous chapter. We're ready to go.

Decoding Data into Messages

Now we can write some protocol code. Let's start with the decoding. We'll write a function, Chat.Protocol.decode_message/1, which decodes a binary into a struct representing the message.

chat/lib/chat/protocol.ex
```elixir
defmodule Chat.Protocol do
  alias Chat.Message.{Broadcast, Register}

  @type message() :: Register.t() | Broadcast.t()

  @spec decode_message(binary()) ::
          {:ok, message(), binary()} | :error | :incomplete
  def decode_message(<<0x01, rest::binary>>), do: decode_register(rest)
  def decode_message(<<0x02, rest::binary>>), do: decode_broadcast(rest)
  def decode_message(<<>>), do: :incomplete
  def decode_message(<<_::binary>>), do: :error

  defp decode_register(<<
         username_len::16,
         username::size(username_len)-binary,
         rest::binary
       >>) do
    {:ok, %Register{username: username}, rest}
  end

  defp decode_register(<<_::binary>>), do: :incomplete

  defp decode_broadcast(<<
         username_len::16, username::size(username_len)-binary,
         contents_len::16, contents::size(contents_len)-binary,
         rest::binary
       >>) do
    {:ok, %Broadcast{from_username: username, contents: contents}, rest}
  end

  defp decode_broadcast(<<_::binary>>), do: :incomplete
end
```

The function returns {:ok, message, rest} if the given binary contains a well-formed message, :incomplete if there is no complete message in the binary, or :error if the data is invalid. The rest value in {:ok, message, rest} is whatever is left of the input binary after parsing a successful message. Returning this leftover data is a common pattern when working with protocols. :incomplete (or something similar) is also common, since messages can look well-formed but be incomplete. It's important to distinguish :error and :incomplete. With errors, for example, a server will do something like terminate the connection, since the data is corrupted. But with incomplete data, the server will have to keep buffering.

Bitstring Syntax

The *bitstring syntax* (<<>>) is a fantastic feature of Elixir and Erlang. It feels like a superpower when constructing or deconstructing sequences of bits. This syntax is powerful and extensible, but the gist is that each comma-separated element within << and >> represents a number of bits—eight by default, but you can specify how many with the ::n modifier, n being the number of bits. ::binary says that that element is a binary number rather than an integer.

This little sidebar is mostly meant to give you some context, but you can check out Elixir's <<>> documentation[a] or Erlang's *Bit Syntax* page.[b]

---

a. https://hexdocs.pm/elixir/Kernel.SpecialForms.html#%3C%3C%3E%3E/1
b. https://www.erlang.org/doc/system/bit_syntax.html

We won't use all of these decode_message/1 return values in our code for the chat server, but that's because we're going to take advantage of the :packet option to lift some weight off our shoulders. Still, it's good to think about these things when working with protocol code. We haven't defined the Chat.Message.Register or Chat.Message.Broadcast yet, so let's do that in the next code snippet.

```
chat/lib/chat/messages.ex
defmodule Chat.Message do
  defmodule Register do
    @type t() :: %__MODULE__{username: String.t()}
    defstruct [:username]
  end

  defmodule Broadcast do
    @type t() :: %__MODULE__{
      from_username: String.t(),
      contents: String.t()
    }

    defstruct [:from_username, :contents]
  end
end
```

We're defining these structs to represent data going through our system. This way, we can work with structured data where field names are well-defined and known at compile time.

Let's write some unit tests for our decoding code.

chat/test/chat/protocol_test.exs

```
Line 1  defmodule Chat.ProtocolTest do
          use ExUnit.Case, async: true

          alias Chat.Message.{Broadcast, Register}
     5
          describe "decode_message/1" do
            test "can decode register messages" do
              binary = <<0x01, 0x00, 0x03, "meg", "rest">>
              assert {:ok, message, rest} = Chat.Protocol.decode_message(binary)
    10        assert message == %Register{username: "meg"}
              assert rest == "rest"

              # Make sure :incomplete is returned when the message is incomplete
              assert Chat.Protocol.decode_message(<<0x01, 0x00>>) == :incomplete
    15      end

            test "can decode broadcast messages" do
              binary = <<0x02, 3::16, "meg", 2::16, "hi", "rest">>
              assert {:ok, message, rest} = Chat.Protocol.decode_message(binary)
    20        assert message == %Broadcast{from_username: "meg", contents: "hi"}
              assert rest == "rest"

              assert Chat.Protocol.decode_message(<<0x02, 0x00>>) == :incomplete
            end
    25
            test "returns :incomplete for empty data" do
              assert Chat.Protocol.decode_message("") == :incomplete
            end

    30      test "returns :error for unknown message types" do
              assert Chat.Protocol.decode_message(<<0x03, "rest">>) == :error
            end
          end
        end
```

We have a test for each message type (lines 7 and 17) and one for invalid messages (line 17). In the first two tests, we make sure of two things. The first is that if there's any data left after the message, decode_message/1 returns it. The second is that if the message we're decoding is incomplete, decode_message/1 returns :incomplete.

Binary Syntax

In the previous two tests, we used different binary syntaxes to express the length of strings. On line 8, we spell out the 2 bytes that make for the length of the string: 0x00 and 0x03. On line 18, we instead use the ::16 modified to encode the number on the left of :: as 16 bits, or 2 bytes. The latter approach is more idiomatic in Elixir and Erlang code. Binary syntax is so expressive that it feels like cheating sometimes, doesn't it?

We should have pretty good coverage with these few lines of tests. You can verify that they pass by running the following command:

```
> mix test
...
Finished in 0.02 seconds (0.02s async, 0.00s sync)
3 tests, 0 failures
```

Fantastic! Now, let's move on to the encoding side.

Encoding with Iodata

Encoding our messages is even simpler than decoding them. That's because we won't need to do any error handling. After all, message structs come from inside rather than outside our system. In general, you should only validate data that comes from outside your system. Let's first have a look at the Chat.Protocol.encode_message/1 function in the following code. You'll probably find the function's return value weird. That's because it returns *iodata*, which we'll discuss right after the code.

```
chat/lib/chat/protocol.ex
@spec encode_message(message()) :: iodata()
def encode_message(message)

def encode_message(%Register{} = msg) do
  [0x01, encode_string(msg.username)]
end

def encode_message(%Broadcast{} = msg) do
  [0x02, encode_string(msg.from_username), encode_string(msg.contents)]
end

defp encode_string(str) do
  [<<byte_size(str)::16>>, str]
end
```

Maybe you expected the return value of encode_message/1 to be a binary—something like this:

```
defp encode_string(str) do
  <<byte_size(str)::16, str::binary>>
end
```

That definitely works, but iodata is more efficient than binary in many cases, both in terms of performance and memory usage. First, let's understand what iodata is. Erlang's documentation defines it this way:

> A binary or list containing bytes and/or iodata. This datatype is used to represent data that is meant to be output using any I/O module. For example: file:write/2 or gen_tcp:send/2.[10]

So, iodata is a *recursive data structure*, since it's defined in terms of iodata itself. The simplest iodata are binaries and lists of bytes, where a byte is an integer in 0..255. For example, these are all valid iodata:

```
"hello"
[?h, ?e, ?l, ?l, ?o]
<<0x01>>
[1]
```

You can nest iodata within itself as deep as you want, and it remains valid iodata. These are only a few examples of how you could write the equivalent of the string "hello" with different combinations of iodata:

```
["hel", "lo"]
[?h, ?e, "ll", ?o]
["he", [?l, [?l, ["o"]]]]
```

You can use IO.iodata_to_binary/1 in Elixir or erlang:iolist_to_binary/1 in Erlang to convert iodata to a binary. For example:

```
IO.iodata_to_binary(["he", [?l, [?l, ["o"]]]])
#=> "hello"
```

Okay, you get what iodata is, but why does it exist? As we touched on before, the short answer is *efficiency*. The BEAM stores binaries as contiguous blocks of memory:

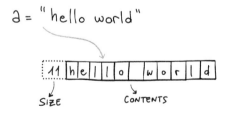

---

10. https://www.erlang.org/doc/man/erlang.html#type-iodata

When you concatenate two binaries, the BEAM creates a new slot in memory to hold the resulting binary. This operation can be costly.

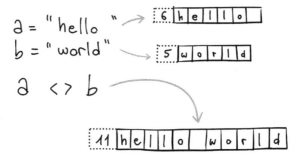

Imagine doing that many times to build payloads like the ones in our Chat.Protocol. Even something as small and simple as encode_message/1 would result in *five* binary concatenations. Iodata can be efficient because putting items together in lists is a cheap operation to do on the BEAM, since lists are represented as linked lists—that is, each element is stored in a different place in memory, and the list itself contains pointers to those memory locations. For example, when you put "hello " and "world" in a list together, the BEAM doesn't reserve a new area of memory for "hello world".

The following image should give you a visual idea of this:

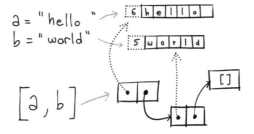

But there's more! As the documentation we quoted earlier states, iodata is particularly useful for data intended for output using any I/O module. If the data you are building is handed over to the OS (as when it's written to a file or sent over the network), the BEAM doesn't need to concatenate the iodata into a binary *at all*. In fact, functions like :gen_tcp.send/2 and File.write/2 accept iodata directly. The native C parts of the Erlang standard library can write iodata directly to OS buffers without creating intermediate binaries. That's generally more efficient than concatenating binaries on the BEAM and handing over a single binary to I/O functions.

Getting the Length of Iodata

 If you have an iodata structure and want to know its length, use IO.iodata_length/1 in Elixir or erlang:iolist_size/1 in Erlang instead of converting the iodata to a binary just to use byte_size/1. Those two functions are implemented in C inside the BEAM, so they're blazing fast (even though they're not constant time, as with byte_size/1).

You'll see the iodata structure everywhere in the standard libraries of Elixir and Erlang, as well as in their ecosystem libraries. When working with network code, iodata is almost always the right choice. If you need to, you can always convert the iodata to a binary (with IO.iodata_to_binary/1) after building it, which is common in tests, for example. As a matter of fact, we can look at the tests for our Chat.Protocol.encode_message/1 function to see this pattern.

chat/test/chat/protocol_test.exs
```
describe "encode_message/1" do
  test "can encode Register messages" do
    message = %Register{username: "meg"}
    iodata = Chat.Protocol.encode_message(message)

    assert IO.iodata_to_binary(iodata) == <<0x01, 0x00, 0x03, "meg">>
  end

  test "can encode broadcast messages" do
    message = %Broadcast{from_username: "meg", contents: "hi"}
    iodata = Chat.Protocol.encode_message(message)

    assert IO.iodata_to_binary(iodata) ==
              <<0x02, 0x00, 0x03, "meg", 0x00, 0x02, "hi">>
  end
end
```

Using IO.iodata_to_binary/1 in our assertions here means that we can assert whatever the end result would be, without having to care *how* our code builds the iodata. Our tests are not brittle—we can freely refactor the code without breaking them, as long as the converted iodata stays the same.

Well, that was the code for our whole protocol. It's all we need to work on our server and client, so let's move on to the server code.

Moving to the Server Side

Back to our regularly scheduled network programming (get it?!). In this section, we'll start working on our chat server. We'll leverage what you learned from the simple echo server in Chapter 2, TCP: Exploring the Basics, on page 9, and build on top of it. Let's create our connection acceptor.

Our acceptor process needs to accept incoming TCP connections, just like the acceptor in the previous chapter. But we'll do things a little differently this time around: we'll *supervise* client connections. This is for a couple of reasons. First and foremost, we want to isolate failures in the processes that handle connections. If one of them crashes, we don't want the acceptor process to exit just because it's linked to it. The other reason to involve a supervisor is to have clean shutdowns. When our application stops, having a supervisor gracefully terminate its children means that we have a chance to drain open connections. We won't do that right away, but it's good to know.

One caveat of using a supervisor in a case like this is that we want to prevent the supervisor from restarting children that crash or terminate gracefully. Once a connection-handling process terminates, the server should not reconnect to the client—the supervisor should just let it go. To achieve this, we'll use the restart: :temporary option for our connection-handling GenServers.

The right supervisor to use for our situation is Elixir's DynamicSupervisor, which is meant to supervise a dynamic number of children—exactly what we want here. Let's see it in action in the code for our acceptor GenServer. We'll look only at the init/1 and handle_info/2 callbacks.

chat/lib/chat/acceptor.ex

```
Line 1   defstruct [:listen_socket, :supervisor]

         @impl true
         def init(options) do
      5    port = Keyword.fetch!(options, :port)

           listen_options = [
             :binary,
             active: :once,
     10      exit_on_close: false,
             reuseaddr: true,
             backlog: 25
           ]

           {:ok, sup} = DynamicSupervisor.start_link(max_children: 20)

           case :gen_tcp.listen(port, listen_options) do
     20      {:ok, listen_socket} ->
               Logger.info("Started chat server on port #{port}")
               send(self(), :accept)
               {:ok, %__MODULE__{listen_socket: listen_socket, supervisor: sup}}

             {:error, reason} ->
               {:stop, reason}
           end
     30   end
```

In the preceding code, we started the dynamic supervisor and gave it a limited number of maximum children. This is an additional security measure to make sure we don't spawn an uncontrolled number of connection-handling processes (even though we'd likely run out of OS sockets first). We're also storing the supervisor in the state so that we can use it later to start connection processes.

The :backlog option (line 12) is a useful addition here. By default, when you use :gen_tcp.accept/2, a :gen_tcp listen socket queues only five clients waiting to be accepted. If more clients attempt to connect, they'll be refused. The number of clients that can wait in the queue is controlled by the :backlog option. For now, we're bumping this to 25. Using this option will matter less later when we accept connections in parallel from multiple processes.

Now, let's look at the handle_info/2 callback, where we handle the internal :accept message and implement our accept loop.

chat/lib/chat/acceptor.ex
```
Line 1  @impl true
   -    def handle_info(:accept, %__MODULE__{} = state) do
   -      case :gen_tcp.accept(state.listen_socket, 2_000) do
   -        {:ok, socket} ->
   5          {:ok, pid} =
   -            DynamicSupervisor.start_child(
   -              state.supervisor,
   -              {Chat.Connection, socket}
   -            )
  10
   -          :ok = :gen_tcp.controlling_process(socket, pid)
   -          send(self(), :accept)
   -          {:noreply, state}
   -
  15        {:error, :timeout} ->
   -          send(self(), :accept)
   -          {:noreply, state}
   -
   -        {:error, reason} ->
  20          {:stop, reason, state}
   -      end
   -    end
```

In this code, on line 6, we start every connection-handling process under the dynamic supervisor. DynamicSupervisor.start_child/2 returns the started child's PID, which we can use to change the socket's controlling process (line 11). We don't want our supervisor to restart the connection-handling processes, regardless of whether they finished or crashed, so we'll use :temporary as the restart strategy when implementing Chat.Connection. Next, let's start the acceptor in our application supervisor.

chat/lib/chat/application.ex
```
children = [
  {Chat.Acceptor, port: 4000}
]
```

We're now ready to start writing our connection-handling code in Chat.Connection.

Registering Clients

In this section, we'll write code to handle register messages from clients. The first thing we'll do is write some code to handle any TCP data that the server receives.

chat/lib/chat/connection.ex
```
Line 1  defmodule Chat.Connection do
  -       use GenServer, restart: :temporary
  -
  -       @spec start_link(:gen_tcp.socket()) :: GenServer.on_start()
  5       def start_link(socket) do
  -         GenServer.start_link(__MODULE__, socket)
  -       end
  -
  -       defstruct [:socket, :username, buffer: <<>>]
  10
  -       @impl true
  -       def init(socket) do
  -         {:ok, %__MODULE__{socket: socket}}
  -       end
  15
  -       @impl true
  -       def handle_info(message, state)
  -
  -       def handle_info(
  20            {:tcp, socket, data},
  -             %__MODULE__{socket: socket} = state
  -           ) do
  -         state = update_in(state.buffer, &(&1 <> data))
  -         :ok = :inet.setopts(socket, active: :once)
  25            handle_new_data(state)
  -       end
  -
  -       ## Helpers
  -
  30      defp handle_new_data(state) do
  -         case Chat.Protocol.decode_message(state.buffer) do
  -           {:ok, message, rest} ->
  -             state = put_in(state.buffer, rest)
  -
  35             case handle_message(message, state) do
  -               {:ok, state} -> handle_new_data(state)
  -               :error -> {:stop, :normal, state}
  -             end
```

```
40        :incomplete ->
            {:noreply, state}

          :error ->
            Logger.error("Received invalid data, closing connection")
45          {:stop, :normal, state}
        end
      end
    end
```

This initial code is similar to the connection-handling code in Chapter 2, TCP: Exploring the Basics, on page 9. As promised, we're using restart: :temporary (line 2) to ensure that these processes never get restarted by their dynamic supervisor. The real difference from the similar code in the previous chapter is in how we write the handle_message/2 function called on line 35. Our protocol specification from Specifying Our Chat Binary Protocol, on page 36, says that a register message *must* be the first message that clients send after connecting. We can enforce this by looking at the :username field at the start of the connection. If it's nil, which is the starting value, then we know that the client didn't send a register message yet—otherwise, we know it's an invalid register message. That's what we're doing in the next piece of code.

chat/lib/chat/connection.ex
```
Line 1  defp handle_message(
            %Register{username: username},
            %__MODULE__{username: nil} = state
          ) do
5      {:ok, put_in(state.username, username)}
      end

      defp handle_message(%Register{}, _state) do
        Logger.error("Invalid Register message, had already received one")
10      :error
      end
```

We now have a basic server that can accept connections and register clients.

Let's hop into a new file and write a basic test for the error case on line 10.

chat/test/chat/integration_test.exs
```
defmodule ChatTest do
  use ExUnit.Case, async: true

  import Chat.Protocol

  alias Chat.Message.{Broadcast, Register}

  test "server closes connection if client sends register message twice" do
❶    {:ok, client} = :gen_tcp.connect(~c"localhost", 4000, [:binary])
❷    encoded_message = encode_message(%Register{username: "jd"})
```

```
❸      :ok = :gen_tcp.send(client, encoded_message)

       log =
         ExUnit.CaptureLog.capture_log(fn ->
❹          :ok = :gen_tcp.send(client, encoded_message)
❺          assert_receive {:tcp_closed, ^client}, 500
         end)

❻      assert log =~ "Invalid Register message"
     end
   end
```

❶ We start a new connection to the server to simulate a client connection.

❷ We create a new register message and encode it to iodata.

❸ We send this message first, which is what a well-behaved client must do.

❹ We send the same register message again, which is invalid behavior.

❺ We assert that the server closes the connection.

❻ We also assert that the server logs the right message.

Fantastic. Let's move on to implementing support for broadcast messages.

Broadcasting

When we get a broadcast message from a client, we need to broadcast it to all other connected clients. But how do we know who the other connected clients are? A possible approach is to get all the current connection processes through the dynamic supervisor, using DynamicSupervisor.which_children/1. It works, but the approach leaves something to be desired. In fact, we'd only be able to get *all the connected* clients but not do things like get the process for a specific client identified by its username. This means, for example, we wouldn't be able to implement direct messages.

A perfect tool for this job is Elixir's Registry.[11] A registry is essentially a key-value process table. You can register processes in a given registry under a key and store some additional values under that key. You can then use functions in the Registry module to look up processes by key, dispatch messages to all processes under a key, and more. The registry takes care of cleaning up processes that stop, regardless of whether they stop gracefully. For now, we'll register all processes under the key :broadcast, which will allow us to implement pub/sub-like dispatching. We'll also start another registry to check for username uniqueness. By registering

---

11. https://hexdocs.pm/elixir/Registry.html

each client process under its username as the key, we'll guarantee that no two users can use the same username.

Using Registry to Check for Uniqueness

 We could have used other tools to check username uniqueness in our code. For example, an Agent[12] would have provided an alternative global storage to store usernames and check for uniqueness. A set ETS table would have also done the job, and likely faster than an agent. The true advantage of using a registry here is that it's tailored to be a process registry, with features such as monitoring the registered processes and de-registering them if they exit. This is perfect for our use case: we don't have to worry about the usernames of users who disconnect being taken. As soon as a connection drops and its connection-handling process exits, the username key gets freed up in the registry and is ready to be taken by another user.

The first thing to do is start the two global registries in the supervision tree of our application. Registries need to have a unique name, so we'll go with Chat.BroadcastRegistry and Chat.UsernameRegistry here.

chat/lib/chat/application.ex
```
children = [
  {Registry, keys: :duplicate, name: Chat.BroadcastRegistry},
  {Registry, keys: :unique, name: Chat.UsernameRegistry},
  {Chat.Acceptor, port: 4000}
]
```

We used the keys: :duplicate option for our broadcast registry so that we can register multiple processes under the same key (:broadcast). For the username registry, we instead had to use the keys: :unique option, since its whole point is to have *unique* usernames registered under it.

We can move on to registering connection processes once they receive a register message from the connected client. We'll modify our existing handle_message/2 helper function to add two calls to Registry.register/3.[13] Registry.register/3 registers the PID of the current process (self()) under the given key. Registries also support storing a *value* associated with each PID-key pair, but in this case we don't have anything to store there, so we went with the atom :no_value.

chat/lib/chat/connection.ex
```
defp handle_message(
```

---

12. https://hexdocs.pm/elixir/Agent.html
13. https://hexdocs.pm/elixir/Registry.html#register/3

```
2        %Register{username: username},
3          %__MODULE__{username: nil} = state
4        ) do
6      {:ok, _} = Registry.register(BroadcastRegistry, :broadcast, :no_value)
7      {:ok, _} = Registry.register(UsernameRegistry, username, :no_value)
9      {:ok, put_in(state.username, username)}
10   end
```

On line 6, we are directly matching on the {:ok, _} return value for the Registry.register/3 call. We're taking a shortcut here. In production code, you should handle this possible case by doing something like sending an error to the user and giving them a chance to try a different username. But that would introduce unneeded complexity in our case, so let's have the connection crash altogether and not worry too much.

We can now handle incoming Chat.Message.Broadcast messages from clients.

chat/lib/chat/connection.ex
```
Line 1  defp handle_message(%Broadcast{}, %__MODULE__{username: nil}) do
   -      Logger.error("Invalid Broadcast message, had not received a Register")
   -      :error
   -    end
5
   -    defp handle_message(%Broadcast{} = message, state) do
   -      sender = self()
   -      message = %Broadcast{message | from_username: state.username}
   -
10        Registry.dispatch(BroadcastRegistry, :broadcast, fn entries ->
   -        Enum.each(entries, fn {pid, _value} ->
   -          if pid != sender do
   -            send(pid, {:broadcast, message})
   -          end
15        end)
   -      end)
   -
   -      {:ok, state}
   -    end
```

The first clause (line 1) handles the case when a client misbehaves by sending a broadcast message before sending the register message. The second clause (line 6) is where we do the broadcasting. Let's take a closer look:

1. On line 8, we add the username of the current connection to the message we're going to dispatch to all connected clients

2. Then, on line 10, we call the Registry.dispatch/3 function to invoke a callback function for processes under the key :broadcast

3. We want to avoid broadcasting to the client that sent the broadcast message in the first place, so we make sure that we don't send to self() (line 12)

4. To broadcast the message, we send a {:broadcast, message} Erlang message (that's a lot of times using the word "message"!) to each connection-handling process on line 13

Now we need to handle the {:broadcast, message} message. Remember that the code in Chat.Connection runs in every connection-handling process, so Chat.Connection is where we want to define the handle_info/2 callback to handle this message. Let's do that next.

chat/lib/chat/connection.ex
```elixir
def handle_info({:broadcast, %Broadcast{} = message}, state) do
  encoded_message = Chat.Protocol.encode_message(message)
  :ok = :gen_tcp.send(state.socket, encoded_message)
  {:noreply, state}
end
```

Piece of cake! In just a couple of lines, we're re-encoding the broadcast message and sending it to the socket in the state with :gen_tcp.send/2. This works because the processes that run this code are all the connection-handling processes, each holding the socket to the connected client in their state. Let's take a moment to write a test to make sure our broadcasting functionality works as expected.

chat/test/chat/integration_test.exs
```elixir
Line 1  test "broadcasting messages" do
          client_jd = connect_user("jd")
          client_amy = connect_user("amy")
          client_bern = connect_user("bern")

     5    # TODO: remove once we'll have "welcome" messages.
          Process.sleep(100)

          # Simulate Amy sending a message.
    10    broadcast_message = %Broadcast{from_username: "", contents: "hi"}
          encoded_message = encode_message(broadcast_message)
          :ok = :gen_tcp.send(client_amy, encoded_message)

          # Assert that Amy doesn't receive the message.
    15    refute_receive {:tcp, ^client_amy, _data}

          # Assert that the other clients receive the message.
          assert_receive {:tcp, ^client_jd, data}, 500
          assert {:ok, msg, ""} = decode_message(data)
    20    assert msg == %Broadcast{from_username: "amy", contents: "hi"}

          assert_receive {:tcp, ^client_bern, data}, 500
          assert {:ok, msg, ""} = decode_message(data)
          assert msg == %Broadcast{from_username: "amy", contents: "hi"}
    25  end
```

```
      defp connect_user(username) do
        {:ok, socket} = :gen_tcp.connect(~c"localhost", 4000, [:binary])
        register_message = %Register{username: username}
30      encoded_message = encode_message(register_message)
        :ok = :gen_tcp.send(socket, encoded_message)
        socket
      end
```

The connect_user/1 helper function (line 27) helps us avoid repetition when setting up a new connection to simulate a user. The rest of the test goes like this:

1. We connect three users
2. We have one of the users (Amy) send a broadcast message
3. We assert that the other two users get that message

It looks like our broadcasting functionality works. That's all we wanted our server to do, so we're ready to work on a better interface for clients.

Chatting with Clients

In this chapter, we won't dive too deep into building reliable, scalable TCP clients. Instead, we'll write a simple terminal-based interface for our chat server, just to see it working in real time. To reuse our protocol code (in Chat.Protocol), we'll build the client right inside the chat project we worked on throughout this chapter. It'll be somewhat of a hack, but we'll write our client as a Mix task. Hop into a new file and let's get started.

chat/lib/mix/tasks/chat_client.ex
```
defmodule Mix.Tasks.ChatClient do
  use Mix.Task

  import Chat.Protocol

  alias Chat.Message.{Broadcast, Register}

end
```

We're starting out with a new Mix task, which by convention we place in the lib/mix/tasks directory. Mix tasks have to define a run/1 function that takes the command-line arguments:

chat/lib/mix/tasks/chat_client.ex
```
Line 1  def run([] = _args) do
          {:ok, socket} =
            :gen_tcp.connect(~c"localhost", 4000, [:binary, active: :once])

     5    user = Mix.shell().prompt("Enter your username:") |> String.trim()

          :ok = :gen_tcp.send(socket, encode_message(%Register{username: user}))

          receive_loop(user, socket, spawn_prompt_task(user))
```

```
10   end

     defp spawn_prompt_task(username) do
       Task.async(fn -> Mix.shell().prompt("#{username}# ") end)
     end
```

Our task doesn't accept any arguments (by matching on the empty list []). You could modify this to take command-line options to select a hostname and port for the server to connect to, but for the sake of our example we're hard-coding those to ~c"localhost" and 4000. If you want to modify the code to take options, have a look at the OptionParser module[14] in the Elixir standard library.

Back to our code. After establishing a TCP connection on line 3, we prompt the user for their username (line 5) and send the initial register message to the server. We then enter our receive loop. The spawn_prompt_task/1 function that we call on line 9 spawns an Elixir task, which prompts the user for a message. We have to do this in a separate process; otherwise, the main process would block waiting for user input and wouldn't be able to receive and display TCP data. Let's look at receive_loop/3 next.

chat/lib/mix/tasks/chat_client.ex
```
Line 1   defp receive_loop(username, socket, %Task{ref: ref} = prompt_task) do
           receive do
             # Task result, which is the contents of the message typed by the user.
             {^ref, message} ->
 5             broadcast = %Broadcast{from_username: username, contents: message}
               :ok = :gen_tcp.send(socket, encode_message(broadcast))
               receive_loop(username, socket, spawn_prompt_task(username))

             {:DOWN, ^ref, _, _, _} ->
10             Mix.raise("Prompt task exited unexpectedly")

             {:tcp, ^socket, data} ->
               :ok = :inet.setopts(socket, active: :once)
               handle_data(data)
15             receive_loop(username, socket, prompt_task)

             {:tcp_closed, ^socket} ->
               IO.puts("Server closed the connection")

20           {:tcp_error, ^socket, reason} ->
               Mix.raise("TCP error: #{inspect(reason)}")
           end
         end
```

We're using receive to receive messages. We handle five messages:

---

14. https://hexdocs.pm/elixir/OptionParser.html

1. Task replies, in the form {ref, reply} (line 4). These messages mean that the user typed something in the prompt, so we send a broadcast message to the server with its contents, then spawn a new prompt task and go back to the loop.

2. :DOWN messages from the prompt task (line 9). These mean something likely went wrong with the task, so we exit with an error message.

3. TCP data (line 12). We hand this over to handle_data/1, set the :active option back to :once as we have done in other cases, and go back to the loop.

4. TCP closed messages. These mean the server closed the connection (line 17). We print a message and exit gracefully.

5. TCP socket errors (line 20). We print these out before exiting with an error.

The last missing piece in our client is the handle_data/1 function. For the sake of keeping our client simple, we're not going to do any real error handling or data buffering here, so this function is very concise.

chat/lib/mix/tasks/chat_client.ex
```elixir
defp handle_data(data) do
  case decode_message(data) do
    {:ok, %Broadcast{} = message, ""} ->
      IO.puts("\n#{message.from_username}> #{message.contents}")

    _other ->
      Mix.raise(
        "Expected a complete broadcast message and nothing else, " <>
          "got: #{inspect(data)}"
      )
  end
end
```

We're using Chat.Protocol.decode_message/1 and only handling the case where the data contains a single, well-formed broadcast message, which we print to the terminal. In any other case, such as protocol errors or incomplete data, we raise an error. We're now done with our client. To see it in action, open a couple of terminal windows and start the client in each one with mix chat_client. Remember to have the server running in another window for this to work, which you can do with mix run --no-halt.

In the first window, where you ran mix chat_client, you'll see something like this:

```
⟨ Enter your username:
⇒ Andrea
⟨ Andrea#
```

In the second window, where you ran mix chat_client, try another username:

```
‹  Enter your username:
⇒  José
‹  José#
⇒  Hello friends!
```

You should see the message "Hello friends!" show up in the first window.

Wrapping Up

You have a working chat system on your hands! We built a functional chat server capable of distributing messages to clients, and we also built clients that can interact with this server. We had the chance to explore binary and textual protocols, the iodata data structure, registry-based routing, and asynchronous message handling.

But our chat system is not a particularly robust or scalable one. For that, we'll have to look at some design patterns and strategies to make use of BEAM features and kick our server's scalability into high gear. That's what the next chapter is about.

## CHAPTER 4

Scaling TCP on the Server Side

By now, you have a foundational understanding of TCP, serialization protocols, and how to build TCP servers capable of handling multiple concurrent clients. But the code for the TCP server in the previous chapter is not production-grade. Real-world TCP servers need to be able to scale up and be resilient to failures. That's what we'll work on in this chapter. You'll learn the final shape of a TCP-server supervision tree. Finally, we'll turn our gaze to the Elixir ecosystem, taking a look at how you can use existing libraries to implement your TCP servers instead of doing it from scratch.

Increasing Scalability with Multiple Acceptors

Up until now, we've always had just one process accepting connections in a loop. This works for the simple use case where there are only a handful of connected clients at a time, but it's not how you'd write a production-grade TCP server on the BEAM. :gen_tcp.accept/2 can in fact be called by multiple processes simultaneously, which increases the possible throughput of accepted connections by introducing some concurrency. When accepting connections, most Elixir and Erlang TCP servers use a pattern commonly referred to as an *acceptor pool*—a set of running processes, each waiting on a :gen_tcp.accept/2 call. When using the acceptor pool pattern, a TCP server's flow is as follows:

1. An initial process calls :gen_tcp.listen/3 to start listening for TCP connections on an address and port combination

2. The listener process starts a pool of acceptor processes, passing the same newly created listen socket to each of them

3. Each acceptor process calls :gen_tcp.accept/2 and spawns a connection-handling process when a client connects, similar to what our Chat.Acceptor does but with multiple acceptors

The following figure is a visual representation of this same set of steps:

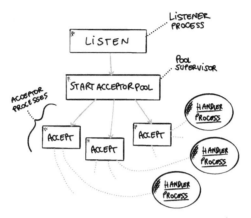

We won't need to make too many changes to our code to implement the acceptor pool pattern. We'll have to split up our Chat.Acceptor process into a single listener process and a pool of acceptor processes. As you learned earlier in this chapter, it's a good idea to supervise OTP processes when possible, so we'll also introduce a new supervisor to supervise the acceptor pool processes, as well as a TCP supervisor to supervise the socket-related processes of our application. We'll discuss all the components of the new supervision tree in this section, but let's start by looking at an overview of the tree:

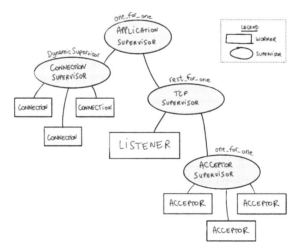

In order to keep the code from previous sections around, we'll stick all the new code in this section under the Chat.AcceptorPool namespace.

Let's start with the new top-level application supervisor.

chat/lib/chat/acceptor_pool/application.ex

```
Line 1  def start(_type, _args) do
   -      children = [
   -        {Registry, keys: :duplicate, name: Chat.BroadcastRegistry},
   -        {Registry, keys: :unique, name: Chat.UsernameRegistry},
   5        {Chat.AcceptorPool.ConnectionSupervisor, []},
   -        {Chat.AcceptorPool.TCPSupervisor, port: 4000}
   -      ]
   -
   -      opts = [strategy: :one_for_one, name: Chat.Supervisor]
   10     Supervisor.start_link(children, opts)
   -    end
```

On line 3, we still start the broadcast registry from the previous section. We also start the supervisor for connection-handling processes (line 5) and the parent supervisor for the TCP-acceptor part of our application (line 6). The order of children under a supervisor matters, since the supervisor starts the children in that order. In this case, we put the connection supervisor first, because we want it to be already available when our TCP acceptors begin accepting connections. This approach works here, because connections have a :temporary restart strategy, so we don't expect the connection supervisor to ever crash.

The code for the connection supervisor itself is short and sweet. It's a dynamic supervisor, just like the one we used in code/chat/lib/chat/acceptor.ex in the previous section.

chat/lib/chat/acceptor_pool/connection_supervisor.ex

```
Line 1  defmodule Chat.AcceptorPool.ConnectionSupervisor do
   -      use DynamicSupervisor
   -
   -      @spec start_link(keyword()) :: Supervisor.on_start()
   5      def start_link(options) do
   -        DynamicSupervisor.start_link(__MODULE__, options, name: __MODULE__)
   -      end
   -
   -      @spec start_connection(:gen_tcp.socket()) :: Supervisor.on_start()
   10     def start_connection(socket) do
   -        DynamicSupervisor.start_child(__MODULE__, {Chat.Connection, socket})
   -      end
   -
   -      @impl true
   15     def init(_options) do
   -        DynamicSupervisor.init(strategy: :one_for_one)
   -      end
   -    end
```

We register the connection supervisor with the name Chat.AcceptorPool.Connection-Supervisor (line 6) so that we can start connections under it from anywhere in our application without having to know its PID. We also added the public start_connection/1 function (line 10) to have an easy-to-call API. As you can see, we start Chat.Connection processes under this supervisor—the exact same processes we used in the previous section.

Let's look at the TCP supervisor next.

chat/lib/chat/acceptor_pool/tcp_supervisor.ex

```
defmodule Chat.AcceptorPool.TCPSupervisor do
  use Supervisor

  @spec start_link(keyword()) :: Supervisor.on_start()
  def start_link(options) do
    Supervisor.start_link(__MODULE__, options)
  end

  @impl true
  def init(options) do
    children = [
      {Chat.AcceptorPool.Listener, {options, self()}}
    ]

    Supervisor.init(children, strategy: :rest_for_one)
  end
end
```

The code for this supervisor does something seemingly different from what we showed in the supervision tree diagram: the only child is the listener process, Chat.AcceptorPool.Listener. There is no acceptor supervisor child (line 12). This is because it doesn't make sense to start a pool of acceptor processes if we don't have a TCP listen socket just yet. We'll start the acceptor supervisor from the listener process once we have a listen socket returned by :gen_tcp.listen/2. We'll look at that in a second, but an important thing to explain here is the :rest_for_one strategy we're using on line 15. When a supervisor uses this strategy and a child crashes, the supervisor shuts down all the children *after* that child under the supervisor and restarts them in the original order. This strategy expresses a useful dependency between children—exactly the dependency we have in our case. Our acceptor supervisor (and acceptor pool) depends on the listener process being alive. If the listener crashes, we lose the TCP listen socket and can't accept new connections. But we don't need to restart the listener if the acceptor supervisor crashes—if we did, we would've had to use the :one_for_all strategy instead.

Next is the code for the listener process.

chat/lib/chat/acceptor_pool/listener.ex

```
Line 1  defmodule Chat.AcceptorPool.Listener do
          use GenServer, restart: :transient

          alias Chat.AcceptorPool.AcceptorSupervisor
5
          require Logger

          @spec start_link(keyword()) :: GenServer.on_start()
          def start_link({options, supervisor}) do
10          GenServer.start_link(__MODULE__, {options, supervisor})
          end

          @impl true
          def init({options, supervisor}) do
15          port = Keyword.fetch!(options, :port)

            listen_options = [
              :binary,
              active: :once,
20            exit_on_close: false,
              reuseaddr: true
            ]

            case :gen_tcp.listen(port, listen_options) do
25            {:ok, listen_socket} ->
                Logger.info("Started pooled chat server on port #{port}")
                state = {listen_socket, supervisor}
                {:ok, state, {:continue, :start_acceptor_pool}}

30            {:error, reason} ->
                {:stop, {:listen_error, reason}}
            end
          end

35        @impl true
          def handle_continue(:start_acceptor_pool, {listen_socket, supervisor}) do
            spec = {AcceptorSupervisor, listen_socket: listen_socket}
            {:ok, _} = Supervisor.start_child(supervisor, spec)

40          {:noreply, {listen_socket, supervisor}}
          end
        end
```

Most of the init/1 callback is similar to our old Chat.Acceptor process from earlier in this chapter, but there are two main differences. The first is that the argument we use to start the listener is now {options, supervisor}, where supervisor is the PID of the TCP supervisor. We use this to start the acceptor supervisor under the TCP supervisor, which we do on line 38. The second difference is that now we're using the *continue* feature of GenServers (line 28). This feature allows us to return from the init/1 callback, which tells the parent supervisor that this GenServer has finished initialization and lets us move on to something else right away. This eliminates the chance of other messages coming to the GenServer before it can start the acceptor pool. The other part of the continue feature is the aptly named handle_continue/2 callback on line 36, where we start the acceptor supervisor.

The code for the acceptor supervisor itself is quite concise. Let's go through it.

chat/lib/chat/acceptor_pool/acceptor_supervisor.ex

```
Line 1   defmodule Chat.AcceptorPool.AcceptorSupervisor do
           use Supervisor

           @spec start_link(keyword()) :: Supervisor.on_start()
    5      def start_link(options) do
             Supervisor.start_link(__MODULE__, options)
           end

           @impl true
   10      def init(options) do
             pool_size = Keyword.get(options, :pool_size, 10)
             listen_socket = Keyword.fetch!(options, :listen_socket)

             children =
   15          for index <- 1..pool_size do
                 spec = {Chat.AcceptorPool.Acceptor, listen_socket}
                 Supervisor.child_spec(spec, id: "acceptor-#{index}")
               end

   20        Supervisor.init(children, strategy: :one_for_one)
           end
         end
```

It's a pretty standard supervisor. In the init/1 callback, we start by reading the :pool_size option and getting the listen socket (lines 11 and 12). We then use the pool size to create that number of Chat.AcceptorPool.Acceptor children (code/chat/lib/chat/acceptor_pool/acceptor.ex) in the for comprehension on line 15, passing the listen socket to each acceptor. A peculiar thing to pay attention to here is the call to Supervisor.child_spec/2 on line 17. We *have to* use that because children under a single supervisor must have different child IDs. If we just used {Chat.AcceptorPool.Acceptor, listen_socket} for the child specifications, we'd have a bunch of children with the same ID. Instead, we use acceptor-<index> as the unique ID for each child. The last thing to mention here is the supervisor's strategy, which is :one_for_one. This is a sensible choice here, since acceptors are independent from each other and an acceptor crashing shouldn't affect other acceptors.

Wow, we just went through all the components of our updated supervision tree. Each was only a handful of lines of code, but there is some complexity in juggling all of them in their different files. So, congratulations on making it to the end!

Sketching Supervision Trees

 When designing non-trivial supervision trees like the one we're dealing with here, I always sketch the supervision tree before writing any code. Having a visual reference makes things significantly easier for me. This is especially true because it's harder to "see" the supervision tree structure by just looking at code and files. I recommend you always do the same.

To validate the changes we made to the architecture of our application, we'll do two things: run tests and verify our supervision tree.

To run tests, we only have to change what supervision tree is the top-level tree in our application. We don't have to modify the tests themselves, which is a testament to the fact that the changes we made were only architectural and not functional. The trick we'll use here is a system-environment variable to determine which application callback module to start in mix.exs. This is what we do in the following code. For now, don't mind the THOUSAND_ISLAND environment variable—we'll use it for similar purposes later in this chapter.

chat/mix.exs
```
def application do
  [
    extra_applications: [:logger],
➤   mod: application_mod()
  ]
end

defp application_mod do
  cond do
    System.get_env("POOL") ->
      {Chat.AcceptorPool.Application, []}

    System.get_env("THOUSAND_ISLAND") ->
      {Chat.ThousandIsland.Application, []}

    true ->
      {Chat.Application, []}
  end
end
```

Now we can run tests with the following:

```
> POOL=true mix test
Generated chat app
```

```
08:44:45.925 [info] Started pooled chat server on port 4000
........
Finished in 0.2 seconds (0.2s async, 0.00s sync)
8 tests, 0 failures

Randomized with seed 934120
```

The other way to verify that we correctly implemented the supervision tree we designed is to use Erlang's Observer,[1] a graphical tool for visually exploring a running BEAM system. To use it, you'll first need to make sure that your Erlang version was compiled with wxWidgets[2] support. Then, add these applications to :extra_applications in your mix.exs file:

```
def application do
  [
-   extra_applications: [:logger],
+   extra_applications: [:logger, :runtime_tools, :wx, :observer],
    mod: application_mod()
  ]
end
```

Now let's start our system with a shell open and use Observer to look at the supervision tree.

```
> POOL=true iex -S mix
iex> :observer.start()
:ok
```

This session should open an Observer window. If you navigate to the Applications tab and click on the chat app on the left-hand side, you should see our supervision tree (arrows and notes added for emphasis), as shown in the screenshot on page 67.

We can recognize the exact same structure we sketched out at the beginning of this section. Fantastic.

This concludes our server-side efforts. Before wrapping up, let's look at how we can use ecosystem libraries to abstract away most of the lower-level complexity in managing connections and pooling.

Rewriting the Server with Thousand Island

Both Elixir and Erlang have well-made, fast, and reliable libraries that provide ways to build scalable TCP servers. In this section, we'll look at Thousand

---

1. https://www.erlang.org/doc/man/observer.html
2. https://www.wxwidgets.org/

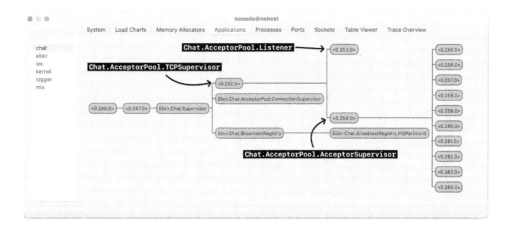

Island,[3] a pure-Elixir socket server. Thousand Island powers the Elixir web server Bandit.[4] Let's start by modifying our mix.exs to include Thousand Island as a dependency.

chat/mix.exs
```
defp deps do
  [{:thousand_island, "~> 1.3"}]
end
```

We're using the version requirement ~> 0.6.4 here because 0.6.4 is the latest version available on Hex[5] at the time of writing.

Thousand Island abstracts the TCP acceptor pooling code we wrote earlier in this chapter, providing an easy way to build reliable, scalable, and highly performant TCP servers. The core component you work on when using Thousand Island is the *handler*, a module that implements the ThousandIsland.Handler behavior. Its job is essentially to handle connections, similarly to what our Chat.Connection process did but without the lower-level details of the TCP connection handling. The ThousandIsland.Handler behavior defines callbacks that correspond to events that happen during the life cycle of the connection, such as data coming from the socket, errors with the connection, and so on.

We'll use the same trick we saw when we worked on the acceptor pool and put all the modules in this section under the Chat.ThousandIsland namespace. Let's write a handler to replace the Chat.Connection process, which we'll call

3.   https://github.com/mtrudel/thousand_island
4.   https://github.com/mtrudel/bandit
5.   https://hex.pm/packages/thousand_island

Chat.ThousandIsland.Handler, starting with a couple of callbacks defined by the ThousandIsland.Handler behavior.

chat/lib/chat/thousand_island/handler.ex

```
defmodule Chat.ThousandIsland.Handler do
  use ThousandIsland.Handler

  defstruct [:username, buffer: <<>>]

  @impl ThousandIsland.Handler
  def handle_connection(_socket, [] = _options) do
    {:continue, %__MODULE__{}}
  end

  @impl ThousandIsland.Handler
  def handle_data(data, _socket, state) do
    state = update_in(state.buffer, &(&1 <> data))
    handle_new_data(state)
  end
end
```

The first callback is handle_connection/2 on line 7. Thousand Island calls this when a new connection is established. Its first argument is a ThousandIsland.Socket struct, which is a thin wrapper around a :gen_tcp (or SSL) socket. The second argument is a list of options you can pass down when starting the server, as we'll see later on, but here we're not passing any. In this callback, we're just returning an empty state using %__MODULE__{}. The {:continue, state} return value tells Thousand Island to keep the connection open.

The second callback is handle_data/3 on line 12. This is called whenever new data comes from the socket. The first argument is the new data, the second is the socket, and the third is the state. In our implementation, we append the new data to the buffer in the state and then call handle_new_data/1, which is almost identical to the version in Chat.Connection.

chat/lib/chat/thousand_island/handler.ex

```
defp handle_new_data(state) do
  case Chat.Protocol.decode_message(state.buffer) do
    {:ok, message, rest} ->
      state = put_in(state.buffer, rest)

      case handle_message(message, state) do
        {:ok, state} -> handle_new_data(state)
        :error -> {:close, state}
      end

    :incomplete ->
      {:continue, state}

    :error ->
```

```
15        Logger.error("Received invalid data, closing connection")
          {:close, state}
      end
  end

20  # «handle_message/2 definition»
```

The only change is that we return slightly different values than the ones we used in Chat.Connection. When we want to keep the connection alive, we return {:continue, state} (line 12). When we want to close the connection, we return {:close, state} (lines 8 and 16). We won't look at the definition for handle_message/2, which we call on line 6, since it's identical to the one in Chat.Connection.

Something to know about Thousand Island handlers is that they're also GenServers, which means we can define all the GenServer callbacks we want. In our case, we'll define handle_info/2 to handle those {:broadcast, message} messages, as we did in Chat.Connection. Let's see that next.

chat/lib/chat/thousand_island/handler.ex
```
Line 1  @impl GenServer
2  def handle_info({:broadcast, %Broadcast{} = message}, {socket, state}) do
3    encoded_message = Chat.Protocol.encode_message(message)
4    :ok = ThousandIsland.Socket.send(socket, encoded_message)
5    {:noreply, {socket, state}}
6  end
```

When you define GenServer callbacks in a Thousand Island handler, Thousand Island passes the state as {socket, state}, which is what we need to return as well (line 5). Instead of using :gen_tcp.send/2 directly, we use the wrapper ThousandIsland.Socket.send/2 here (line 4).

That does it for our handler. You can see the library abstracting the lower-level network details in it. There's no need to deal with :gen_tcp messages or manage TCP sockets: Thousand Island takes care of all that, letting us focus on our business logic. The only thing left to get this working is start a Thousand Island server in our application's supervision tree. We'll use a different application module, just as we did for the acceptor pool earlier in the chapter.

chat/lib/chat/thousand_island/application.ex
```
Line 1  @impl true
  def start(_type, _args) do
    children = [
      {Registry, keys: :duplicate, name: Chat.BroadcastRegistry},
5     {Registry, keys: :unique, name: Chat.UsernameRegistry},
      {ThousandIsland,
       port: 4000,
       handler_module: Chat.ThousandIsland.Handler}
    ]
```

```
      opts = [strategy: :one_for_one, name: Chat.Supervisor]
      Supervisor.start_link(children, opts)
15  end
```

We start the two registries like we did in Chat.AcceptorPool.Application. The difference is on line 6, where we pass ThousandIsland as a child of our supervisor. The options are self-explanatory: :port specifies the port to listen for connections on, while :handler_module tells Thousand Island which callback module to use for handling connections. We can verify that the behavior of our server stayed the same by running tests against the new supervision tree.

```
> THOUSAND_ISLAND=true mix test
Generated chat app
........
Finished in 0.2 seconds (0.2s async, 0.00s sync)
8 tests, 0 failures

Randomized with seed 93200
```

Still works. Congratulations!

Homework

 Take a look again—and with fresh eyes—at the Chat.Connection module from Chapter 3, Designing a Chat Protocol and Its TCP Server, on page 33, to see how it compares with this new Thousand Island version.

Libraries such as Thousand Island can help you get away from a lot of the complexity of working with TCP (or TLS/SSL, for that matter, as we'll see later in the book). They also get a lot of corner cases right, letting you focus on the logic specific to your application.

Wrapping Up

It took some time to cover all the pieces of a TCP server, but we wrote everything from scratch, using only standard-library components. We now have a resilient, concurrent system with a relatively small amount of code. That is a remarkable feat of the BEAM.

Awesome job getting to the end of our journey across TCP servers! We started the previous chapter with an overview of different kinds of network protocols, focusing on the difference between binary and textual protocols, then coming up with a protocol of our own. We then wrote a TCP-based chat server using only tools from the Elixir and Erlang standard libraries, and we threw together a client for that as well. In this chapter, we made our server more scalable by building a TCP acceptor pool. Finally, we used a library called Thousand Island to simplify the task of building TCP servers.

In these past few chapters, we laid many of the foundations that we will use throughout the rest of the book. It was worth taking the time to go through binary protocols, registries, pooling, and more, since you will encounter most of those again at some point. TCP is also likely the most commonly used network protocol out there, so understanding how it works is a great investment.

After spending a lot of time on the server side of TCP, we'll explore advanced techniques for building TCP clients in the next chapters.

## CHAPTER 5

Building TCP Clients

So far, we've mostly focused on the server side of TCP. But chances are you'll end up writing your fair share of TCP clients as well. Sometimes, those clients will even end up as part of your server application. For example, many modern web applications run both sides of TCP within the same application. On the server side, you have your HTTP server accepting client connections and requests. That web server often connects to a database of some sort to retrieve data, and those database connections are TCP clients. This figure might help you visualize this.

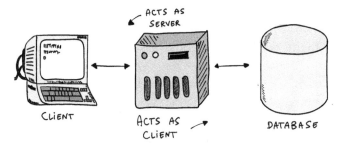

The client side of TCP presents different challenges from the server side, but they are challenges nonetheless. Servers generally concern themselves with the reliability of the whole server rather than a single connection. Clients, however, usually have to put strategies in place to make connections as stable and resilient as possible. Another challenge unique to clients is *pooling*: opening multiple TCP connections to a server to improve reliability and scalability.

In this and the next chapters, we'll explore all aspects of TCP clients and how to write robust and performant ones. Your learning project will be a toy client for the Redis key-value data store. We'll start by looking at Redis's network protocol. Then, we'll build a simple client to talk to it. In the next chapter, we'll take things to the next level and explore how to scale and optimize such TCP clients.

The Redis Protocol

Redis[1] is a widely used key-value data store that runs in memory. It communicates with its clients through a textual protocol called RESP. The protocol is easy to use and understand, letting us focus on the TCP client aspects. We'll work inside a new redis_client application, so run the following to scaffold it:

```
> mix new redis_client
* creating README.md
* creating .formatter.exs
* creating .gitignore
* creating mix.exs
* creating lib
* creating lib/redis_client.ex
* creating test
* creating test/test_helper.exs
* creating test/redis_client_test.exs

Your Mix project was created successfully.
You can use "mix" to compile it, test it, and more:

    cd redis_client
    mix test

Run "mix help" for more commands.
```

Our finished client will let us establish connections to a Redis server, run commands, and receive responses. The next IEx session shows what we'll be able to do: it uses the SET Redis command to set the how_cool_you_are key to 9 and the INCR command to increase the value of that same key by 1. It does this through the RedisClient module we'll write and its command/2 function.

```
iex> {:ok, client} = RedisClient.start_link(host: ~c"localhost", port: 6379)
iex> RedisClient.command(client, ["SET", "how_cool_you_are", "9"])
{:ok, "OK"}
iex> RedisClient.command(client, ["INCR", "how_cool_you_are"])
{:ok, 10}
```

RESP stands for REdis Serialization Protocol. It's well-documented on the Redis website.[2] RESP is a textual protocol. We explored the difference between textual and binary protocols in Binary Protocols and Textual Protocols, on page 34. This protocol defines only five data types: simple strings, errors,

---

1.   https://redis.io
2.   https://redis.io/docs/reference/protocol-spec/

integers, bulk strings, and arrays. Every protocol message starts with a single byte containing a character that identifies the data type of the message.

Data Type	First Byte	Example	Elixir Representation
Simple string	+	+OK\r\n	"OK"
Error	-	-ERR bad!	%Redis.Error{message: "ERR bad!"}
Integer	:	:42\r\n	42
Bulk string	$	$11\r\nhello world\r\n	"hello world"
Array	*	*3\r\n+OK\r\n:1\r\n:2\r\n	["OK", 1, 2]

For bulk strings, the number after $ is the number of bytes that make up the string, followed by \r\n and the bulk itself. Arrays are similar: after *, you have the number of elements in the array and \r\n, then each element followed by \r\n as well.

Symmetrical Protocols

RESP is a *symmetrical* protocol, meaning that clients and servers encode and decode data in the same way. This is especially useful when working on clients or servers, because you will end up with code to both encode and decode. You can use this to your advantage: for example, if you are implementing a client, you can use the same protocol code to implement a mock server for testing. Many protocols are symmetrical, since client-server communication usually goes both ways, so both parties have to encode *and* decode.

We don't need to go through each data type, since we won't dive too deep into the protocol code and we should avoid digressing too much. The first four types in this table are types that represent simple data structures. The array type is the only *composite* type, meaning it contains other simple or composite types. All types are terminated with a CRLF (Carriage Return Line Feed) sequence of bytes—that is, the bytes \r\n.

We can represent most of these types as Elixir/Erlang native types. We'll use strings to represent simple and bulk strings, integers for integers, and lists for arrays. The only custom struct we'll introduce is %Redis.Error{message: message}, which we'll use to represent RESP errors.

Okay, we got the data types down. A Redis server's response is always a single term represented by one of the five data types we just looked at. The good news is that requests that clients send to a Redis server are always made of a single array containing only bulk strings. This simplifies clients and removes the ambiguity that would happen, for example, when having to encode an

Elixir/Erlang string, which could be encoded as a simple string or a bulk string.

Let's move on to implementing encoding and decoding for RESP. We don't need to dive into the code that we'll use to do that, because it's outside the scope of networking itself, but you can find the whole source in the book's resources if you're curious, in the code/redis_client/lib/redis_client/resp.ex file. The code is mostly taken from Redix,[3] an Elixir client for Redis. In this chapter, we'll only look at the API provided by our protocol code. If you're following along, start an IEx session in the code/redis_client directory with iex -S mix.

To encode a list of Elixir terms into an RESP array, we can use RedisClient.RESP.encode/1, which takes a list of terms that can be converted to strings (through the String.Chars Elixir protocol) and returns iodata. We discussed iodata in depth in Encoding with Iodata, on page 43. Let's try this function out in our running session:

```
iex> iodata = RedisClient.RESP.encode(["OK", 1, 2])
[
  42,
  "3",
  '\r\n',
  [
    [[[], [36, "2", '\r\n', "OK", '\r\n']], [36, "1", '\r\n', "1", '\r\n']],
    [36, "1", '\r\n', "2", '\r\n']
  ]
]
iex> IO.iodata_to_binary(iodata)
"*3\r\n$2\r\nOK\r\n$1\r\n1\r\n$1\r\n2\r\n"
```

The iodata is difficult to parse visually, but it should make more sense when converted to a regular binary with IO.iodata_to_binary/1. The encoded string also looks cryptic. Let's break it down:

```
iex> iodata |> IO.iodata_to_binary() |> IO.puts()
*3  # Array with three elements
$2  # First element, a string with 2 bytes
OK  # The string
$1  # Second element, a string with 1 byte
1   # The string (remember, even integers are encoded as bulk strings)
$1  # Third element, a string with 1 byte
2   # The string
```

Decoding has slightly more complexity to it. Our decoder has to be able to handle both encoding errors and incomplete data. Errors are not a real concern

---

3. https://github.com/whatyouhide/redix

with Redis, since we can safely assume that Redis encodes its messages correctly, but they could be a concern with other RESP servers. But incomplete data is something we have to deal with because of how TCP splits and sends data packets, as you learned in Decoding Data into Messages, on page 40.

Our decoder's approach to incomplete data is based on *continuations*. Returning only something like :incomplete means the decoder has to throw away everything it parsed until that point, only to parse it again when new data arrives. For example, imagine you have the following data to decode:

```
"*3\r\n:1\r\n:2\r\n"
```

Decoding this, we see that it starts with a * byte, so it's an array. The following 3 means it has three elements. After that, only two elements follow, so the data is incomplete. But at this point our decoder has already done the work of decoding two out of three elements. To avoid that work going to waste, RedisClient.RESP implements a pattern called *continuations*. When data is incomplete, it returns {:continuation, cont} where cont is a function that takes more data and continues parsing where it left off. You can see it in action in the next IEx session:

```
iex> {:continuation, cont} = RedisClient.RESP.decode("*3\r\n:1\r\n:2\r\n")
{:continuation, #Function<13.122536824/1 in RedisClient.RESP.take_elems/3>}
iex> cont.(":3\r\n")
{:ok, [1, 2, 3], ""}
```

When we feed the last element (:3\r\n) to the continuation, we get back a complete and correct response. The third element of the :ok tuple returned by decode/1 is whatever data is left after a complete response.

Incomplete Data

Packets that are not whole are a major headache for network programmers in my experience. Data can be split at any point, and you have to be able to handle all those possible cases.

The good news is that parsing data is not a problem unique to networks, and parsers are a whole field of computer science. You'll find a lot of resources and techniques to deal with parsers if you look around the Internet. To start digging into that rabbit hole, check out parser combinators,[4] LALR parsers,[5] and Erlang's parsetools.[6]

---

4. https://en.wikipedia.org/wiki/Parser_combinator
5. https://en.wikipedia.org/wiki/LALR_parser
6. https://www.erlang.org/doc/apps/parsetools/

That's it for our exploration of RESP. RESP is a fantastic real-world example of a textual protocol, which is why we took the time to explore it. You now know about this protocol that we can use to talk to Redis, so you're ready to learn more about TCP clients by building a Redis client.

Building Our First Client

Let's lay the foundations for our client. We'll start with just using a TCP socket directly, and then we'll gradually build on top of that. We'll add a process around the TCP socket whose job is to manage that socket and keep it alive. Then, we'll add functionality to check in and check out the socket, as well as to queue requests. Finally, we'll add some failure handling. The following figure is a simplified view of what our client will look like:

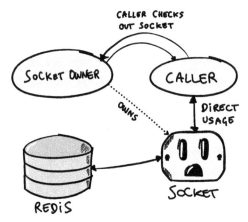

From now on, we'll refer to this type of Elixir/Erlang TCP client as *checkout clients*.

To follow along with the examples in this section, you should have a Redis server instance running on your local machine on port 6379. The Redis installation page[7] will help you get Redis up and running.

At the core of every TCP client is the TCP socket that the client uses to communicate with the server. A gen_tcp client socket works almost the same as a gen_tcp server socket (the socket returned by :gen_tcp.accept/2). Let's start playing around with client sockets by firing up an IEx session. In these first few examples, we'll just get a feel for the protocol, without working on a module. Hop into an IEx session inside code/redis_client (iex -S mix) and run the following:

```
iex> options = [:binary, active: false]
iex> {:ok, socket} = :gen_tcp.connect(~c"localhost", 6379, options, 5000)
```

---

7. https://redis.io/docs/getting-started/installation/

If your Redis server is running, you shouldn't see any errors. We've already used :gen_tcp.connect/3 in Writing a TCP Client with the gen_tcp Module, on page 12, and at this point you're familiar with the options we're using here.

Now, let's encode a command and send it to the server. Commands are just lists of strings. We'll try out the PING command, which Redis responds to with the string "PONG":

```
iex> encoded_command = RedisClient.RESP.encode(["PING"])
[42, "1", '\r\n', [[], [36, "4", '\r\n', "PING", '\r\n']]]
iex> :gen_tcp.send(socket, encoded_command)
:ok
```

RedisClient.RESP.encode/1 returns iodata. This is yet another example of using iodata directly to write data to the socket without converting it to a binary. Until we receive new data, nothing really happens. Let's use :gen_tcp.recv/3 to get the response from Redis:

```
iex> {:ok, response_data} = :gen_tcp.recv(socket, 0, 5000)
{:ok, "+PONG\r\n"}
iex> RedisClient.RESP.decode(response_data)
{:ok, "PONG", ""}
```

We're receiving *all available data* by passing 0 as the second argument to :gen_tcp.recv/3, and we can see that the decoded response is exactly what we expect—that is, the string "PONG". This is a great start!

We could keep going in this direction and wrap the whole interaction in a function. Users of our Redis client would call this function to send a command and get a response. But we'd run into quite a few issues right away, the biggest being that, for most use cases, this approach is awfully inefficient. Opening a new TCP client socket every time we want to exchange some information with a server goes directly against one of the fundamental properties that characterize TCP itself: TCP is a stateful, *connection-oriented* protocol. It's built from the ground up to work with longer-lived connections, which only perform the initial handshake once and can then exchange data back and forth. TCP sockets also take up operating-system resources, so opening new sockets isn't free. Last but not least, the TCP handshake itself has a non-negligible cost in terms of computation and network round trips, as explained in more detail in Appendix 2, TCP Protocol Details, on page 225.

For all these reasons, what we would ideally do is reuse TCP client sockets for multiple exchanges with the server. To do that, we need to store the TCP socket somewhere while it's not being used for requests. On the BEAM, that somewhere is a *process*.

Holding TCP Sockets Inside Processes

The approach we'll take for the client is this:

1. Start a process to hold on to the socket
2. Open the socket once when we start this client process
3. The client process will lend the socket to callers that want to use it—to put it another way, callers will *check out* the socket, use it, and then check it back in

We'll model our socket process as a GenServer. Create a new file, and let's start from the start_link/1 function.

```elixir
redis_client/lib/redis_client_no_queue.ex
defmodule RedisClient do
  use GenServer

  @spec start_link(keyword()) :: GenServer.on_start()
  def start_link(options) do
    GenServer.start_link(__MODULE__, options)
  end
end
```

Run-of-the-mill stuff here. We'll use a struct to hold the state of this GenServer, which we can see in the next piece of code.

```elixir
defstruct [:host, :port, :socket, :caller_monitor]
```

:host and :port are in the state so that we can use them again when reconnecting, in case the connection goes down for some reason. :socket holds the gen_tcp socket, or nil if there's no connected socket. :caller_monitor is a reference returned by Process.monitor/1. We'll talk more about that a bit later on.

Next, let's define the init/1 callback. We'll use a trick that we have seen before: the GenServer.handle_continue/2 callback to connect asynchronously. This way, our start_link/1 function will return before connecting to the server, and then our client will attempt to connect.

```elixir
Line 1  @impl true
     2  def init(options) do
     3    initial_state = %__MODULE__{
     4      host: Keyword.fetch!(options, :host),
     5      port: Keyword.fetch!(options, :port)
     6    }
     7
     8    {:ok, initial_state, {:continue, :connect}}
     9  end
```

We build an initial state and then return {:continue, :connect} on line 8 so that the handle_continue/2 callback is invoked just after returning from init/1 with :connect as the first argument. The code for handle_continue/2 is next.

```elixir
@impl true
def handle_continue(:connect, %__MODULE__{} = state) do
  tcp_options = [:binary, active: :once]

  case :gen_tcp.connect(state.host, state.port, tcp_options, 5000) do
    {:ok, socket} ->
      {:noreply, %{state | socket: socket}}

    {:error, reason} ->
      Logger.error("Failed to connect: #{:inet.format_error(reason)}")
      Process.send_after(self(), :reconnect, 1000)
      {:noreply, state}
  end
end
```

We've seen :gen_tcp.connect/4 in action a few times by now. If we establish a successful connection, we update the state and return from the callback (line 7). If there's an error, we log it and send a delayed :reconnect message to self() before returning. This gives us a chance to *back off* before attempting to reconnect so that the client eventually reconnects but not right away—otherwise, tight reconnect loops could overload the server.

We're using the active: :once option here when connecting to the server—but not because we want to *receive* data on the socket. After all, Redis won't send us any data unless it's in response to a command that our client sends. We want the socket to be in active mode because we want our client to receive :tcp_closed and :tcp_error messages in case the connection is interrupted. Since that's bound to happen at some point, let's define the handle_info/2 callback clauses to handle those cases.

```elixir
@impl true
def handle_info(message, state)

def handle_info(
      {:tcp_closed, socket},
      %__MODULE__{socket: socket} = state
    ) do
  Process.send_after(self(), :reconnect, 1000)
  {:noreply, %{state | socket: nil}}
end

def handle_info(
      {:tcp_error, socket, _reason},
      %__MODULE__{socket: socket} = state
    ) do
```

```
  Process.send_after(self(), :reconnect, 1000)
  {:noreply, %{state | socket: nil}}
end
```

Let's also define one more handle_info/2 clause to handle the :reconnect message. We already connect in our handle_continue/2 callback, so we can just return {:continue, :connect} to tell the client to reconnect.

```
def handle_info(:reconnect, state) do
  {:noreply, state, {:continue, :connect}}
end
```

This is amazingly concise.

Okay, we now have a GenServer that wraps a TCP client socket and reconnects in case the connection closes for any reason. It's time to implement commands.

Checking Out the Socket

At this point, we're faced with two possible ways to implement commands. One approach is as follows:

1. Callers send the command to our connection process

2. The connection process sends the command to the Redis server over TCP

3. The connection process blocks while receiving new data containing the response to the command

4. Once the response arrives, the connection process forwards it to the caller

This approach works but turns out to be cumbersome here. One reason is that we'd be blocking the connection process while waiting for the response to the command, which prevents the process from getting system messages. We could get around that by storing the waiting caller in the state while we wait for :tcp messages, but it would introduce more complexity to make sure no other callers try to send commands until we get a response for the in-flight one. In the next section, we'll dig deeper into this approach to clients and solve these issues, but for now let's focus on another possible approach: checking out the socket.

With this approach, callers temporarily borrow the socket from the connection process, use it to send the command and receive the response, and then give it back to the connection process. By doing this, the caller can block directly while receiving data, and the connection process is left alone. An additional advantage of this design is that the caller and the connection process exchange less data through BEAM messages, since they only pass the socket around.

This can potentially lower memory usage, given that sending messages generally creates copies of the data being sent.

Let's first take a look at the command/2 function that exposes this functionality.

redis_client/lib/redis_client_no_queue.ex

```
Line 1  @spec command(GenServer.server(), [String.t()]) ::
              {:ok, term()} | {:error, term()}
        def command(client, command) do
          case GenServer.call(client, :checkout) do
     5      {:ok, socket} ->
              result =
                with :ok <- :gen_tcp.send(socket, RESP.encode(command)),
                     {:ok, data} <- receive_response(socket, &RESP.decode/1) do
                  {:ok, data}
    10          else
                  {:error, reason} -> {:error, reason}
                end

              GenServer.call(client, :checkin)
    15          result

            {:error, reason} ->
              {:error, reason}
          end
    20  end

        defp receive_response(socket, continuation) do
          case :gen_tcp.recv(socket, 0, 5000) do
            {:ok, data} ->
    25        case continuation.(data) do
                {:ok, response, _rest = ""} ->
                  {:ok, response}

                {:continuation, new_continuation} ->
    30            receive_response(socket, new_continuation)
              end

            {:error, reason} ->
              {:error, reason}
    35    end
        end
```

The idea is this: the caller checks out the socket (line 4), sends the encoded command (line 7), receives the response (line 8), and checks the socket back in before returning the result (line 14). The :checkout call might return an error, such as when the client is temporarily not connected, so we only do all of this if the call returns {:ok, socket}.

receive_response/2 is a recursive function. It calls :gen_tcp.recv/3 and receives all available data. It tries to parse that data, and it returns it if it succeeds (line 27). If parsing returns {:continuation, continuation}, we call receive_response/2 recursively with the new continuation (line 30). If receiving data returns an error, we bubble up the error and return it (line 34).

Let's take a look at how to handle the :checkout and :checkin calls.

```
Line 1  def handle_call(:checkout, _from, %__MODULE__{socket: nil} = state) do
          {:reply, {:error, :not_connected}, state}
        end

     5  def handle_call(:checkout, {pid, _ref}, %__MODULE__{} = state) do
          caller_monitor = Process.monitor(pid)
          :ok = :inet.setopts(state.socket, active: false)
          state = %{state | caller_monitor: caller_monitor}
          {:reply, {:ok, state.socket}, state}
    10  end

        def handle_call(:checkin, _from, %__MODULE__{} = state) do
          Process.demonitor(state.caller_monitor, [:flush])
          :ok = :inet.setopts(state.socket, active: :once)
    15    {:reply, :ok, %{state | caller_monitor: nil}}
        end
```

First things first, if the client is not connected (which we can see when the :socket in the state is nil), we return {:error, :not_connected} on line 2.

To implement the :gen_tcp.recv/3 approach we just looked at, we need to change the mode of the socket to passive when checking it out so that the caller can use :gen_tcp.recv/3 to receive the data. We can change the mode back to active once we check the socket back in. When a socket is in passive mode, any process can call :gen_tcp.recv/3, not just the controlling process. This means we don't need to change the controlling process of the socket when checking it out. We do this in the handle_call/3 clause on line 5.

Now, let's discuss the Process.monitor/1 call on line 6. We monitor the process that wants to check out the socket because it could exit for any reason *before* it's able to send our client the :checkin call. In that case, we still want our client to know that the socket is not in use by any client anymore. If the caller checks the socket in successfully, we call Process.demonitor/2 to cancel the monitor (line 13). We also use the [:flush] option so that the BEAM takes care of race conditions with the :DOWN message. Speaking of the :DOWN message, we also have to handle that, which we see in the next piece of code.

```
def handle_info(
      {:DOWN, ref, _, _, _},
      %__MODULE__{caller_monitor: ref} = state)
```

```
  do
  :ok = :inet.setopts(state.socket, active: :once)
  {:noreply, %{state | caller_monitor: nil}}
end
```

This clause handles the :DOWN message for the current monitored client. We only set the socket back in active mode.

There's one more thing to talk about when it comes to this sort of error handling. What happens if the connection drops (for any reason) while the socket is checked out? The caller will see the error because :gen_tcp.send/2 or :gen_tcp.recv/3 will return {:error, reason}, but we also want our client to know that the connection is down so that it can reconnect. Luckily, OTP makes this a breeze. As it turns out, setting a passive closed socket back to active mode (with :inet.setopts/2) delivers a {:tcp_closed, socket} message to the controlling process! This means that if a caller checks in a closed socket, our client process will set it to active mode and then immediately receive a :tcp_closed message. This is a very desirable behavior. It mirrors the behavior of Process.monitor/1, which delivers the :DOWN message right away if the given PID is the PID of an already-dead process.

Wow, that was a lot of content. The good news is that we're ready to try out the first version of our client. Run iex -S mix to open an IEx session in the project, and type in the following:

```
iex> {:ok, client} = RedisClient.start_link(host: ~c"localhost", port: 6379)
{:ok, #PID<0.177.0>}
iex> RedisClient.command(client, ["SET", "mykey", "it works!"])
{:ok, "OK"}
iex> RedisClient.command(client, ["GET", "mykey"])
{:ok, "it works!"}
```

It works! But you won't like what happens if two processes call command/2 at the same time: one of the two errors out. Let's figure out why.

Queuing Requests

Right now, our client can't deal with two callers checking out the socket simultaneously. We're about to address this issue.

First and foremost, let's verify that this is an actual issue. We can use Task to spawn two processes that send a command to Redis through the client at the same time.

Fire up IEx and type this in:

```
iex> {:ok, client} = RedisClient.start_link(host: ~c"localhost", port: 6379)
iex> for _ <- 1..2 do
```

```
...>   Task.async(fn -> RedisClient.command(client, ["PING"]) end)
...> end
```

You will likely see some error, such as a FunctionClauseError or a CaseClauseError. Our client code is full of race conditions that occur when dealing with multiple callers!

The problem is that we're allowing multiple callers to check out the socket at the same time. When this happens, we run into cases where multiple callers call :gen_tcp.send/2 to send their commands, which results in multiple responses being sent by Redis. Remember that only one process can be calling :gen_tcp.recv/3 at any given time on a socket. This means you'll likely see one of the two tasks get both responses from the :gen_tcp.recv/3 call, while the other sees an {:error, :ealready} error.

These issues make sense, though. If we want to check out the TCP socket to callers, we must only hand the socket to one caller at a time. We could return an error if a caller tries to check out the socket when it's already checked out, but that would make for a pretty awkward API. *Queuing requests* are the most common approach to handle this problem.

Implementing a Simple Queue (That Doesn't Handle Reconnections)

Let's implement a simple and naive caller queue. You can go ahead and edit the current RedisClient module or copy it to a new module—the source code for the book has this code in RedisClientQueued (code/redis_client/lib/redis_client_queue.ex).

For now, we'll completely ignore error states—that is, what happens when the connection gets interrupted for some reason. We'll dig deeper into that in the next chapter, where we'll come up with strategies to handle reconnections and pending requests. So, let's go ahead and focus on the queuing for now. We'll start by changing the state to include a queue of callers. Erlang's standard library provides a queue module[8] that we can use.

```
-defstruct [:host, :port, :socket, :caller_monitor]
+defstruct [:host, :port, :socket, :caller_monitor, queue: :queue.new()]
```

The elements of this queue will be the from tuples that we get in the handle_call(:checkout, from, state) callback. Those are a good choice because we can then use GenServer.reply/2 to reply to callers once the socket is available, instead of returning {:reply, {:ok, socket}, state} from handle_call/3. This allows callers to block waiting for a reply, while our GenServer continues to handle requests and wait for data from Redis.

---

8. https://www.erlang.org/doc/man/queue.html

Now, we need to queue callers when handling checkout calls if the socket is already checked out. We'll do two things. First, we'll *enqueue* the new caller. Then, we'll call a helper function that takes the first caller out of the queue and hands it the socket. We're using a helper function because we can reuse it in other parts of the client, as you'll see in a moment. Let's look at the code to handle the :checkout call.

```
redis_client/lib/redis_client_queue.ex
def handle_call(:checkout, _from, %__MODULE__{socket: nil} = state) do
  {:reply, {:error, :not_connected}, state}
end

def handle_call(:checkout, from, %__MODULE__{} = state) do
  # First, queue the new caller.
  state = update_in(state.queue, &:queue.in(from, &1))

  # Then, check out the next queued caller.
  state = checkout_if_waiting(state)
  {:noreply, state}
end
```

The helper function we mentioned is checkout_if_waiting/1, which we define as follows:

```
redis_client/lib/redis_client_queue.ex
Line 1   # If there is already a caller which checked out the socket,
     -   # leave the state alone.
     -   defp checkout_if_waiting(%__MODULE__{caller_monitor: ref} = state)
     -         when is_reference(ref) do
     5     state
     -   end
     -
     -   # If we can hand the socket to a waiting caller, we do that. If there
     -   # are no callers waiting, we just return the state.
    10   defp checkout_if_waiting(%__MODULE__{} = state) do
     -     case :queue.out(state.queue) do
     -       {:empty, _empty_queue} ->
     -         state
     -
    15       {{:value, {pid, _ref} = from}, new_queue} ->
     -         ref = Process.monitor(pid)
     -         :ok = :inet.setopts(state.socket, active: false)
     -         GenServer.reply(from, {:ok, state.socket})
     -         %{state | queue: new_queue, caller_monitor: ref}
    20     end
     -   end
```

Most of this code is made of pieces of code we already saw in this section. In this helper function, we use :queue.out/1 to get the next element out of the callers queue on line 11. The return value of :queue.out/2 is either {:empty, queue}, if the queue is empty, or {{:value, item}, new_queue}, with item being the next item in the queue. On line 18, you can see how we call GenServer.reply/2 to hand the socket over to the waiting from caller.

We can modify how we handle :checkin calls as well. The only difference is that we need to check if there are waiting callers in the queue once the current caller checks in the socket. Luckily, we can reuse the checkout_if_waiting/1 helper we just saw. Let's look at the code for the handle_call/3 clause in question.

redis_client/lib/redis_client_queue.ex
```elixir
def handle_call(:checkin, _from, %__MODULE__{} = state) do
  Process.demonitor(state.caller_monitor, [:flush])
  state = %{state | caller_monitor: nil}
  state = checkout_if_waiting(state)
  {:reply, :ok, state}
end
```

Our client can now handle a queue of callers waiting for their turn to check out the socket. But this means that if the connection is interrupted for some reason, then we likely want to also notify the waiting callers about it. We can define a helper for this that we'll call when handling :tcp_closed and :tcp_error messages. Here's the code:

```elixir
# If the socket is closed, we reply to all the waiting callers,
# because we don't know if we'll ever reconnect. Callers can always
# retry if needed.
defp flush_queue(state) do
  Enum.each(:queue.to_list(state.queue), fn from ->
    GenServer.reply(from, {:error, :disconnected})
  end)

  %{state | queue: :queue.new()}
end
```

The idea is to reply to all the waiting callers with {:error, :disconnected} if the connection goes down so that they can decide what to do next. For example, some callers might retry the command they were trying to send, while others might give up. Here's an example of using flush_queue/1 when handling :tcp_closed messages:

redis_client/lib/redis_client_queue.ex
```elixir
def handle_info(
      {:tcp_closed, socket},
      %__MODULE__{socket: socket} = state
    ) do
  state = flush_queue(state)
  Process.send_after(self(), :reconnect, 1000)
  {:noreply, %{state | socket: nil}}
end
```

If you try to run the previous Task example with this new version of our client, it should go just fine. We've now got a working Redis client that can queue requests from callers and handle Redis commands. Awesome job! Let's end this section with a short overview of what we built and some thoughts on this check-out/check-in kind of client.

Pros and Cons of Checkout Clients

Let's look back at how we got here. Our goal was to build a basic Redis client. To do that, we went with an approach where our client is essentially a BEAM process that controls a TCP client socket. Other processes can use the client to interact with Redis. The way they do that is to check out the TCP socket from the client and interact with it directly for as long as needed before checking it back in.

After the first pass at this approach, we added request queuing. Our final client can also serve multiple processes interacting with Redis by queuing their requests and passing the socket to one client at a time. We also baked a resilient approach to error handling into the Redis client. The client is able to deal with disconnections by notifying waiting callers and attempting to reconnect after a short backoff period. Our client can also deal with callers crashing by monitoring the current caller and going through a reconnection cycle if the current caller goes down.

The main advantage of this approach to TCP clients on the BEAM is that we move the *TCP socket* around instead of the *data*. On the BEAM, sending a message from one process to another generally means copying the data being sent from the memory of the sending process to the memory of the receiving process. The only case where this is not true is for binaries larger than 64 bytes, which live in a common memory space. This is a desirable property for a virtual machine like ours, because it allows processes to be completely isolated and allows the VM to garbage-collect processes individually. But a TCP client like the one we built mostly sends messages to and from caller processes, so the memory overhead of always copying those messages can be significant. Moving the socket around, instead, means that callers can read from and write to the OS socket buffer directly, without copying data within the BEAM.

This approach, however, has one drawback when it comes to data: our client is not taking advantage of *TCP multiplexing*. Multiplexing is a property of TCP that allows a TCP socket to send *and* receive data simultaneously. In our client, we only ever send *or* receive data, since we always send a command with :gen_tcp.send/2 and only then start receiving a response with :gen_tcp.recv/3.

> ## How the BEAM Stores Binaries in Memory
>
> Most Erlang terms live in the memory of each process using them. One exception is binaries. Small binaries less than 64 bytes in size are stored in the process heap (*heap binaries*), but binaries larger than that are stored in a shared memory area. These are called *refc binaries* (*reference-counted binaries*) because they are referenced by processes using them. The BEAM counts these references so that it knows when to garbage-collect these binaries. Another representation of binaries on the BEAM is *sub binaries*, which are terms that can reference only part of a refc or heap binary. You can use :binary.referenced_byte_size/1[a] to get the size of the referenced binary if it's a sub binary. Knowing this information about binaries is important when designing the process architecture of your application and planning how your processes will exchange messages. For example, if you expect most messages exchanged with a TCP server to be large binaries, then you could avoid passing the socket around, since the binaries will likely be refc binaries anyway. That means sending them across processes will only send references to shared memory, which could entail a simpler implementation and lower memory usage in some cases.
>
> You can read detailed information about binaries and their performance in the Erlang efficiency guide.[b]
>
> ---
>
> a.   https://www.erlang.org/doc/man/binary.html#referenced_byte_size-1
> b.   https://www.erlang.org/doc/efficiency_guide/binaryhandling.html

This is fine for the way our client operates, since we only ever give the socket to one caller at a time, but we could take advantage of TCP multiplexing if we allowed multiple clients to send their commands concurrently. To do that, however, we'd have to receive all data in a single process and dispatch the right responses to the right callers. This is a viable alternative approach, and we'll explore it in the next chapter.

A second drawback, related to resilience, is the potential size of the callers queue. As a general rule, whenever your system has a queue, you'll likely want to enforce an upper bound on its size. Not doing so could result in memory leaks. In our client, we could choose to limit the size of the callers queue and either drop older callers or stop accepting new ones until more caller requests are served.

While it took us a good while to go through the code for the Redis client, we managed to get a resilient client working in under two hundred lines of code (including comments!). But in a real-world system you'd be unlikely to use a client like this directly. This is due to one main reason: performance. Whenever your system is interacting with an external system (such as Redis), you'll likely want to connect to that system using a *pool* of connections. This is the same idea as the TCP acceptor pool that we explored in Increasing Scalability with Multiple Acceptors, on page 59. We'll explore pooling TCP client sockets in the next chapter.

Wrapping Up

We already explored a lot in this chapter, but our journey through TCP clients on the BEAM is only halfway complete. We laid the groundwork for understanding how to build great TCP clients on the BEAM, we looked at a real-world network protocol (for Redis), we played around with raw TCP sockets, and we built our first *checkout client*. In the next chapter, you'll level up your knowledge of TCP clients on the BEAM by learning about different pooling techniques as well as strategies to handle high request loads. You'll also learn about an alternative approach to TCP clients based on state machines. Exciting times ahead.

## CHAPTER 6

Scaling and Optimizing TCP Clients

You got your feet wet with TCP clients on the BEAM, but we didn't write production-ready code. The simple client we put together is missing a few fundamental features, such as handling disconnections and high request loads through pooling. Now we'll focus on how to make TCP clients that are fast, scalable, and reliable. This is the kind of client you see in libraries and production codebases.

You'll start by learning about *pooling* clients, which is a way to make your application more reliable and scalable. These pooling strategies will be helpful in different use cases. After this, you'll learn about a whole different approach to building TCP clients, based on a *state machine* process. Finally, you'll look at one more pooling strategy tailored to state-machine clients.

Pooling TCP Client Sockets

The client we built in the previous chapter works and can queue multiple callers, but it's still operating *sequentially*—that is, it can only serve one request at a time. In a real-world system, this can work for some use cases, but most of the time you'll want to be able to send requests *concurrently* as well. This is where pooling connections come into play. We'll explore a couple of possible approaches to pooling.

The idea is to have a pool of multiple TCP client sockets connected to Redis and to choose a strategy to check out sockets from the pool when needed. We can implement this in several ways, and each may be a better fit for different use cases. Since we already have a working process-based Redis client, let's start by using that as the foundation for our pooling.

Pooling Processes with Poolboy

Poolboy[1] is an open-source pooling library for Elixir and Erlang. Its job is to keep a pool of workers running and allow callers to check out workers from the pool when necessary. A worker can be any sort of process, such as our client GenServer. The following figure gives you a visual idea of what a Poolboy pool looks like:

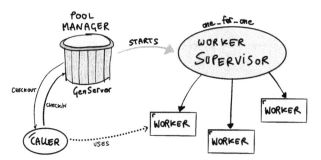

Poolboy has a small API. Other than a bunch of functions to start and stop a pool, the only functionality it provides is to check out a worker from the pool and check a worker back into the pool. It also exposes a convenience function, :poolboy.transaction/2, which checks out a worker, executes the given function, and then checks the worker back in.

To introduce Poolboy in our Redis client, first add it to your dependencies:

redis_client/mix.exs
```elixir
defp deps do
  [
    {:poolboy, "~> 1.5"},
  ]
end
```

Now, create a new module, RedisClient.Pool, which we'll keep in the file lib/redis_client/pool.ex. We'll only have two functions: one to start a pool of clients and one to execute a command through a worker in the pool. Let's take a look at start_link/1 first.

redis_client/lib/redis_client/pool.ex
```elixir
def start_link(worker_args) do
  pool_args = [worker_module: RedisClientQueued, size: 5]
  :poolboy.start_link(pool_args, worker_args)
end
```

---

1. https://github.com/devinus/poolboy

Our start_link/1 function is essentially delegating to :poolboy.start_link/2, which takes two arguments: the pool options and the arguments to start workers with. We're only using two pool options. The first, :worker_module, specifies which module to use as the workers—this should be a module that can be started with start_link/1. The second option, :size, controls the number of workers to start in the pool. We went with a hard-coded number here, but it would be straightforward to make this customizable. The return value of :poolboy.start_link/2 is the PID of the pool.

The second function we need has an API that is almost identical to our command/2 function from the client itself. Let's take a look at it.

redis_client/lib/redis_client/pool.ex
```
def command(pool, command) do
  :poolboy.transaction(pool, fn client ->
    RedisClientQueued.command(client, command)
  end)
end
```

While we could use :poolboy.checkout/1 and :poolboy.checkin/1, we can keep things even more concise with :poolboy.transaction/2. The first argument to this function is the pool's name or PID, and the second argument is a callback function. The pool executes this function with a checked-out worker as its argument. In the callback function we're passing, we're only calling the command/2 function from our client.

That's mostly it when it comes to pooling with Poolboy. Given its simplicity and small API surface, Poolboy is a great tool to reach for when you want to scale something up by adding copies of the worker process.

Poolboy is especially useful when the workers you want to pool are not built for multiple concurrent caller requests. That's exactly the case of our Redis client, which can only serve a single caller at a time. When your workers can serve requests concurrently, Poolboy might limit the throughput of the workers. In those cases, there are better pooling techniques we can use, which we'll discuss in depth later in this chapter.

Our Redis client is a process, but it's mostly wrapping a TCP socket and passing it around to other processes. We can think of that TCP socket as a *resource*. When it comes to pooling resources, Poolboy is not the perfect choice, since it's optimized for pooling processes. In our example so far, we have a pool manager (Poolboy) that returns pooled processes to callers, only for those pooled processes to then give direct access to the TCP client socket.

db_connection

We should also mention another library called db_connection.[a] This library provides something similar to the Poolboy-based solution we just explored, but it's specifically intended for writing database clients (not even necessarily based on TCP). Its core idea is once again to have a pool of processes managing connections to a database and to check those connections in and out for callers to use. db_connection also provides specific functions for common database features such as cursors and transactions. It wouldn't be a great fit for our Redis client, but it's a fantastic library. It powers many of the most widely used database adapters for Elixir, such as Postgrex[b] and MyXQL.[c]

---

a. https://github.com/elixir-ecto/db_connection
b. https://github.com/elixir-ecto/postgrex
c. https://github.com/elixir-ecto/myxql

There's an alternative pool built specifically for this sort of use case. Let's take a look at it next.

Pooling Resources Directly with NimblePool

NimblePool[2] is a small open-source library focused on writing *pools of resources*. The idea behind the library is this: if you want to pool resources, it might be enough to have a single process managing all of those resources and handing them out to callers. This works in many cases, because the bulk of the work is done in the callers. That's the case with our Redis client, since the caller is the one encoding the command, sending it over the wire, waiting for a response, and then decoding the response. Let's take a look at a visual representation of what a NimblePool-based Redis client could look like:

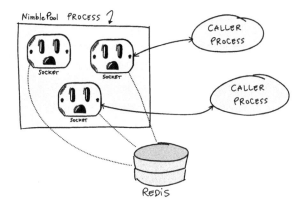

---

2. https://github.com/dashbitco/nimble_pool

NimblePool is a *behavior*, but an unusual one at that: the callbacks it defines are not executed in a single process, like what happens with GenServer, for example. With NimblePool, some callbacks are executed in the single pool process, while others are executed in the callers.

Before using NimblePool, add it to your dependencies—you can either replace :poolboy or add it after that.

redis_client/mix.exs
```
defp deps do
  [
    {:nimble_pool, "~> 1.0"},
  ]
end
```

Now, let's look at some code. Let's create a new file, lib/redis_client/socket_pool.ex, and start with the behavior definition and a start_link/1 function.

redis_client/lib/redis_client/socket_pool.ex
```
defmodule RedisClient.SocketPool do
  @behaviour NimblePool

  def start_link(options) when is_list(options) do
    NimblePool.start_link(worker: {__MODULE__, options}, pool_size: 5)
  end
end
```

In this code, we call NimblePool.start_link/1. The :worker option defines what the callback module should be and passes some arguments that we can use to initialize the pool. The first callback we'll look at is init_worker/1. NimblePool calls this to initialize a worker, which is the resource we're pooling. A worker is *not* a process—it's just some state, in our case the socket. A single Nimble-Pool process manages all the workers in its state.

redis_client/lib/redis_client/socket_pool.ex
```
@impl NimblePool
def init_worker(options) do
  host = Keyword.fetch!(options, :host)
  port = Keyword.fetch!(options, :port)
  parent = self()

  connect_fun = fn ->
    case :gen_tcp.connect(host, port, [:binary, active: :once], 5000) do
      {:ok, socket} ->
        :ok = :gen_tcp.controlling_process(socket, parent)
        socket

      {:error, _reason} ->
        nil
    end
```

```
  end

  {:async, connect_fun, _pool_state = options}
end
```

The init_worker/1 callback executes in the pool process and blocks it, so you should avoid doing lengthy work in it. That's why we return :async on line 18. The connect_fun here executes in a different temporary process so that the resource initializes asynchronously. The return value of connect_fun is the state of the worker, which in our case is the gen_tcp socket itself (or nil if the connection doesn't succeed). Since this function executes in a different process, we have to change the controlling process of the socket to give ownership back to the pool process, which we do on line 10. As you can see on line 8, we keep the TCP sockets in active mode. We do this so that we can get :tcp_closed and :tcp_error messages in the pool if the sockets are not checked out. Let's look at handle_info/2, which is executed for each worker when the pool receives a message.

redis_client/lib/redis_client/socket_pool.ex

```
@impl NimblePool
def handle_info({:tcp_closed, socket}, socket) do
  {:remove, :closed}
end

def handle_info({:tcp_error, socket, reason}, socket) do
  {:remove, reason}
end

def handle_info(_other, socket) do
  {:ok, socket}
end
```

If we receive :tcp_closed or :tcp_error, we make sure the socket is the same as the worker handle_info/2 is being invoked on. If it is, we return :remove to remove that worker from the pool. Otherwise, we return {:ok, socket} to leave the worker alone (on line 11).

Okay, we got a few callbacks out of the way. Now for the interesting parts: checking workers in and out and using the TCP socket. Let's look at the handle_checkout/4 callback, which is called when checking out the resource to a caller.

redis_client/lib/redis_client/socket_pool.ex

```
@impl NimblePool
def handle_checkout(:command, _from, socket, pool_state) do
  :ok = :inet.setopts(socket, active: false)
  {:ok, _client_state = socket, _worker_state = socket, pool_state}
end
```

The first argument is what we'll see passed down in NimblePool.checkout!/3 in a little while. The only thing we're doing here is setting the socket to passive mode for the caller, calling :gen_tcp.recv/3, and avoiding messages altogether. The return value of handle_checkout/4 contains the client state, which is what gets passed to the callback in NimblePool.checkout!/3, as well as the updated worker state and pool state. Now, let's see the command/2 function, where the caller interacts with the socket.

redis_client/lib/redis_client/socket_pool.ex
```
def command(pool, command) do
  NimblePool.checkout!(pool, :command, fn _from, socket ->
    with :ok <- :gen_tcp.send(socket, RESP.encode(command)),
         {:ok, data} <- receive_response(socket, &RESP.decode/1) do
      {{:ok, data}, {:ok, socket}}
    else
      {:error, reason} ->
        {_result = {:error, reason}, _client_state = {:error, reason}}
    end
  end)
end
```

This is the most complex piece of code in the pool. NimblePool.checkout!/3 takes the pool, a term (:command) that it passes down to handle_checkout/4, and a callback function. The callback function is invoked with a from argument (similar to GenServer.handle_call/3) and the client state returned by handle_checkout/4. We interact with the socket the same way we did in previous examples. The only difference is the return value of the callback, which is {result, client_state}—they're both set to {:error, reason} here. result is the return value of NimblePool.checkout!/3. client_state is passed in as the first argument to the handle_checkin/4 callback, so let's take a look at that.

redis_client/lib/redis_client/socket_pool.ex
```
Line 1  @impl NimblePool
     2  def handle_checkin({:ok, socket}, _from, socket, pool_state) do
     3    :ok = :inet.setopts(socket, active: :once)
     4    {:ok, socket, pool_state}
     5  end
     6
     7  def handle_checkin({:error, reason}, _from, _worker_state, pool_state) do
     8    {:remove, reason, pool_state}
     9  end
```

If the client state is {:ok, socket}, we set the socket to active mode again (line 3). If it's {:error, reason}, we remove the worker from the pool, since this happens if there was an error with the socket. We can close the TCP socket in the terminate_worker/3 callback.

```
redis_client/lib/redis_client/socket_pool.ex
@impl NimblePool
def terminate_worker(_reason, socket, pool_state) do
  :gen_tcp.close(socket)
  {:ok, pool_state}
end
```

That's all. We now have a working resource pool managed by a single process. This can be a resource-efficient choice in cases like this, but there's one thing to take into consideration here: the single process might become a bottleneck if the pool is large and a lot of check-ins and check-outs are expected. A good way to mitigate this is to start multiple NimblePool-based pools, effectively resulting in a pool of resource pools. That's quite the inception, isn't it? For example, you could start one RedisClient.SocketPool per *scheduler* (see System.schedulers_online/0).[3] You could also use Registry for this use case. We will look at Registry-based pools later in this chapter.

As we mentioned a while ago, the clients and pooling strategies we looked at are the right choice in some cases, but they do limit the concurrency offered by protocols such as TCP. So, let's look at some alternatives.

Building State-Machine-Like TCP Clients

Let's look at an approach for building clients based on the client process modeled as a state machine. A client process built in this way handles everything related to the socket: keeping it alive, reconnecting, sending data, and receiving data. This kind of TCP client gives up some efficiency when it comes to copying data around and sending messages, but it's better at taking advantage of an important property of TCP: being full-duplex.

TCP is a *full-duplex* protocol. This means the protocol is bidirectional—that is, data can flow both ways. It also means that data can flow both ways *at the same time*, as opposed to a half-duplex protocol, where data can only flow in one direction at a time, as shown in the following figure.

The clients we built so far do not take advantage of the full-duplex property of TCP. The exchange of data always looked more or less like this:

---

3. https://hexdocs.pm/elixir/System.html#schedulers_online/0

1. Caller checks out the socket from the client (whether directly or through the pool)

2. Caller sends some data through the socket to Redis

3. Caller blocks and waits for data from the socket (sent by Redis)

4. Caller checks the socket back in to the client (or the pool)

In the type of interaction just described, we see that we never send and receive data at the same time through the socket. We also don't take advantage of the ability to send data while the TCP server is computing the answer to other requests.

Now, on to an alternative approach. We'll work on a new version of our Redis client, this time focused on taking advantage of the full-duplex property of TCP. We want to use a state-machine-like process that manages a socket and deals with sending data to and receiving data from the Redis server. We'll send data for a request even before receiving the response to a previous request. By doing this, we'll keep a stream of data going out and data coming in, taking full advantage of the full-duplex property.

State Machines

The state machine is a well-known model in computer science. You'll find plenty of resources to learn more about it, if you want to dig deeper. In short, we can use state machines to model systems that have different states, and in which events can happen that potentially cause the state machine to transition between those states.

A subset of state machines is called *finite* state machines. These have a discrete, finite number of possible states, as opposed to potentially infinite states. For example, a light switch has two discrete states, on and off, so we could easily model it as a finite state machine.

If you want to read more about state machines, start with the dedicated Wikipedia page.[a]

---

a.   https://en.wikipedia.org/wiki/Finite-state_machine

Let's dive in and build our state-machine client.

gen_statem to the Rescue

We can model most TCP clients as *finite state machines*. Finite state machines (FSMs) are a way to model the behavior of systems using states and state transitions. An FSM can be in only one state at any given time, and the number of states is finite (hence the name). Events can cause the FSM to transition from one state to another.

TCP clients can usually be modeled as FSMs with just two states: connected and disconnected. Visual representations are a great tool to help us understand FSMs, so let's take a look at what an FSM for a TCP client would look like.

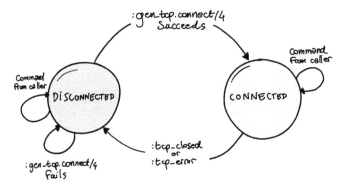

The transitions between the connected and disconnected states are straightforward. The client starts in the disconnected state. If the client establishes a TCP connection, it transitions to the connected state. Once in the connected state, any TCP error causes the client to transition back to the disconnected state. The remaining events are interesting: while they don't cause any state transitions, they still result in some action being performed by the FSM. Here are the events that we want our FSM to be able to deal with:

- A caller asks our client to send a command to Redis
- Our client receives some data from Redis
- The backoff timeout fires, telling our connection to reconnect (more on this later)

This is when having a well-modeled FSM shines: we can handle the same event differently in each state.

To understand all of this better, let's take a look at some code. Erlang ships with a behavior called gen_statem[4] that you can use to implement state-machine processes. gen_statem is a powerful behavior that lets you implement potentially complex processes, but it's not the easiest to grasp due to its vast API surface. The good news is that we'll only use a few of the features it provides in our examples. Let's kick things off with a new module, RedisClient.StateMachine, in

---

4.	https://erlang.org/doc/man/gen_statem.html

lib/redis_client/state_machine.ex. Similarly to what you'd do for a GenServer, we'll define a start_link/1 function next. But this time we call :gen_statem.start_link/3.

redis_client/lib/redis_client/state_machine.ex
```
defmodule RedisClient.StateMachine do
  alias RedisClient.RESP

  require Logger

  def start_link(options) do
    :gen_statem.start_link(__MODULE__, options, _gen_statem_options = [])
  end
end
```

The :gen_statem behavior can act in two different ways, depending on how you want to represent the state. If you want to represent it as just a single atom (such as :connected or :disconnected), and you want to implement the handling of all events separately based on the state, then you can use the *state functions* mode. In this mode, you define functions such as connected/3 or disconnected/3, which represent event handling in different states. The other possible mode is the *handle event mode*, in which you define a single handle_event/4 callback function (with many clauses) that takes the state as the first argument. In this mode, you're not limited to using atoms for the state—you can use any term. You choose which mode to use through the mandatory callback_mode/0 callback, so let's start by coding that up.

redis_client/lib/redis_client/state_machine.ex
```
@impl :gen_statem
def callback_mode, do: [:state_functions, :state_enter]
```

Let's go with :state_functions here, since we only have two states and they're easily represented by the atoms :connected and :disconnected. As you can see, we're returning a list from callback_mode/0, with the second atom being :state_enter. This is a way to tell the :gen_statem behavior to fire *state enter* events when entering every state. We'll see how that's useful to us later on.

State and Data

 When using :gen_statem, you'll need to revisit your terminology. In GenServers and most other behaviors, you'll use state to refer to the data that your process holds in memory and acts on. But when using :gen_statem, the term *state* refers to the state of the state machine. Because of this, you'll usually refer to the process's internal data as *data*. This is a good choice, since it's what the :gen_statem documentation uses as well.

Okay, let's move on to more interesting stuff. The next function we want to implement is the init/1 callback. It works similarly to GenServer.init/1, but instead of just returning {:ok, _}, it needs to return the initial state of the state machine as well as the data. We're also including the defstruct that defines the data here.

redis_client/lib/redis_client/state_machine.ex
```elixir
# The "data" (that is, the equivalent of the "state" in a GenServer).
defstruct [:host, :port, :socket, :continuation, queue: :queue.new()]

@impl :gen_statem
def init(options) do
  data = %__MODULE__{
    host: Keyword.fetch!(options, :host),
    port: Keyword.fetch!(options, :port)
  }

  actions = [{:next_event, :internal, :connect}]
  {:ok, :disconnected, data, actions}
end
```

In this code, we build the data from the options and then return :disconnected as the second element of the return tuple. This tells :gen_statem that we want to start in the disconnected state. The last element of the return tuple—that sneaky actions—is part of the magic of :gen_statem. Every :gen_statem callback can return a list of actions that the state machine applies before continuing its process loop. Actions allow you to do many things, such as set timers, fire events, reply to calls, and more. In this case, we're using the :next_event action. This fires an internal event, which gets processed before messages, calls, casts, or any other event arriving at the state machine. It's sort of analogous to returning a :continue tuple from GenServer.init/1.

So, we're starting in the disconnected state and firing this :connect event. Its purpose is to tell our state machine to establish a connection. The :connect event will fire in the disconnected state, so let's define a disconnected/3 clause to handle that.

redis_client/lib/redis_client/state_machine.ex
```elixir
def disconnected(:internal, :connect, data) do
  options = [:binary, active: :once]

  case :gen_tcp.connect(data.host, data.port, options, 5000) do
    {:ok, socket} ->
      data = %{data | socket: socket}
      {:next_state, :connected, data}

    {:error, reason} ->
      Logger.error("Failed to connect: #{:inet.format_error(reason)}")
      timer_action = {{:timeout, :reconnect}, @backoff_time, nil}
      {:keep_state_and_data, [timer_action]}
  end
end
```

This is run-of-the-mill stuff at this point, but the interesting snippet here is line 7. By returning :next_state, we're telling :gen_statem that we want to switch state and move to the connected state. If there's an error establishing the connection, we can instead return :keep_state_and_data, which leaves both data and state alone (line 12). Here, we're also using the :timeout action, which sets up a timeout that will fire after a specified interval. We're entering the realm of connections and reconnections.

Connections and Reconnections

Let's write another disconnected/3 clause, this time to handle the timeout itself.

redis_client/lib/redis_client/state_machine.ex
```
def disconnected({:timeout, :reconnect}, nil, _data) do
  actions = [{:next_event, :internal, :connect}]
  {:keep_state_and_data, actions}
end
```

The beauty of :gen_statem! We can just fire the good old :connect internal event and we'll go right back to attempting to connect. Instead of just using nil as the timeout data, we could embellish the event and the timeout with more information. For example, we could keep track of the timeout value and implement exponential backoff.

Now, on to dealing with callers. If a caller wants to send a command, but we're in the disconnected state, we'll just return an error right away. Let's type this up, alongside the function that sends the call to our process.

redis_client/lib/redis_client/state_machine.ex
```
def command(pid, command, timeout \\ 5000) do
  :gen_statem.call(pid, {:command, command}, timeout)
end

def disconnected({:call, from}, {:command, _command}, _data) do
  actions = [{:reply, from, {:error, :disconnected}}]
  {:keep_state_and_data, actions}
end
```

We use the :reply action to reply to the caller with an error. But such a call could come to our process in the connected state as well, so let's implement the same event handling but in that state.

redis_client/lib/redis_client/state_machine.ex
```
def connected({:call, from}, {:command, command}, data) do
  :ok = :gen_tcp.send(data.socket, RESP.encode(command))
  data = update_in(data.queue, &:queue.in(from, &1))
  {:keep_state, data}
end
```

The rest of the code in this module deals with buffering data from Redis and sending responses to the queued clients when we get them. The only thing left to look at is that :state_enter value we returned from callback_mode/0. With that, :gen_statem fires an event of type :enter when entering states. This is useful in our case, because one of the things we can do is *cancel* the reconnection timer whenever we enter the connected state. Here's how that looks.

```
redis_client/lib/redis_client/state_machine.ex
def connected(:enter, _old_state = :disconnected, _data) do
  actions = [{{:timeout, :reconnect}, :cancel}]
  {:keep_state_and_data, actions}
end
```

Connection Storms and Backoffs

In the code for disconnected(:internal, :connect, data), on line 11, we used a hard-coded @backoff_time timeout of one second. This is fine for the purposes of this small example, but this strategy could cause issues for a real-world TCP client. The problem here is as follows. Imagine you have many instances of a client like this running on your system, all connected to the same TCP server. If the server restarts, for example, then all the clients will disconnect at the same time, and all the clients will attempt to reconnect at the same time. This will likely cause strain on the server, which now has to accept many connections all at once. This phenomenon is sometimes referred to as a *connection storm.*

To mitigate connection storms, a common strategy is to introduce a bit of *jitter* to the backoff time. This jitter is a small random percentage of the backoff time that gets added to or removed from the backoff time itself. For example, instead of having a fixed backoff time of one second, we could have a backoff time of one second plus or minus half a second. In our code, this would be as simple as the following:

```
jitter = div(Enum.random(-@backoff_time..@backoff_time), 2)
backoff_time = @backoff_time + jitter
timer_action = {{:timeout, :reconnect}, backoff_time, nil}
```

You can do the math in many ways. Here, we're taking the backoff time and adding or subtracting a random number in the interval -@backoff_time / 2 to @backoff_time / 2. This randomized backoff has the effect of spreading out reconnections instead of getting surges of them in the given interval.

Another technique often used to mitigate the effects of connection storms is to combine jitter with *exponential backoffs*. Using exponential backoffs means increasing the backoff time every time a reconnection attempt fails by multiplying the backoff time by a factor. This results in clients that try to reconnect fast initially, then progressively slow down to lower resource consumption on both the server and the client. Implementing exponential backoffs is a matter of multiplication, as you can see in this piece of code.

```
backoff_time = previous_backoff_time * 2
jittered = add_jitter(backoff_time)
timer_action = {{:timeout, :reconnect}, jittered, backoff_time}
```

This assumes we're passing the backoff time around in the timeout (the third element of the tuple) and using it to calculate the new timeout by multiplying by two.

We've got a working state-machine-based client now. It can handle disconnections and reconnections, queue requests, and take advantage of the full-duplex nature of TCP by sending multiple requests *and* receiving responses asynchronously. As our final foray into TCP clients, let's look at how we can scale this type of client up through pooling.

Pooling Connections Through Registry

We saw how to pool client connections through something like poolboy earlier in this chapter. All the benefits of pooling client connections apply to state-machine clients as well. While a single state-machine client can handle multiple callers, you'll still want to add pooling to make the system more reliable (if a client crashes, there are other clients operating) and scalable. There's an additional pooling strategy that doesn't work well with the clients we've seen before, but it fits like a glove when it comes to state-machine clients. Let's look at it.

The pooling strategies we've already explored are not a good fit for state-machine clients. They work, but they're not optimal. We put a bunch of effort into making our state-machine Redis client multiplexed and able to serve callers concurrently, but by using a checkout pool like poolboy we'd be letting go of that advantage completely, since a caller would still check out a client and use it exclusively until done with its request.

An alternative pooling strategy that fits this new type of client better is based on Registry. We've used Registry[5] in Chapter 3, Designing a Chat Protocol and Its TCP Server, on page 33, already, but the gist of it is that it's a process you can use to register other processes. We can use Registry to build a pool where

---

5.   https://hexdocs.pm/elixir/Registry.html

we have a supervisor that starts a bunch of our TCP clients. Each client can register itself in a registry. Callers can get all the registered clients and choose any strategy to execute their requests. Let's visualize the supervision tree for this pool in the following diagram.

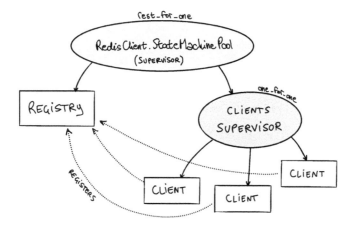

Every client that the pool starts must register under the same key in a registry that has duplicate keys. In registries with duplicate keys, multiple processes can register under the same key. Let's use :client as the key here and add a small modification to our client's start_link/1 function, which you can see in this code.

redis_client/lib/redis_client/state_machine.ex
```elixir
@impl :gen_statem
def init(options) do
  if registry = options[:registry_name] do
    {:ok, _} = Registry.register(registry, :client, :no_value)
  end

  data = %__MODULE__{
    host: Keyword.fetch!(options, :host),
    port: Keyword.fetch!(options, :port)
  }

  actions = [{:next_event, :internal, :connect}]
  {:ok, :disconnected, data, actions}
end
```

If the client gets a :registry_name option, it registers itself in that registry under the key :client. The registry handles everything else for us, such as process crashes and restarts.

We can now create a new module for our pool.

Create lib/redis_client/state_machine_pool.ex and type the following in it.

```
redis_client/lib/redis_client/state_machine_pool.ex
Line 1  defmodule RedisClient.StateMachinePool do
          @spec start_link(keyword()) :: Supervisor.on_start()
          def start_link(options) do
            name = Keyword.fetch!(options, :name)
     5      registry_name = registry_name(name)

            client_specs =
              for index <- 1..Keyword.fetch!(options, :pool_size) do
                child_options = Keyword.put(options, :registry_name, registry_name)
    10
                %{
                  id: {:redis, index},
                  start: {RedisClient.StateMachine, :start_link, [child_options]}
                }
    15        end

            children = [
              {Registry, keys: :duplicate, name: registry_name},
              %{
    20          id: :clients_supervisor,
                start: {
                  Supervisor,
                  :start_link,
                  [client_specs, [strategy: :one_for_one]]
    25          }
              }
            ]

            Supervisor.start_link(children, strategy: :rest_for_one, name: name)
    30    end

          defp registry_name(pool_name) do
            Module.concat(pool_name, Registry)
          end
    35  end
```

That's a lot of code, but the start_link/1 function is only creating the supervision tree that we visualized earlier. On line 4, we require a :name option
for the pool. We use that on the next line to create a name for the pool's
registry (which is just the pool name plus .Registry). Then, we inject the
:registry_name option for each client we start (on line 9). On line 18, we start
the registry, then the supervisor which owns the client processes. The
top-level supervisor for the pool is a :rest_for_one supervisor (line 29),
because we want a registry crash to bring down the client supervisor
too—but not the other way around, since the registry is fine if no clients
are alive, while the opposite is not true.

All that's left is to send commands to Redis. The pool's job is just to pick a client to route the command through. Let's look at the code for the command/2 function in the pool.

redis_client/lib/redis_client/state_machine_pool.ex
```
Line 1  def command(pool_name, command) do
     2    case Registry.lookup(registry_name(pool_name), :client) do
     3      [] ->
     4        {:error, :no_connections_available}
     5
     6      pids ->
     7        {pid, _value} = Enum.random(pids)
     8        RedisClient.StateMachine.command(pid, command)
     9    end
    10  end
```

Short and to the point. If no clients are in the registry, we return an error (line 4). Otherwise, we pick a random client and go through that one (line 7). That's all!

Let's quickly mention something about the *random client* strategy we're using here. It's not great. First, it'll happily pick clients that are disconnected. We could amend that by having code in RedisClient.StateMachine that *unregisters* the process when entering the :disconnected state (Registry.unregister/2)[6] and *registers* it when entering the :connected state instead of only registering in init/1. :gen_statem makes it straightforward to do that when entering states. Second, randomness is not always the best strategy, because it doesn't account for factors such as the latency of each client or the amount of requests each client has in its queue. We won't dig into how to solve these issues here (a good homework assignment for you, dear reader!), but you could use the value each process registers itself under to keep track of information. For example, you could store the number of queued requests for each client and route to the client with the smallest queue. Take a look at the documentation for Registry.update_value/3[7] for inspiration.

Wrapping Up

Well, our journey through the magical realm of TCP on the wings of the BEAM is complete. In this chapter, we chewed through a lot of advanced information around TCP clients. We started with a couple of different approaches to pooling. Then, we explored a completely different approach to clients based

---

6.   https://hexdocs.pm/elixir/Registry.html#unregister/2
7.   https://hexdocs.pm/elixir/Registry.html#update_value/3

on the state machine abstraction. Finally, we looked at yet another pooling strategy based on the Registry Elixir module.

If you want real-world examples of TCP clients on the BEAM, you're in luck: most database drivers are TCP clients at the end of the day. Good codebases to explore include Redix,[8] Postgrex,[9] Mint,[10] and Finch.[11]

Before we move on to the other widely used network protocol, UDP, we'll talk a bit about securing TCP traffic.

8.   https://github.com/whatyouhide/redix
9.   https://github.com/elixir-ecto/postgrex
10. https://github.com/elixir-mint/mint
11. https://github.com/sneako/finch

## CHAPTER 7

Securing Protocols: TLS

Networks and network protocols have this tendency to expose our digital fingerprints. Every connection sends out signals that can be intercepted and analyzed. This was okay in the early days of the Internet, when users might have been a few academics talking about public research. But the more people started using the Internet, the more it became clear that we needed a way to hide and secure traffic between peers to avoid data being intercepted by third parties.

In this chapter, we'll explore what has become the most widely used securing mechanism for network protocols: *TLS*. TLS is a way to secure traffic for several protocols, but it's most commonly used on top of TCP—think of how HTTP, which is based on TCP, uses TLS to secure communication and turn into HTTPS.

UDP (and other datagram-based protocols) get their encryption from a close relative of TLS, DTLS.[1] DTLS essentially emulates for UDP what TLS does for TCP, adding some packet-ordering guarantees but essentially achieving the same goal. Because of this, we won't talk about DTLS in this book, and we will focus all our attention on TLS.

We'll start with a short overview of what TLS is and how it works. We'll then move on to explore the ssl Erlang application.[2] Finally, we'll look at some practical examples of TLS in action by securing the chat application we built in the previous chapters.

---

1. https://en.wikipedia.org/wiki/Datagram_Transport_Layer_Security
2. https://www.erlang.org/doc/apps/ssl/ssl.html

Understanding How TLS Works

TLS is a generic way of securing traffic that happens in network protocols like TCP. It stands for Transport Layer Security, because its job is to secure traffic on the transport layer (Appendix 1, The OSI Model, on page 223). It's mostly used with TCP and its applications: HTTP (with HTTPS), VoIP, email, and more.

What About SSL?

You've probably also heard of *SSL*. SSL (Secure Socket Layer) was a proprietary security scheme developed by Netscape[a] in the mid-'90s. Around 1999, the *Internet Engineering Task Force,*[b] IETF, built on top of version 3.0 of SSL and created the first version of TLS in RFC 2246.[c]

In most circumstances, you'll see the names SSL and TLS used interchangeably. TLS is the technically correct name to use, but many languages and libraries still use the name SSL for historical reasons—and Erlang is one of them.

---

a.   https://isp.netscape.com
b.   https://www.ietf.org/
c.   https://datatracker.ietf.org/doc/html/rfc2246

TLS takes care of three main pillars of security:

- *Encryption*: hiding the content of the data being exchanged so that it can only be deciphered by the sender and the receiver

- *Authentication*: making sure that both ends of the connection are who they say they are

- *Integrity*: checking that the data being exchanged has not been modified or tampered with by anyone

It does all that by using *public-key cryptography*.[3] Public-key cryptography (or asymmetric cryptography) is a cryptography field based on a two-key system—a public key and a private key. If each communicating party has a private and public key pair, you can achieve two-way encryption, authentication, and integrity checking. The way it works is elegant. Let's use Alice and Bob, traditional example names in the cryptography world, as the two people trying to communicate securely.

Alice can encrypt something through her private key, and Bob can use Alice's public key to decrypt it. This isn't useful for hiding data, but it assures Bob

---

3.   https://en.wikipedia.org/wiki/Public-key_cryptography

that the data was indeed encrypted by Alice. Now, Bob can encrypt something with Alice's public key, and only Alice can decrypt it—through her private key. Flip this both ways, and you have two-way secure communication *and* authentication. Integrity checks can be achieved through *signatures*, which are a way to guarantee that the signed data hasn't been tampered with.

This is a pretty short overview of public-key cryptography, but it was necessary to understand how TLS does its job.

TLS only uses public-key cryptography during its *handshake* phase, which happens when two peers connect. During the handshake, client and server end up with a *secret* they then use to encrypt all exchanged data for the duration of the connection. The following figure shows a sketch of the TLS handshake up to TLS v1.2. The circled numbers tell you the order of operations.

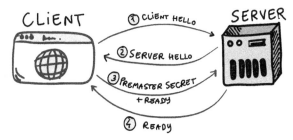

TLS v1.3 is all about making this handshake *quicker* by collapsing some operations. The changes boil down to the client and server communicating more information that allows them to agree on the encryption secret through fewer steps. It more or less looks like this:

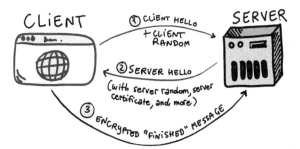

We now have a decent picture of how TLS works. One of the most appealing aspects of TLS, though, is *using* it in practice is usually trivial. Generally speaking, you use TLS in place of the underlying transport protocol. So, instead of using TCP directly, you use TLS. That's how most language libraries for TLS operate: they wrap the TCP implementation and add the TLS handshake and encryption to it. That's what Erlang's standard library does as well, so let's take a look at that.

The ssl Application

Most of the functionality you need when it comes to TLS in Elixir and Erlang is contained within Erlang's ssl application.[4] ssl exposes the concept of a *TLS socket*, which is just a wrapper around a TCP socket with some metadata about the TLS handshake and shared secret.

TLS Sockets and the OS

 We referred to *TLS sockets*, but that's not an operating-system concept the way TCP or UDP sockets are. Operating systems only know about TCP and UDP sockets. But most language ecosystems choose to provide a similar socket-based API for TLS connections, so they wrap the OS socket in a language-specific data structure. Erlang is no exception.

If you want to see this in practice, open a TCP socket and a TLS socket and call inspect/1 on each of them: you'll see that there's a TCP socket nested inside the TLS socket!

If you do some spelunking through ssl's API, you'll see that many functions mirror the functions in gen_tcp, including connect/4, listen/2, send/2, and recv/3. These behave just like their gen_tcp counterparts, but they encrypt and decrypt data when necessary.

We talked a lot. Let's start to play with some code. Most websites use HTTPS, which is based on TLS, so we can establish a TLS connection to any of those—usually HTTPS runs on port 443. In an IEx shell (just type iex in your terminal), type the following:

```
iex> {:ok, _} = Application.ensure_all_started(:ssl)
iex> :ssl.connect(~c"erlang.org", 443, [:binary])
{:error,
 {:options, :incompatible, [verify: :verify_peer, cacerts: :undefined]}}
```

Uh-oh. Actually, that error is fantastic news. It's telling us that the default value for the :verify option (:verify_peer) is incompatible with the :cacerts option being :undefined. Those are a lot of new words, but the gist is this: :ssl.connect/3 tried to verify the certificate provided by erlang.org, but we didn't provide any *root certificate*, so validation failed.

We have two ways to fix this error: either we skip validation or we use valid certificates. Skipping validation, which you can do by passing verify: :verify_none, defeats the whole point of TLS, since you won't know which server you're

---

4.   https://www.erlang.org/doc/apps/ssl/ssl.html

Root Certificates and Certificate Chains

The way TLS certificates work is elegant. There are a few root Certificate Authorities (CA), such as Verisign.[a] They're like the ultimate authority figures that everyone else in the trust network looks up to. We build *certificate chains* that are signed using other certificates, all the way up to the root certificates.

We won't dive into this topic. You can find plenty of information online, but we recommend DNSimple's documentation[b] as a great starting point.

_____

a.   https://www.verisign.com/
b.   https://support.dnsimple.com/articles/what-is-ssl-certificate-chain/

talking to. So, let's use valid certificates instead. Since OTP 25, Erlang ships with a way to fetch your operating system's default TLS certificates, which are usually a good choice. You use public_key:cacerts_get/0[5] to do that:

```
iex> certs = :public_key.cacerts_get()
iex> {:ok, socket} =
...>    :ssl.connect(~c"erlang.org", 443, [:binary, cacerts: certs])
{:ok,
 {:sslsocket, {:gen_tcp, #Port<0.6>, :tls_connection, :undefined},
  [#PID<0.141.0>, #PID<0.140.0>]}}
```

Success! That's a convoluted data structure, but you don't have to know what's going on inside: you always just pass it around as the TLS socket.

Certificates Before Erlang/OTP 25

If you find yourself needing up-to-date certificates, but you're running an older Erlang version—or you want to avoid falling back to OS certificates for any reason—you can use CAStore.[6] It's an Elixir library that ships with trusted certificates (from Mozilla), maintained by two Elixir core team members, including the author of this book.

If you leave IEx idle for a while, you'll probably end up with an {:ssl_closed, socket} message (call flush() to see it). In active mode, ssl mirrors the messages used by gen_tcp:

- {:ssl, socket, data} for new data
- {:ssl_error, socket, reason} for errors
- {:ssl_closed, socket} when the socket gets closed

_____

5.   https://www.erlang.org/doc/apps/public_key/public_key.html#cacerts_get/0
6.   https://github.com/elixir-mint/castore

There's one more way you can set up TLS connections: by *upgrading* existing TCP connections. To do that, you start with a normal gen_tcp socket and then pass it to :ssl.connect/2:

```
iex> {:ok, tcp_socket} = :gen_tcp.connect(~c"erlang.org", 443, [:binary])
{:ok, #Port<0.14>}
iex> :ssl.connect(
...>    tcp_socket,
...>    cacerts: :public_key.cacerts_get(),
...>    server_name_indication: ~c"erlang.org"
...> )
{:ok,
 {:sslsocket, {:gen_tcp, #Port<0.14>, :tls_connection, :undefined},
  [#PID<0.182.0>, #PID<0.181.0>]}}
```

:ssl.connect/2,3,4 options can be complex and easy to mess up. Here, for example, we had to use :server_name_indication because without the option the upgrade wouldn't work. We won't look at any more options, but the ssl Erlang documentation is a great reference when needed.

Well, that was a short tour of ssl in Erlang. There's not much more to it: most of the complexity usually lies in making sure we are using it *safely*, which depends on use cases and the servers we're connecting to. Luckily, higher-level libraries that take care of protocols like HTTPS—which is based on TLS—usually take care of the security aspect for you, as we'll see in Chapter 11, Talking the Internet Protocol: HTTP/1.1, on page 175.

Now, let's take a moment to see ssl in practice by securing the chat server we built a few chapters ago.

Securing Our Chat System

All the way back in Chapter 3, Designing a Chat Protocol and Its TCP Server, on page 33, we started working on a chat system that we then iterated on. When we left it in Chapter 4, Scaling TCP on the Server Side, on page 59, our chat system was able to support multiple clients connected at the same time and sending messages to each other. Our goal here is to *secure* that chat system by encrypting in-flight data through TLS. We'll do that by changing the chat system code to use ssl rather than gen_tcp and tweaking it for some TLS-specific stuff. You can follow along by modifying the chat application in code/chat. For the sake of keeping resources separated, the source code for the version of the chat application that uses TLS will live in code/chat_tls.

Since TLS secures traffic *on top* of TCP, we don't need to make any changes to our chat protocol (Chat.Protocol). The same goes for the data structures we used to represent messages in code/chat/lib/chat/messages.ex. We'll only change the places where we used gen_tcp to adapt them to use ssl.

Let's start with an annoying part of all this: certificates.

Generating Self-Signed TLS Certificates

It's TLS, so we'll need some certificates. We're running all this locally, however, so we'll generate and self-sign some certificates. We'll need a public certificate and private key for the server and the same for the client. We'll also want to combine those into a PEM-encoded Certificate Authority (CA) certificate chain. This is not stuff you usually do yourself, so we won't go too deep. To follow along, you'll need OpenSSL[7] installed—that's a standard tool for this sort of thing.

Why You Usually Don't Generate Certificates

The reason you don't generally go through generating client/server certificates and CA certificates is that it would somewhat defeat the point of certificates on the Internet. If anybody could self-sign certificates, then it would be hard to trust the certificates. So, it usually works like this:

- If you're a server, you request a domain certificate from a trusted registered provider, receive the certificate, and can then use it

- If you're a client, you usually use certificates that ship with your OS or from a trusted source, such as Mozilla's CA Certificate List,[a] which already knows how to verify certificates signed through registered providers

---

a. https://wiki.mozilla.org/CA/Included_Certificates

In a terminal, create a priv directory inside code/chat and cd into it:

```
mkdir priv
cd priv
```

Start by generating a key for our simulated certificate authority and then a self-signed certificate from that key:

```
> openssl genrsa -out ca.key 2048
> openssl req -new -x509 -key ca.key -out ca.pem -days 365 -subj "/CN=MyCA"
```

Now, you need to generate a server key and a server certificate request. This step is an implementation detail, but to generate a certificate you need to first generate a request and then sign it.

---

7. https://www.openssl.org/

```
> openssl genrsa -out server.key 2048
> openssl req -new -key server.key -out server.csr -subj "/CN=localhost"
```

Now that you have the request, you can get a certificate by signing that request with the CA:

```
> openssl x509 -req \
    -in server.csr -CA ca.pem -CAkey ca.key -CAcreateserial \
    -out server.crt -days 365
```

We now need to repeat the same process for the client: generate a key and a certificate request, then sign that request with the CA.

```
> openssl genrsa -out client.key 2048
> openssl req -new -key client.key -out client.csr -subj "/CN=client"
> openssl x509 -req \
    -in client.csr -CA ca.pem -CAkey ca.key -CAcreateserial \
    -out client.crt -days 365
```

You should now have the following:

- priv/ca.pem: the CA
- priv/server.key and priv/server.crt: the server's key and certificate
- priv/client.key and priv/client.crt: the client's key and certificate

cd back into code/chat and we're ready to move on!

Following Along

 All the following code snippets reference code/chat_tls (rather than code/chat) so that we could keep all application versions in the book resources. But if you're following along, making modifications to your copy of code/chat would be the way to go.

Listening for TLS Connections

The first thing we can update is our *listener*. Remember, a listener is a GenServer process that opens a listen socket and listens for connections (it's in code/chat/lib/chat/acceptor_pool/listener.ex). The only thing we need to change here is the call to :gen_tcp.listen/2, which we swap for :ssl.listen/2. We also need some additional options in there for passing in certificates and whatnot (they're highlighted).

chat_tls/lib/chat/acceptor_pool/listener.ex
```
listen_options = [
  :binary,
  active: :once,
  exit_on_close: false,
  reuseaddr: true,
```

```
➤    cacertfile: Application.app_dir(:chat, "priv/ca.pem"),
➤    certfile: Application.app_dir(:chat, "priv/server.crt"),
➤    keyfile: Application.app_dir(:chat, "priv/server.key")
  ]

case :ssl.listen(port, listen_options) do
  # Same as before
```

The acceptor supervisor (code/chat/lib/chat/acceptor_pool/acceptor_supervisor.ex) stays exactly the same: it keeps spawning acceptor processes. For those, we need to replace the call to :gen_tcp.accept/2 with :ssl.transport_accept/2, and :gen_tcp.controlling_process/2 with :ssl.controlling_process/2.

chat_tls/lib/chat/acceptor_pool/acceptor.ex
```
case :ssl.transport_accept(listen_socket, 2_000) do
  {:ok, socket} ->
    Logger.debug("Accepted TLS connection")
    {:ok, pid} = ConnectionSupervisor.start_connection(socket)
    :ok = :ssl.controlling_process(socket, pid)
    __accept_loop__(listen_socket)
```

The last step on the server side is the connection itself in code/chat/lib/chat/connection.ex. :ssl servers need to perform one additional operation on the socket compared to :gen_tcp to accept a client: they need to call :ssl.handshake/1. This performs the TLS handshake and verifies parameters.

chat_tls/lib/chat/connection.ex
```
def init(socket) do
➤  case :ssl.handshake(socket) do
    {:ok, socket} ->
      {:ok, %__MODULE__{socket: socket}}
```

We do this when the connection initializes in the init/1 callback so that we terminate the connection if the client's certificates or validation are invalid. We could perform the handshake in the acceptor as well, *before* spawning a connection, but the Erlang documentation itself[8] says the following:

> ssl:transport_accept/1 and ssl:handshake/2 are separate functions so that the handshake part can be called in a new Erlang process dedicated to handling the connection.

The remaining changes to Chat.Connection are trivial:

- We replace :tcp, :tcp_error, and :tcp_closed messages with the corresponding :ssl, :ssl_error, and :ssl_closed messages

- We replace :gen_tcp.send/2 with :ssl.send/2

- :inet.setopts/2 becomes :ssl.setopts/2—different function, exact same behavior

---

8.   https://www.erlang.org/doc/apps/ssl/using_ssl.html#basic-connection

The server side is good to go. You can start the new TLS server the same way you did for the TCP server:

```
> POOL=true mix run --no-halt
10:05:42.302 [info] Started TLS pooled chat server on port 4000
```

The client's going to be even easier.

Connecting to Our TLS Server

Changing the client in code/chat/lib/mix/tasks/chat_client.ex to support connecting via TLS boils down to changing some options when connecting, similarly to what we did on the server. We'll need to add some options to :ssl.connect/3:

```
chat_tls/lib/mix/tasks/chat_client.ex
{:ok, socket} =
  :ssl.connect(~c"localhost", 4000, [
    :binary,
    active: :once,
    verify: :verify_peer,
    cacertfile: Application.app_dir(:chat, "priv/ca.pem"),
    certfile: Application.app_dir(:chat, "priv/client.crt"),
    keyfile: Application.app_dir(:chat, "priv/client.key")
  ])
```

These options set the CA certificate to the same public certificate that's on the server, then use the client certificate and key we generated earlier. The rest of the changes consist in replacing :gen_tcp.send/2 calls with :ssl.send/2, replacing :tcp messages with :ssl messages, and replacing :inet.setopts/2 with :ssl.setopts/2—just as we did for the server's Chat.Connection.

You're ready to test out our chat system now. With the server running in one terminal, start two chat sessions in two separate terminals:

```
> mix chat_client
```

You'll see it behaves exactly as our TCP chat client did, but this time traffic is encrypted!

```
→ mix chat_client
Enter your username: Andrea
Andrea#
Eric> Encrypted traffic 😈
```

```
→ mix chat_client
Enter your username: Eric
Eric#  Encrypted traffic 😈
Eric# █
```

Homework

Want to feel like you're a hacker in a movie? Play around with Wireshark[9] and analyze traffic for our chat system—first the TCP version, then the TLS. To start, you'll probably want to capture packets on the lo0 network interface and use at least the filter tcp.port == 4000.

You'll see that TCP traffic is in plain text: you can inspect anything that gets sent between server and client. On the other hand, for TLS traffic, Wireshark will just say "Encrypted Application Data".

Wrapping Up

This chapter was a bit shorter than others in the book. TLS is a fundamental thing to know about when working with networks, but you'll mostly use it transparently over TCP and focus on other networking aspects of your applications. But you still got to know the fundamentals of how TLS works, played around with the ssl Erlang application, and converted the chat system from previous chapters to use TLS.

This chapter concludes our journey into TCP. Next, we venture into the realm of UDP.

---

9. https://www.wireshark.org/

Part II

UDP

UDP is the "other" Internet protocol. It powers hostname resolution with DNS, real-time communication applications such as VoIP and video streaming, and more.

CHAPTER 8

Same Layer, Different Protocol: Introducing UDP

TCP is the right choice for most applications. After all, the backbone of everything we do on the Internet is TCP: the web, instant messaging, streaming, downloads, and more. But there are times when we need more control. Maybe you just need to get as close to the network as you can, maybe you don't need persistent connections, or maybe you don't need network packets to always be delivered in order (or at all). That's when we reach for UDP.

UDP (*User Datagram Protocol*) is a simple and efficient network protocol often used as the foundation of more complex applications. TCP is like a cake mix: throw in a few wet ingredients, such as eggs and milk, and you've got yourself a nice cake. It's hard to mess up the process, because the cake mix gives you a nice guarantee. UDP is like baking completely on your own. You have more control over the quality of each ingredient and the proportions, but it requires you to do a lot more.

Reach for UDP only when you absolutely need to squeeze everything out of the performance of the protocol and when you can get away with fewer guarantees. For example, video-conferencing protocols usually rely on UDP. This makes sense for that use case because missing or out-of-order frames can be dealt with—you may have choppier video streams or artifacts, but you still get a usable experience.

We'll start our UDP chapter with a quick review of the protocol. Then, you'll start working on a simple but nifty little application that relies on UDP. We'll build a rudimentary metric-collection system, and then we'll iterate on it, gradually adding features as we go. Let's get started.

The Basics of the Protocol

In this section, you'll learn about the basics of UDP. We'll use Erlang's standard library to have two UDP peers exchange some packets—just to dip our feet in the ocean. Rather than starting from scratch, let's explore UDP by comparing it to TCP and looking at the differences.

As a protocol, UDP sits at the same OSI layer as TCP—that is, the transport layer (layer 4). For a quick guide to the OSI model, see Appendix 1, The OSI Model, on page 223. Just like TCP, UDP is also responsible for packaging, routing, and carrying bytes across the network. It routes those packets to the right peers.

The biggest difference between UDP and TCP is that UDP is *stateless*, while TCP is *stateful*. TCP connections are persistent and represent a stateful relationship between the two peers. UDP, on the other hand, doesn't even deal with the concept of a connection. UDP relies on sockets and their addresses to send and receive data. When you open a UDP socket, all you're doing is getting a handle on the UDP address and port combination. To send data to another UDP socket, you just have to specify its address and port combination. This all sounds a bit abstract, but we'll get our hands dirty soon. First, let's look at a quick recap of the differences between the two protocols in the following table.

TCP	UDP
Stateful connection	No connection
Packets cannot get lost	No delivery guarantees
Packets are always delivered in order	No order guarantees

One key characteristic of UDP, which is a product of its statelessness, is that there are almost *no guarantees*. At all. You can't know whether your socket is connected. You can't know if the data you send reaches its destination. If the data you send makes it to its destination, you can't assume that it reached it in the order it was sent. But there's a reason for all this: efficiency. Thanks to the lack of any handshake to initiate connections, and thanks to not having to keep track of sent and received for ordering purposes, UDP stays fast and lightweight. Like most things in the software world, you give something up (guarantees) to get something back (efficiency)—it's all about compromises and use cases. We'll explore how to deal with this lack of guarantees throughout this chapter. For now, let's dive in and look at some UDP in action.

Sending Some Data via UDP

Hop into a terminal and start a simple UDP server through netcat,[1] a networking utility that ships with most Unix-based operating systems. The command shown next starts a UDP echo server—that is, a server that receives packets and prints them back on the terminal.

```
> nc -u -l 9001
```

The -u flag tells netcat to use UDP instead of TCP (TCP is the default). -l tells it to listen for packets (you can also use netcat as a client). Lastly, 9001 specifies the port we want to listen on. You won't see any output when you run this command, because this server hasn't received any data yet. Let's fix that by sending it some data from the BEAM. Fire up an IEx session and send the bytes "hello" to the netcat server using the following commands:

```
iex> {:ok, sending_socket} = :gen_udp.open(9002, [:binary])
iex> :gen_udp.send(sending_socket, ~c"localhost", 9001, "hello")
:ok
```

If you kept an eye on the running nc command, you should have seen the string hello printed on the terminal. So, something must be working!

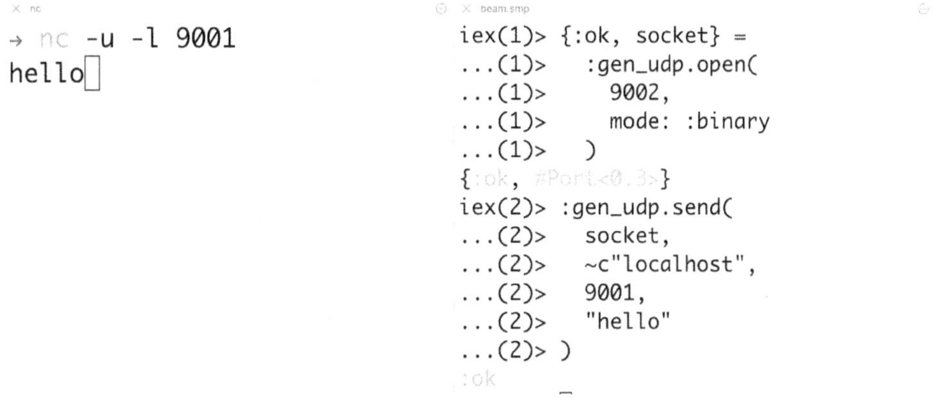

```
✕  nc
→  nc -u -l 9001
hello
```

```
✕  beam.smp
iex(1)> {:ok, socket} =
...(1)>    :gen_udp.open(
...(1)>       9002,
...(1)>       mode: :binary
...(1)>    )
{:ok, #Port<0.3>}
iex(2)> :gen_udp.send(
...(2)>    socket,
...(2)>    ~c"localhost",
...(2)>    9001,
...(2)>    "hello"
...(2)> )
:ok
```

Let's unpack what we just saw. This is our first encounter with the gen_udp module.[2] As you might assume, it's the UDP counterpart to the gen_tcp module that we've used extensively in the previous chapters. It also ships with the Erlang standard library and exposes an API that closely resembles the gen_tcp one.

The first function we used is :gen_udp.open/1. This function returns a UDP socket. There's an important difference between UDP sockets and TCP sockets.

---

1. https://en.wikipedia.org/wiki/Netcat
2. https://www.erlang.org/doc/man/gen_udp.html

In TCP, a socket needs a peer to connect to. In UDP, however, a socket lives a life of its own—there's no concept of an established connection. When you open a UDP socket, what you're in fact doing is hooking into the OS UDP socket listening on the given port. Here, we chose port 9002. :gen_udp.open/2 is the equivalent of :gen_tcp.connect/4, but the name difference is a clear indication of what we just talked about.

We can send UDP data to another UDP socket through the one we opened. That's what we do with the call to :gen_udp.send/4. As you can see in the IEx session, we specify a host-and-port combination right in the send/4 call, without the need for connecting first. If we wanted to send data to another UDP peer, we could do it through the same socket. All we'd need to do is use a different host-and-port combination. This is not possible in TCP, where a specific socket is permanently connected to a specific peer.

The next two figures show the difference between TCP and UDP when it comes to the flow of opening a socket and sending data. In the following figure, you can see the TCP flow that you know by now: the client initiates the connection, the server accepts the connection, and the new socket is opened and can be used to exchange data.

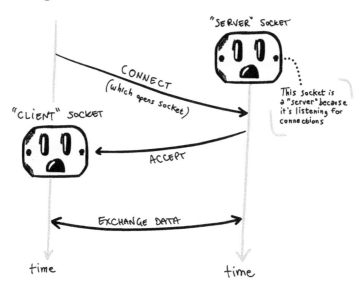

Compare that with the figure shown on page 131, which shows what you can do with UDP sockets. The first step is to open the UDP socket on port 9002. That's also the *only* step when it comes to opening the socket! Once that socket is open, we can use it to send data to any UDP socket on any other peer. The numbers in that figure show you the order of operations, but all that matters is that opening the socket comes first.

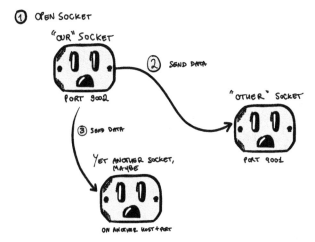

Receiving Data

There's even more to our humble UDP socket. It doesn't just send data—it also *receives* data. To see that in action, let's switch the role of netcat and use it to send some data to our open Erlang socket. Leave the previous IEx session running and exit out of the nc command that you used before—a Ctrl-c will do. Then, run the following command to open a netcat session, where you'll be able to send data to our UDP socket, and type the words hello and world, each followed by Return:

```
> nc -u 127.0.0.1 9002
hello
world
```

We just sent the strings hello\n and world\n to our Erlang UDP socket. In the IEx session, you can use the flush() helper[3] to display the messages received by the shell process. We opened the UDP socket with :gen_udp.open/1, which defaults to a socket in active mode (see Active and Passive Modes for Sockets, on page 14)—that's why the shell process gets the data delivered as Erlang messages.

```
iex> flush()
{:udp, #Port<0.3>, {127, 0, 0, 1}, 63827, "hello\n"}
{:udp, #Port<0.3>, {127, 0, 0, 1}, 63827, "world\n"}
```

The #Port<...> number might be different for you, as might the fourth element of the tuple, which is the source port. The messages you see here look somewhat like the {:tcp, socket, data} messages we got used to in previous

---

3. https://hexdocs.pm/iex/IEx.Helpers.html#flush/0

chapters, but there's more information here. The structure of these new messages is as follows:

```
{:udp, udp_socket, source_address, source_port, data}
```

When comparing this to the {:tcp, socket, data} messages that the :gen_tcp module uses, the only two additional elements are source_address and source_port. Why include those in the message? Because the UDP socket is *stateless* and not connected to any particular address and port. This means that it can receive data from *any other UDP socket*. You can verify that by exiting out of netcat (again, just Ctrl - c), starting it again, and sending more data.

```
> nc -u 127.0.0.1 9002
more data
```

If you check the received messages in IEx now, you'll see a new :udp message but with a different source port—64927 here instead of the old 63827.

```
iex> flush()
{:udp, #Port<0.3>, {127, 0, 0, 1}, 64927, "more data\n"}
```

Once again, the source_port will likely look different for you. That's just the port that the OS allocates to the running netcat command. The second element of the tuple, however, will look exactly the same as the previous messages, showing you that the UDP socket that received the data is the same.

> ## UDP Sockets
>
> For all intents and purposes, UDP sockets are pretty much the same as TCP sockets when it comes to OS abstractions. As we explained in Sockets, on page 10, OS sockets are independent of network protocol: whether they give an interface for UDP or TCP traffic is decided by a flag in the socket data structure itself.

In this section, you got a general idea of how UDP works, especially as compared to TCP. UDP is stateless and not connection-oriented. Sending and receiving data works similarly to how it does for TCP, but it accounts for the socket being stateless: you have to specify where to send data every time, and incoming data is tagged with its source peer. Now that we've got the basics of UDP down, we can move on to building something that leverages the protocol.

Building a Metrics Ingestion Daemon

It's time to start working on the application that you'll use to learn UDP. Let's take a moment to describe the use case. In real-world systems, you usually want to report metrics about what your system is doing: counters (numbers of web requests), gauges (how much memory your system is using), timings (how long something usually takes), and more. A common architecture and set of tools for this consists of a daemon running in the background and listening for metrics, paired with the application sending metrics to it. The daemon's job is to collect metrics, aggregate them, and eventually send them over to some data storage. The silly figure here gives you a visual idea of this architecture.

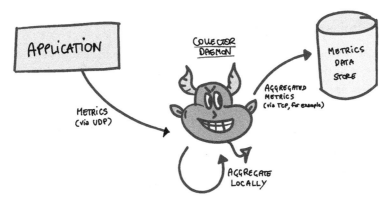

What's UDP got to do with all this? As you can see in the image, UDP tends to be the protocol that applications and these metric-collecting daemons communicate through. There are multiple reasons for the choice of protocol for this use case:

1. *Performance*: In most cases, you want reporting metrics to be as efficient as possible, since it's usually not critical to the business domain of the application. Additionally, there's a good chance that applications will report huge amounts of metrics. As we saw, UDP doesn't need a handshake when establishing connections, there is no packet format overhead, and there are no receiving acknowledgments. All this amounts to a faster protocol overall.

2. *Reliability*: Since metrics tend to not be "fundamental" data, it's okay to lose a few here and there. If you want to get a more-or-less accurate overview of HTTP traffic to your system, you're likely not going to care about the *exact* number of HTTP requests. If that were a business-critical measure to keep track of, you'd keep track of it in your business logic, not in your metrics system.

3. *Resource efficiency*: UDP sockets have a small footprint, since they're not persistent connections. This is useful here, because metrics are secondary data—so, using fewer resources for reporting them is ideal.

Throughout the rest of this chapter, we'll build part of what we just described. We'll code the *reporter*, which is the thing that reports data to the daemon, and the *daemon*, which ingests and aggregates data. Instead of having the daemon store data in an external metrics storage, we'll have it print the aggregated data on the terminal for the sake of simplicity.

Let's start with the basics. As in previous chapters, we'll kick things off with a brief description of the text protocol we'll use.

Getting Familiar with the Protocol

Let's briefly talk about the protocol we'll use to encode and decode data. This protocol is a subset of the protocol used by one of the most widely adopted metric-collecting daemons, StatsD.[4] You can consult the full specification of the protocol,[5] but we're only going to focus on two metric types: counters and gauges.

> ### Metric Types: Counters and Gauges
>
> We glossed over what these metric types are about, but let's take a second to define them.
>
> *Counters* are exactly what they sound like: they count something. Your application increments counters when an interesting event happens, such as a request completing. The collector daemon keeps track of the counter and resets it every time it flushes the current value to the external storage.
>
> *Gauges* measure the current value of something. For example, the current used disk space is usually measured with a gauge. Every time the collector daemon flushes, it will send the latest value of the gauge metric over to the external storage.

This protocol is a textual protocol (Binary Protocols and Textual Protocols, on page 34), just like the one in The Redis Protocol, on page 74. It's also a *line-based protocol*, meaning that each message is delimited by a single newline character (\n). This makes it easier for tools such as nc to work with the protocol. A protocol message looks like this:

```
<metric-name>:<metric-value>|<metric-type>\n
```

The metric name (<metric-name>) can be any name and must be followed by a colon character (:) to separate it from the value. The value (<metric-value>) must be a number—integer or float, positive or negative. The metric type (<metric-type>)

---

4. https://github.com/statsd/statsd
5. https://github.com/b/statsd_spec

can only assume two values: c for counters, g for gauges. Any other metric type is invalid in our simplified protocol.

Starting with an example of a counter metric, let's say that the collector is keeping track of a counter called total_requests, which is now 0. The collector receives the following three metrics:

```
total_requests:3|c
total_requests:1|c
total_requests:1|c
```

Newlines

 In the previous and subsequent code snippets, we don't always show the newline character explicitly (\n). Instead, we visually separate the lines to make it easier to look at for you, dear reader.

The collector's value for total_requests is now 5. When the collector flushes metrics to the external storage, total_requests will go back to 0.

As for gauges, here's an example of a couple of updates to the disk_used_mb metric:

```
disk_used:102.92|g
disk_used:103.02|g
disk_used:101.00|g
```

After these three metric updates, the collector's value for disk_used would be the latest value, 101.00 (even after flushing).

Well, that's it when it comes to the protocol. We won't write the code for it here, but you can find working code for encoding and decoding in the code/xstats/lib/xstats/protocol.ex file. We'll only care about the two public functions in the XStats.Protocol module defined there: parse_metrics/1 and encode_metric/1. Let's represent the metrics as three-element tuples, {type, name, value}, in the following example:

```
{:gauge, "disk_used", 101.0}
{:counter, "total_requests", 1}
```

Notice that parse_metrics/1 takes a string and parses all the *valid* metrics from it, ignoring malformed lines. This behavior is different from the approach we took in the protocols we used in previous chapters. With those protocols, parsing functions would generally parse the next well-formed piece of data and return something like {:ok, parsed, rest}. Here, parse_metrics/1 returns {metrics, errors} and consumes all the data given to it. The reason for this change in behavior will become apparent later in this chapter—but a small spoiler: it boils down to the fact that UDP doesn't guarantee ordering of packets.

The other protocol function, encode_metric/1, takes a metric and returns the encoded line. You can try out the functions by navigating to the code/xstats directory and firing up an IEx console with iex -S mix, as shown here.

```
iex> metric = {:gauge, "disk_used", 2020.83}
iex> iodata = XStats.Protocol.encode_metric(metric)
iex> data = IO.iodata_to_binary(iodata) <> "cruft"
"disk_used:2020.83|g\ncruft"
iex> XStats.Protocol.parse_metrics(data)
{[{:gauge, "disk_used", 2020.83}], ["invalid line format: \"cruft\""]}
```

Next, we'll build the collector daemon.

Building the Collector Daemon

Let's code up the metric-collector daemon next. We'll use a GenServer process for the daemon. Our process will open a UDP socket when starting, then listen for metric packets coming in on that socket. Every few seconds, it will also flush the collected metrics by printing them to standard output.

Later, we'll write some code for reporting metrics. For the sake of simplicity, we'll keep both the daemon and the reporter in the same directory and Mix project, which you can find in code/xstats. In the real world, you might have the reporter embedded and running in your application, with the daemon running as a separate application alongside it. The following figure shows how that would look:

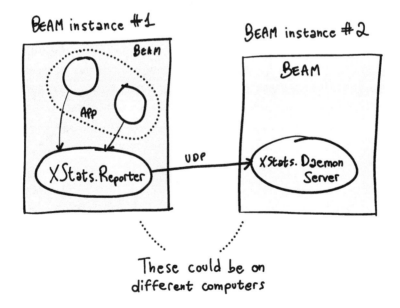

So, back to our GenServer collector. By now, you know the general shape of a GenServer, so we'll gloss over a few details. Let's start by focusing on the init/1 callback. Its job is to open the UDP socket and start the flush timer. The code for init/1 is shown next.

xstats/lib/xstats/daemon_server.ex

```
Line 1  @flush_interval_millisec :timer.seconds(15)

-       @impl true
-       def init(options) do
5         port = Keyword.fetch!(options, :port)
-         flush_io_device = Keyword.get(options, :flush_io_device, :stdio)

-         case :gen_udp.open(port, [:binary, active: true]) do
-           {:ok, socket} ->
10            :timer.send_interval(@flush_interval_millisec, self(), :flush)
-             {:ok, %__MODULE__{socket: socket, flush_io_device: flush_io_device}}

-           {:error, reason} ->
-             {:stop, reason}
15        end
-       end
```

We're keeping the options we pass to :gen_udp.open/2 simple: :binary to send and receive data as binaries, and active: true to keep the socket in active mode. active: :once would probably be a better idea, as you learned in Being More Precise with Active Sockets, on page 28, but we're keeping things simple here. The call to :timer.send_interval/3 on line 10 sets up a timer that periodically sends the :flush message to the GenServer.

The only reason we're passing in a :flush_io_device option (line 6) is to make it easier to test this GenServer. In normal usage, this option keeps its defaults of :stdio, meaning that flushed metrics get printed to standard output as expected. We'll look at testing in a bit.

Next, let's look at how our daemon processes UDP data coming in. All we need is a handle_info/2 callback clause to process the {:udp, ...} messages.

xstats/lib/xstats/daemon_server.ex

```
Line 1  def handle_info(
2         {:udp, socket, _ip, _port, data},
3         %__MODULE__{socket: socket} = state
4       ) do
5         {metrics, _errors} = XStats.Protocol.parse_metrics(data)
6         state = Enum.reduce(metrics, state, &process_metric/2)
7         {:noreply, state}
8       end
```

We're not doing much here. We parse the metrics using our XStats.Protocol.parse_metrics/1 function and ignore all the returned errors for the sake of simplicity. We then go through all the returned metrics and call process_metric/2, which collects each metric into the state. Let's look at the code for process_metric/2 next.

xstats/lib/xstats/daemon_server.ex

```
Line 1  defp process_metric({:gauge, name, value}, %__MODULE__{} = state) do
          put_in(state.metrics[name], {:gauge, value})
        end

     5  defp process_metric({:counter, name, value}, %__MODULE__{} = state) do
          case state.metrics[name] || {:counter, 0} do
            {:counter, current} ->
              put_in(state.metrics[name], {:counter, current + value})

    10      _other ->
              state
          end
        end
```

We pattern match on the metric type. For gauges, we always override the value of the gauge in the state with the provided value (line 2). For counters, we add the provided value to the current value, or to 0 if the counter is not there (that's what the || {:counter, 0} part is for).

A quick note about resiliency: we went through this a few times already, but you never want collecting metrics to cause any issues. Because of this, as you can see, we never raise any errors in our collector. Instead, we simply ignore bad metrics. You can see this on line 5, where we ignore malformed metrics, and on line 10, where we parse counters: we ignore the new counter metric if the metric that's already in the state is not a counter metric. These are all choices we're making to keep our collector alive and not cause any issues to the reporting application.

There's one last thing the collector needs to do: every once in a while, it needs to flush the collected metrics somewhere. We'll have our collector flush the metrics by printing them to an output (defaulting to standard output). We already set up the recurring :flush message in the init/1 callback, so all that's left is to implement a handle_info/2 clause to handle that.

xstats/lib/xstats/daemon_server.ex

```
Line 1  def handle_info(:flush, %__MODULE__{} = state) do
          IO.puts(state.flush_io_device, """
          ================
          Current metrics
     5    ================
          """)
```

```
     state =
       update_in(state.metrics, fn metrics ->
10       Map.new(metrics, fn
           {name, {:counter, value}} ->
             IO.puts(state.flush_io_device, "#{name}:\t#{value}")
             {name, {:counter, 0}}

15         {name, {:gauge, value}} ->
             IO.puts(state.flush_io_device, "#{name}:\t#{value}")
             {name, {:gauge, value}}
           end)
         end)

20
     IO.puts(state.flush_io_device, "\n\n\n")

     {:noreply, state}
   end
```

The idea here is to go through all the metrics in the state, print their values, and reset them. For counters, resetting means returning them to 0 (line 13), while gauges are left at their current value (line 17).

That's all there is to the collector. Instead of writing tests for it, let's quickly put together the code for our reporter, and then we'll write some integration tests using both.

Reporting Metrics

Our reporter will be short and sweet. We'll use a GenServer here as well, because we want to keep a UDP socket around for sending the encoded metrics.

Could We Share a UDP Socket Across Processes?

 Funny you ask! Yes, we could. As long as there's one process that owns the UDP socket, other processes can just send data straight through the socket instead of having to cast to the reporter GenServer. This slightly different behavior requires you to make the socket publicly available, but you can do that by putting the socket in a public or protected ETS table, for example.

If you're up for a fun challenge, try to implement that on your own. The goal is to report metrics without interacting with the reporter process.

The interface for our reporter will be made of just two functions: one to report counters and one to report gauges.

xstats/lib/xstats/reporter.ex
```
@doc """
Increments the given counter by the given value.
"""

@spec increment_counter(GenServer.server(), String.t(), number()) :: :ok
def increment_counter(server, name, value) do
  GenServer.cast(server, {:send_metric, {:counter, name, value}})
end

@doc """
Sets the given gauge to the given value.
"""

@spec set_gauge(GenServer.server(), String.t(), number()) :: :ok
def set_gauge(server, name, value) do
  GenServer.cast(server, {:send_metric, {:gauge, name, value}})
end
```

We're using GenServer.cast/2 on purpose to perform a *fire-and-forget* operation. This is in line with the philosophy of having metrics be a non-disruptive side concern.

Initializing our reporter GenServer is a matter of opening the UDP socket, as you can see in the next piece of code.

xstats/lib/xstats/reporter.ex
```
@impl true
def init(options) do
  dest_port = Keyword.fetch!(options, :dest_port)

  case :gen_udp.open(0, [:binary]) do
    {:ok, socket} ->
      state = %__MODULE__{socket: socket, dest_port: dest_port}
      {:ok, state}

    {:error, reason} ->
      {:stop, reason}
  end
end
```

There's just one more piece of the puzzle. Let's look at how our reporter handles the {:send_metric, metric} casts and reports metrics to the collector.

xstats/lib/xstats/reporter.ex
```
@impl true
def handle_cast({:send_metric, metric}, %__MODULE__{} = state) do
  iodata = XStats.Protocol.encode_metric(metric)
  _ = :gen_udp.send(state.socket, ~c"localhost", state.dest_port, iodata)
  {:noreply, state}
end
```

There should be no surprises here. We encode the metric with XStats.Protocol.encode_metric/1 and then send it over to the reporter with :gen_udp.send/2. We're ignoring the return value of :gen_udp.send/2, because we don't want to cause issues in the reporting application if there's an error.

Next, we'll wire up what we've built through some testing.

Testing Out Our Collector and Reporter

Let's start by running our daemon and reporter and testing things out manually, then take a look at automated tests.

Manual Testing

Hop into the code/xstats directory. To show how the components of our app are communicating through UDP, we'll start two separate instances of the app. We'll start the daemon in one and the reporter in the other.

In one terminal window, run iex -S mix to jump into a console inside our application, and start the daemon with the following:

```
iex> XStats.DaemonServer.start_link(port: 9034)
{:ok, #PID<0.142.0>}
```

You can use whatever port you like, as long as you use the same one when starting the reporter. The returned PID will likely look different for you.

In a different terminal window, run another iex -S mix console, start the reporter, and send in some metrics:

```
iex> {:ok, reporter} = XStats.Reporter.start_link(dest_port: 9034)
{:ok, #PID<0.142.0>}
iex> XStats.Reporter.set_gauge(reporter, "udp_knowledge", 90)
:ok
iex> XStats.Reporter.increment_counter(reporter, "metrics_sent", 1)
:ok
iex> XStats.Reporter.increment_counter(reporter, "metrics_sent", 1)
:ok
iex> XStats.Reporter.increment_counter(reporter, "metrics_sent", 1)
:ok
```

Depending on how quick you are at typing the preceding commands, you'll see different results. At some point, anyway, you should see a report printed out in the first terminal, where the daemon reporter is running:

```
================
Current metrics
================

metrics_sent:   3
udp_knowledge:  90
```

Fantastic! We incremented the metrics_sent counter by 3 overall and set our udp_knowledge gauge to 90. If you wait a little more, you'll see the next flush happen:

```
===============
Current metrics
===============

metrics_sent:    0
udp_knowledge:   90
```

Just what we expected: the metrics_sent counter has been reset to 0 since there were no increments to that counter in this interval. The udp_knowledge, being a gauge, stayed at the same value as in the previous interval.

Manual testing is a valuable way to sanity-check the application and observe that it behaves correctly, but it's not as reproducible as automated testing and is generally more time-consuming. Let's introduce some automated tests next.

Automated Testing

Automated tests are not particularly interesting to look at. You can see the only test file for this application in code/xstats/test/integration_test.exs. The one neat trick we're using is StringIO,[6] a module that ships with Elixir's standard library and behaves as an input/output device. In tests, we pass a StringIO device when we start our collector server so that the server writes output to that device. We can fetch it and assert on it later on. Here's the code our tests use for starting the StringIO device and daemon:

```
xstats/test/integration_test.exs
{:ok, string_io} = StringIO.open("")

assert {:ok, daemon} =
        start_supervised(
          {DaemonServer, port: @port, flush_io_device: string_io}
        )
```

In tests, we can then use StringIO.flush/1 to get the current contents of the device:

```
xstats/test/integration_test.exs
assert StringIO.flush(string_io) =~ "reqs:\t5\n"
```

Sit back and relax: we now have a working metric-collecting and metric-reporting pipeline that communicates via UDP. If you want to tinker with this a bit, you could try adding support for reporting metrics on a collector that runs on a different host. In your code, the reporter is hard-coded to send

---

6. https://hexdocs.pm/elixir/StringIO.html

packets to localhost. You can try changing that as well as the :gen_udp.open/2 call in XStats.DaemonServer to listen to other network interfaces. Then, you can start the reporter and collector on different hosts (maybe using Docker, maybe on different computers—it's up to you!) and test things out. Given that we're using UDP, which is a network protocol, things should work.

Wrapping Up

We got to know UDP throughout this chapter. It's a different beast compared to TCP. You learned about their differences and started to play around with UDP. To do that, we built an application to collect metrics, made of clients and a server communicating via UDP. This exercise showed us how to use the gen_udp Erlang module and how to perform basic operations such as sending and receiving data.

We covered a lot of ground in this chapter, but we still need to improve our metric-collecting application to handle some of the more challenging properties of UDP, such as packets not being necessarily ordered or guaranteed to arrive at the destination. Take a break, and when you're ready, turn the page and dive in.

## CHAPTER 9

Adding Guarantees to UDP

In the previous chapter, we built a solid foundation to understand UDP and its advantages and disadvantages. UDP is essentially a *simpler* protocol compared to TCP. This simplicity comes from not doing many of the things that TCP does: UDP doesn't keep state, it doesn't perform handshakes upon connecting, and it doesn't maintain packet order. These characteristics make it more memory- and resource-efficient, but not all use cases can tolerate these properties.

Sometimes you'll have to make sure, for example, that at least the packets are ordered, or that you can detect missing packets. In this chapter, we'll explore how to add guarantees to UDP so that you can have the precise control you might need in whatever use case you choose it for.

Ordering, Splitting, and Dropping Packets

Let's start by understanding the effects of UDP's lack of guarantees when it comes to our protocol and application. Then, we'll take a look at ways to overcome these challenges.

UDP is not into guarantees at all. The protocol provides you with a way to route packets from one peer to another and not much else. The only real guarantee you have is that the packets don't end up at the wrong destination, but that's about it. When you look at it from an application developer's perspective, these are the main things to be aware of (that result from this lack of guarantees):

- Packets can be dropped
- Packets can be delivered in any order

These two characteristics, once combined, lead to a third: larger packets, which may be split up by the network, cannot easily be reconstructed at the destination without additional information. Take a look at the following figure.

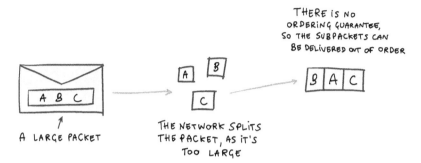

The large packet, represented as ABC, can get split by the network. The split sub-packets can then be delivered in any order, and some of them might not be delivered at all. How can the receiver reconstruct the original ABC packet if the network can split that packet in a number of ways? We'll start from this point and see how it applies to our application. We'll then tackle packets being dropped or delivered out of order.

Avoiding Split Packets

If you happened to dig through the StatsD documentation (you nerd), you might have stumbled upon a section in a page about metric types called "Multi-Metric Packets."[1] This section explains how the protocol we're using supports multiple metrics in a *single packet*. That means the following is a valid packet that the reporter can send:

```
mem_used_mb:1023|g\nmem_free_mb:94782|g\nmem_total_mb:95805|g\n
```

The packet contains three metrics, separated by newlines. Our collector daemon is perfectly equipped to handle this and collect all the metrics present in the packet. But some confusion might start to creep in: what happens if the packet gets split in the middle of a metric? Let's say the reporter gets the preceding metrics as two packets in the following order:

1. First, it gets mem_used_mb:1023|g\nmem_f
2. Then, it gets ree_mb:94782|g\nmem_total_mb:95805|g\n

Fear not! In the TCP chapters, you learned about buffering data and all that jazz, right? Well, not so much. Remember, there's no guaranteed ordering of

1.   https://github.com/statsd/statsd/blob/7c07eec4e7cebbd376d8313b230cea96c6571423/docs/metric_types.md#multi-metric-packets

packets in UDP, and there are no delivery guarantees either, which means the reporter might just as easily receive the two packets swapped like this:

```
ree_mb:94782|g\nmem_total_mb:95805|g\nmem_used_mb:1023|g\nmem_f
```

That's just a bunch of nonsense data now. Or it might receive only one of the two packets, which also leads to nonsense. The trick here is in that same section in the StatsD protocol documentation:

> Be careful to keep the total length of the payload within your network's MTU.

So, the way to deal with packet ordering and delivery guarantees is essentially this: don't rely on ordering, and *never split packets*. If you have to send more metrics than you can fit in a single packet, use multiple well-formed packets.

What Does "MTU" Mean?

MTU stands for Maximum Transmission Unit. What that means is that the MTU is the size of the largest piece of data that can be communicated in a single network layer transaction. The MTU depends on the network properties. For example, the default MTU for Ethernet devices is 1500 bytes,[a] of which 1492 are usable by the sender. Some networks allow a larger MTU—up to 9000 bytes—but a safe size for accommodating *any* network is 520 bytes (512 usable bytes).

If your protocol keeps packets within the MTU of the network being used, the network guarantees that the packet won't be split. But there are still no ordering or delivery guarantees.

---

a.   https://en.wikipedia.org/wiki/Maximum_transmission_unit

Never splitting packets means that our reporter's job is to never construct packets larger than the network's MTU. We shouldn't encounter this problem, because our reporter is not *aggregating* metrics before sending them to the collector daemon. Aggregating, in this context, would mean buffering metrics locally before flushing them via UDP. Our reporter instead sends each metric in its own packet, but we still have to make sure the packet won't be split up. Let's keep things simple and just make sure the packet is below 512 bytes, a conservative value. To do that, let's change the reporter to check the packet size and log an error if it exceeds 512 bytes, rather than sending it. We'll change the handle_cast/2 callback that sends the metric. The new version is in the next snippet.

xstats/lib/xstats/reporter.ex
```elixir
@mtu 512

@impl true
def handle_cast({:send_metric, metric}, %__MODULE__{} = state) do
```

```
  iodata = XStats.Protocol.encode_metric(metric)

  if IO.iodata_length(iodata) > @mtu do
    Logger.error("Metric too large to send: #{inspect(metric)}")
  else
    _ = :gen_udp.send(state.socket, ~c"localhost", state.dest_port, iodata)
  end

  {:noreply, state}
end
```

This was not a big change for our application, but it was necessary to understand the *why* of the change. Next, let's look at how to deal with packets that don't get delivered at all or that get delivered out of order. Spoiler alert: this is not an issue for our little application.

Ignoring Missing or Out-of-Order Packets

For our specific application, missing packets might not be a big issue after all. As we've said a few times in this chapter, metrics are often treated as something that happens on the side, so it follows that precision and accuracy are not strict requirements. For example, say your application is reporting a counter metric called total_requests that counts the number of HTTP requests the application is handling. A few missing requests would likely not change the overall picture of the system. While UDP gives no delivery guarantees, it's usually safe to assume that the majority of packets are not dropped. So, our metric-reporting application can just ignore the fact that UDP might drop packets. This is how real-world metric-collector daemons, such as StatsD or Telegraf,[2] behave.

Now, on to out-of-order packets. Our application supports only two metric types: counters and gauges. For counters, there's more good news: we don't care about packet order. After all, addition is commutative (that is, a + b = b + a), so the end result of the same counter metrics arriving in a different order is the same. The only corner case where order might affect counters is when counter metrics arrive at the collector right around the time the collector is flushing the metrics. In those cases, you might end up reporting a different total counter result, based on which metric came before or after the flush. But once again, *who cares*? The overall behavior of the system you're monitoring through counter metrics is not going to be influenced significantly by when metrics get reported.

Gauges are pretty similar. In most cases, applications tend to report each gauge at a consistent interval. This means that if UDP swaps the order of two metric

---

2. https://www.influxdata.com/blog/telegraf-socket-listener-input-plugin/

packets containing a measure of the same gauge, the mistake will eventually correct itself once another measurement for the same gauge comes in.

Well, that was a pretty easy way to deal with the "shortcomings" of UDP: just ignore 'em! But this approach no longer works if your application needs to send data that doesn't neatly fit in one packet, or if it depends on order, and so on. In the next section, we'll talk about techniques to deal with the lack of guarantees. We're leaving our metric-focused application behind to explore these techniques in isolation.

Adding Guarantees

As you learned at the beginning of this chapter, UDP lacks most guarantees that TCP provides. With UDP, you don't know if packets will be delivered in the right order or delivered at all. Let's quickly go over some strategies and patterns to add guarantees to UDP. These strategies will enable you to tackle some or all of the following situations:

- Out-of-order packets
- Missing packets
- Data that needs to be split into multiple packets

We won't do this for our metric-collecting application, but you'll need to know how to deal with these things if you're working on an app that uses UDP.

As you'll see, the number of strategies you need to have in your tool belt is not large. There's only a handful of techniques to know. Plus, those techniques sometimes handle more than one guarantee. Let's start with a simple yet effective change: adding a timestamp to our packets.

Ordering Messages with Timestamps

One of the easiest approaches to dealing with out-of-order packets is adding a timestamp to the protocol being used. The timestamp can be, for example, the number of microseconds since the Unix epoch[3] (January 1, 1970). It should be set by the sender and represent the time at which the sender stamped the packet. For example, in the metric-collecting application we built earlier in this chapter, the timestamp could be the time at which a gauge measurement occurred, as shown in the figure on page 150.

The utility of the timestamp is simple: it lets the receiver keep track of the order that the sender sent packets in. The receiver can put the pieces back

---

3. https://en.wikipedia.org/wiki/Unix_time

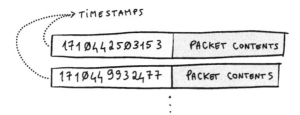

together in the right order when receiving data. But this technique only addresses the ordering guarantee. Packets can still go missing, for example.

There's one important disclaimer to make about timestamps: measuring precise and reliable time in distributed systems is challenging, to say the least. As long as you have a single sender, like in our example application, this is a viable approach. But when you have multiple senders running on different machines in a network, timestamping might lead to issues as the current time measured by different machines drifts. *Clock drift*, as this phenomenon is generally called, is a well-known issue in distributed systems, and there's plenty of literature[4] on how to deal with it. Most computers nowadays mitigate clock drift by relying on NTP,[5] a network protocol used to synchronize clocks. We won't go any deeper into this topic since there are many learning resources out there.

Let's move on to *missing* packets.

Using Counters to Detect Missing Packets

A simple way to detect missing packets is to add a counter to the packets that identifies them, as in the following figure. Each packet gets an ID, and the sender increments that ID by one for every new packet it sends.

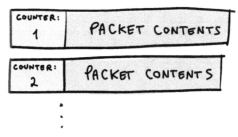

The logic here is that the receiver can keep track of the current counter and detect missing packets if any IDs are skipped among the incoming ones. For

---

4.   https://en.wikipedia.org/wiki/Clock_drift
5.   https://en.wikipedia.org/wiki/Network_Time_Protocol

example, if the last-received packet had an ID of 120 and the next packet that arrives has ID 123, the receiver can infer that two packets (with IDs 121 and 122) were dropped at some point.

This strategy doesn't only address missing packets. Using counters also addresses out-of-order packets, as long as there's only one sender or the sender includes its address/port information in the packet—so that different senders can essentially keep their own counters going.

Detecting missing packets is not hard—*what to do* in case of missing packets is. This is the first time since we started exploring UDP that we need to think about *two-way communication*. The simplest approach to dealing with missing packets would be to ask the sender to send those missing packets again. An example of this is shown in the following picture, where packet 2 gets lost and the receiver asks the sender to send it again.

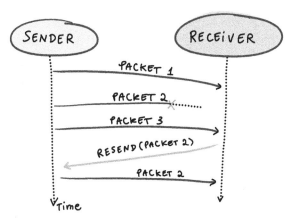

But this is a pretty naive approach. First, these resend request packets going from the receiver back to the sender can also get lost. You might be starting to get a sense of how few guarantees UDP provides! Even if the number of dropped packets (in both directions) is tiny, this approach can easily lead to out-of-control loops: sender and receiver can keep sending and resending each other messages, but there's no guarantee that the receiver will ever be able to get all the packets. To tackle this issue, protocols have to introduce more two-way communication in the form of *acknowledgments*. Let's explore that in the next section.

Acknowledgments and Redeliveries

If you're talking to someone and they say something that you don't quite catch, you'll usually throw them a confused "huh?" If you want to make sure they know you understood, you'll say something like "got it." The following figure shows a pretty common conversation.

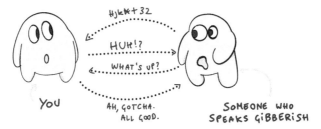

Well, that's all you need to know to understand acknowledgments. To deal with missing packets, you can implement a similar system of "huh"s and "got it"s. In the case of UDP, you can introduce an *acknowledgment message* into your protocol. Receivers can send this message to senders to tell them they received a specific message or set of messages. If our protocol were to use counters, like we explored in the previous section, then the acknowledgment message might include the highest counter that the receiver received and processed. The following figure helps visualize this type of interaction.

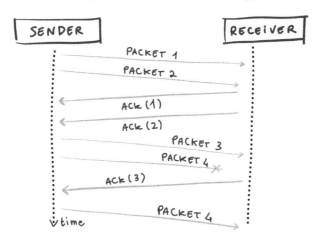

Instead of an *ack* message (or alongside it), you could introduce a message that lets receivers ask senders to *resend* some messages.

We've got a chicken-and-egg problem here. What if the acknowledgment message or the request-to-resend message itself gets lost? Fortunately, this is the bread and butter of distributed systems—there are solutions and plenty of literature. The most common approach is to introduce timeouts practically everywhere. For example, if the sender doesn't receive an ack message within a certain time window, it will consider the packets lost. If the receiver doesn't receive packets for a while, it can ask the sender to resend them.

Last but not least, with the techniques we just explored, you're bound to end up with duplicate messages on both sides. For example, a receiver could get message A and send an ack back for it, but the ack might get lost. So, after a timeout, the sender would send message A again, potentially delivering the same message to the receiver twice (or more, if this keeps going). In the next and last section, you'll learn how to deal with this scenario.

Dealing with Duplicate Packets

The key to dealing with duplicate messages is *idempotence*.[6] This fancy word just means that receiving the same message multiple times should have the same effect as receiving it once. Idempotence can be achieved in many ways. Let's look at a couple:

- You can ensure you can *process* the same message more than once. For example, gauge metrics naturally have the property that if you receive the same value for a gauge, and you mark messages with timestamps, then setting the same gauge to the same value at the same timestamp will have no effect.

- You can avoid processing duplicated messages altogether. A common way to do that is to give messages a unique ID, then store a table of received messages on each side. When receiving a message, you can discard it if it's already in the table. To keep that table from growing endlessly, you can store message IDs in it for only a certain amount of time. What if, for some reason, a very old message gets redelivered after you already purged its ID from the table? You could ignore very old messages, but this depends on the properties of your system.

This is the last of the missing guarantees we're going to explore. Let's conclude the chapter with some thoughts about when to use UDP.

Wrapping Up

Now, you might be thinking, "Wow, all this work to implement guarantees in UDP. Isn't there a protocol that provides them out of the box?" Well, of course there is: it's TCP. As we mentioned when we started our UDP journey, your default choice of protocol should be TCP, unless you're sure that UDP's fewer guarantees are worth it for your use case.

---

6. https://en.wikipedia.org/wiki/Idempotence

In this chapter, you learned more about the challenges that surround UDP. We explored techniques and strategies that you can use to deal with out-of-order, dropped, or split packets. This is important knowledge to have when it comes to UDP. Depending on the use case, you might need to guarantee a subset of these things—for example, you might be okay with dropped packets, but you might require packets to at least be ordered. You should now have the tools to pick and choose how to use UDP based on your requirements.

Hey, you made it! We've talked a lot about UDP and its lack of guarantees. It was quite a ride. But we didn't look at many examples of UDP in the real world. That's because the next chapter will dive into what is possibly the most common use of UDP in the wild: DNS. These past two chapters were packed with information, but you can take a breath and relax a bit, because the next chapter is going to be a breeze to go through.

## CHAPTER 10

UDP in the Wild: DNS

DNS is the first protocol we'll explore that sits one layer above TCP and UDP. It's a somewhat simple but ubiquitous protocol, so knowing how it works will give you a better understanding of networks in general. It's also *very* flexible. While the DNS protocol is not necessarily tied to UDP, the vast majority of DNS traffic happens over it. DNS was designed to work over both TCP and UDP protocols, but it's generally recommended that standard DNS queries happen over UDP and only fall back on TCP for larger packets and some other cases. With DNS, you'll see how a real-world protocol makes accommodations for UDP's lack of guarantees, which we explored in the past couple of chapters.

This chapter is a bit different from the other ones in this book. In the previous chapters about TCP or UDP, and in the next chapters about HTTP, there's always a focus on characteristics of the BEAM or design patterns for network applications. In this DNS chapter, our focus will be on the DNS protocol itself. DNS is not a protocol you will often use directly in your applications, but anyone working with networks will absolutely benefit from knowing its inner workings. You'll understand exactly what happens when you translate a domain name to an IP address—and chances are, that's something you rely on frequently. You'll also learn what else DNS can do, and you'll get to flex your Elixir/Erlang networking skills by experimenting with it.

We're going to dig (pun intended and explained later) into how DNS does what it does by writing our own little DNS client in Elixir. This will show you how simple the protocol is and reinforce how nice it is to work with binary protocols on the BEAM. Then, we'll explore some fun DNS use cases, including a few that are pretty out there. No spoilers. You'll also get a short overview of inet_res,[1]

---

1. https://www.erlang.org/doc/man/inet_res.html

a simple DNS client included in the Erlang standard library. Finally, to conclude the chapter, we'll write a simple DNS server.

Understanding How DNS Works

Computers route packets to each other on networks by knowing the IP addresses of their peers. IPs are essentially large numbers represented with different notations depending on the IP version—for example, 142.251.209.46 is an address in IPv4's notation. Of course, users don't go around typing IP addresses or memorizing the address of every computer on the Internet. We're used to a cozy system of *domain names*. We only need to remember elixir-lang.org rather than the IP for the server that hosts the website. That's where DNS comes in: its job is to translate domain names to IP addresses, as its name—*Domain Name System*—implies.

At its core, DNS is a distributed key-value database. Like other key-value databases, it maps keys to values. In the case of DNS, keys are domain names, such as elixir-lang.org, and values are information—often IP addresses, such as 185.199.108.153. These key-value pairs are called *resource records*, or just *records*.

The purpose of records is to store the information associated with a name, such as the IP address, so that a *resolver* can translate the name into the corresponding IP. This is called *resolving a name*. *Resolving* is just DNS lingo for *translating*—fetching a key from the key-value database.

Let's look at the structure of domain names for a second.

DNS Domain Names and Internet Domains

DNS is tightly coupled with the world of Internet domains and domain registration. This connection is so strong that it's hard to see where one ends and the other begins.

DNS is mostly used to resolve public domain names—that is, Internet domain names—into their IP addresses. For this reason, it is important to understand the structure of an Internet domain name.

A name is made of three main parts, separated by dots, reading from right to left:

- The *TLD* (Top Level Domain) is the right outermost part. For Internet names, it has a restricted set of values (such as .com and .io). DNS doesn't have this restriction at the protocol level.

- The *parent domain* is the second part of the name, which generally corresponds to the part of the domain that you can register (such as github and apple).

- An optional *subdomain* is the third part of the name. It can be composed of zero or more levels. For example, gist is the subdomain in gist.github.com. elixir-lang.com has zero subdomain levels, while sheets.docs.google.com has two (sheets.docs is the subdomain).

The following figure illustrates the domain sheets.docs.google.com.

The parent domain combined with the TLD make up the *registrable domain*, which is what individuals and companies can register (buy) and control. For example, Apple owns apple.com and the author of this book owns andrealeopardi.com. When you register a domain, you control the domain and all the subdomains. So, Apple also controls support.apple.com, whatever.apple.com, and so on.

Now, before digging into the protocol details, let's quickly look at how DNS resolution works—it's a fascinating topic.

Resolving a DNS Record

Imagine you're visiting https://gist.github.com in your browser. The first step is for your browser to figure out the address of the server hosting the requested website—this is *DNS resolution*. More often than not, DNS resolution is a recursive process. You don't reach out directly to the DNS server that hosts the record for gist.github.com. Instead, you reach out to a series of servers that get closer to—and eventually find—that server. Let's see that in more detail.

Resolution starts with a *recursive DNS resolver*. This is a DNS server whose job is to resolve DNS records by performing the full resolution process. Often, your ISP provides the recursive DNS resolver. Another well-known example is Google Public DNS,[2] a public recursive DNS resolver maintained by Google—the notorious 8.8.8.8. Any DNS server can resolve recursively and cache resolved records—DNS is quite the decentralized protocol. If the recursive DNS server holds the requested record in its cache, it can return it

---

2. https://developers.google.com/speed/public-dns

to the client and resolution halts. The interesting part, however, is what happens when the record isn't in the cache.

The first thing our recursive DNS resolver has to figure out is where all the records for the requested TLD (.com, in our example) are hosted. For that, we need to turn to a *root nameserver*. Root nameservers map each TLD, such as .com or .net, to a corresponding TLD nameserver.

Who Watches the Watchmen?

 Root nameservers are maintained by the Internet Assigned Numbers Authority (IANA).[3] IANA maintains a list of root nameservers[4] that can be used to start the DNS resolution process.

Okay, our recursive DNS resolver now knows where the TLD nameserver for .com is. Once we have the IP address of the TLD server, we can ask that DNS server about the specific domain. In this case, that's github.com, which is indexed (or *stored*) by an *authoritative nameserver*, the DNS resolver's last stop. The authoritative nameserver for github.com is responsible for github.com and all its subdomains, including gist.github.com. So, the recursive DNS resolver can now ask the authoritative nameserver for github.com for the IP address of gist.github.com. The following figure illustrates the process of DNS resolution.

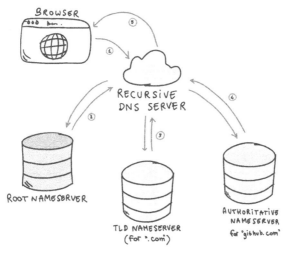

If you want to play around with DNS resolution, a great tool is dig.[5] There are alternatives out there, but dig is commonly shipped with Unix systems. Also, it's the punchline for the pun at the beginning of this chapter!

---

3. https://www.iana.org/
4. https://www.iana.org/domains/root/servers
5. https://en.wikipedia.org/wiki/Dig_(command)

Type this in your terminal to perform the DNS resolution for gist.github.com:

```
> dig gist.github.com +short
140.82.121.3
```

The +short option instructs dig to show you only the resolved IP address. When working with DNS, dig is your Swiss Army knife. It can take a bit of time to learn it, but it's a powerful tool.

Tracing DNS Resolution

 Want to see DNS resolution at work? You can pass the +trace flag to dig, and it will show you all the DNS servers it contacts and their answers. Try it out with dig gist.github.com +trace.

You now have an idea of how DNS resolution works, and you know what the *purpose* of DNS is. Let's move on to DNS records.

The Shape of DNS Records

A DNS record has four main properties:

1. *Type*: indicates what the value of the record represents—for example, an IPv4 address, an IPv6 address, or another domain name

2. *Name*: the key in the key-value database—for example, www or mail (a name convention is the value @, which generally represents the empty subdomain, such as apple.com rather than <subdomain>.apple.com)

3. *Data*: a collection of one or more values, depending on the type—for example, IPv4 for the A type or structured data for the CAA type

4. *TTL* (Time To Live): specifies how long DNS clients can cache the record for

The following figure is a visual example of what a DNS record could look like.

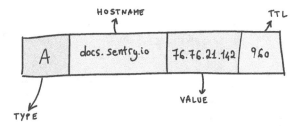

The type of a DNS record is what gives the protocol its flexibility. The table on page 160 shows you a few common types, alongside their purposes and some examples.

Type	Value	Purpose	Example Name	Example Value
A	IPv4 address	Maps a name to an IPv4 address	@	102.39.11.0
AAAA	IPv6 address	Maps a name to an IPv6 address	www	2001:db8:...
CNAME	Another name	Maps a name to another name	blog	foo.github-pages.io
ALIAS	Another name	Same as CNAME but non-standard and without limitations	@	myapp.fly.io
TXT	Any string	Stores arbitrary text	info	Some text
MX	Another name	Specifies the server that handles email associated with the domain	@	imap.fastmail.com
CAA	Certificate authority data	Specifies rules for issuing domains	example.com	issue "letsencrypt.org;validation-methods=dns-01"

The types in this table are not a comprehensive list. In fact, there are dozens of possible record types.[6] These are just a few common ones.

IPv4 vs. IPv6

IPv4 and IPv6 are the two versions of the Internet Protocol (IP). For the purposes of what you're learning here, you don't need to know much about them.

One of the main and most important differences is the sizes of IPv4 addresses and IPv6 addresses. IPv4 addresses are encoded with four bytes, which are the four numbers you see in the a.b.c.d notation. With four bytes you can only encode around four billion values (2^{32}). But the Internet is such a big place that in 2011 unallocated IPv4 addresses became exhausted. Enter IPv6. IPv6 addresses are encoded with 16 bytes, for a total of 2^{128} possible addresses. That's a lot of digits. For all practical use cases, IPv6 addresses are considered inexhaustible.

If you want to know more, AWS has a short and useful breakdown.[a]

---

a.   https://aws.amazon.com/compare/the-difference-between-ipv4-and-ipv6/?nc1=h_ls

To see DNS record types in action, we can once again make use of dig. Let's ask our recursive DNS server to resolve elixir-lang.org. Type the following command:

---

6.   https://en.wikipedia.org/wiki/List_of_DNS_record_types

```
> dig elixir-lang.org

; <<>> DiG 9.10.6 <<>> elixir-lang.org
;; global options: +cmd
;; Got answer:
;; ->>HEADER<<- opcode: QUERY, status: NOERROR, id: 33913
;; flags: qr rd ra; QUERY: 1, ANSWER: 4, AUTHORITY: 0, ADDITIONAL: 1

;; OPT PSEUDOSECTION:
; EDNS: version: 0, flags:; udp: 4095
;; QUESTION SECTION:
;elixir-lang.org.                IN      A

;; ANSWER SECTION:
elixir-lang.org.        377     IN      A       185.199.109.153
elixir-lang.org.        377     IN      A       185.199.110.153
elixir-lang.org.        377     IN      A       185.199.108.153
elixir-lang.org.        377     IN      A       185.199.111.153

;; Query time: 151 msec
;; SERVER: 100.100.100.100#53(100.100.100.100)
;; WHEN: ...
;; MSG SIZE  rcvd: 108
```

The output is pretty long and dense with information. Parts of it will look different for you. By the end of this chapter, you'll know what most of it means, but let's focus on the highlighted part for now. In it, you can see four A records for elixir-lang.org., each with a different IP address. Remember that A records hold IPv4 addresses, which is what you see in this output.

Let's take a short detour into the DNS protocol before we start to work on our client.

The DNS Protocol: A Short Overview

DNS uses a *binary protocol* (Binary Protocols and Textual Protocols, on page 34). This book provides you with the code to work with that protocol, but in case you want to explore it on your own, check out code/xdig/lib/xdig/protocol.ex.

The DNS protocol is based on DNS messages. The protocol is symmetrical—that is, messages have the same shape for both directions (client to server and server to client). The direction is identified by a flag contained in each message, called the QR flag. If set to 0, it identifies a query message. If set to 1, it identifies a reply message.

DNS messages are formed by a header and a body. The header is 12 bytes long, and the rest of the message is the body. As you might remember from Avoiding Split Packets, on page 146, it's wise to keep packets small when working with UDP, and that's exactly what DNS does. This means that anything after the

12-byte header until the end of the packet is the body of the message. The following figure is a visual representation of a DNS message.

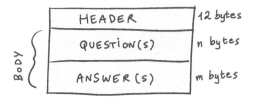

Questions are what DNS clients want to know from DNS servers. *Answers* are, as you might have guessed, the answers from the servers. The header contains information needed to understand the direction of each message, its ID, the number of questions and answers in the message, and more.

DNS Message IDs

Each DNS message contains a 2-byte client-generated ID. Servers include this ID in responses to clients so that clients can match their responses to the original request, which can otherwise be tricky with UDP since the protocol is stateless and doesn't guarantee order.

Well, you know enough about DNS to be dangerous. You've been introduced to what DNS is, some terminology and components that make up the protocol, and a few examples here and there. Now, let's use the network a bit to play with DNS and the BEAM.

Writing a Simple DNS Client

Let's write a funky little Elixir client that works as a (small) subset of dig. Since our imagination knows no bounds, we'll call it xdig. We've got our protocol code in XDig.Protocol from the previous section, so let's focus on the network parts. All the code is in code/xdig.

The first thing we need is a DNS server to connect to. There are many to choose from, such as Google's 8.8.8.8, but we're going to use 1.1.1.1,[7] a neat alternative from the folks at CloudFlare and APNIC.

Our client needs to do the following:

1. Open a UDP socket
2. Build a DNS query message made of a header, one question, and zero answers
3. Send the encoded message over UDP to the 1.1.1.1 DNS server

---

7. https://one.one.one.one/dns/

4. Await a reply from the server
5. Decode the reply

We'll code all this up in a single function, lookup/3. Let's sketch it out using some helper functions that we'll define in a second.

xdig/lib/xdig.ex
```
Line 1  def lookup(server_address, record_type, hostname) do
          message_id = :crypto.strong_rand_bytes(2)

          encoded_dns_message =
     5      encode_dns_message(message_id, record_type, hostname)

          {:ok, socket} = :gen_udp.open(0, [:binary, active: false])

          :gen_udp.send(socket, server_address, 53, encoded_dns_message)
    10
          {:ok, {^server_address, 53, packet}} = :gen_udp.recv(socket, 0, 5000)

          :ok = :gen_udp.close(socket)

    15    decode_dns_message(message_id, packet)
        end
```

The function starts by generating a new message ID using two random bytes on line 2. We need these to identify the query message and its reply later on. After that, we encode the message. Then, it's time for the UDP part: we open a new socket on any available port (that's what port 0 means on line 7), send the encoded DNS query message (line 9), and receive all available bytes on the UDP socket (line 11). Once we get the reply message, we just decode it with another helper function on line 15.

Let's try it. Hop into the code/xdig directory and start an IEx session with iex -S mix.

```
iex> XDig.lookup({1, 1, 1, 1}, :a, ["elixir-lang", "org"])
[
  %XDig.Protocol.Answer{
    name: ["elixir-lang", "org"],
    type: :a,
    class: 1,
    ttl: 300,
    rdata: {185, 199, 110, 153}
  },
  %XDig.Protocol.Answer{
    name: ["elixir-lang", "org"],
    type: :a,
    class: 1,
    ttl: 300,
    rdata: {185, 199, 111, 153}
  },
```

```
%XDig.Protocol.Answer{
  name: ["elixir-lang", "org"],
  type: :a,
  class: 1,
  ttl: 300,
  rdata: {185, 199, 108, 153}
},
%XDig.Protocol.Answer{
  name: ["elixir-lang", "org"],
  type: :a,
  class: 1,
  ttl: 300,
  rdata: {185, 199, 109, 153}
}
]
```

That's pretty similar to what dig showed us earlier in the chapter. The 1.1.1.1 DNS server returned four answers, each containing one A record for one IPv4 address that elixir-lang.org resolves to.

The encode_dns_message/3 and decode_dns_message/2 helper functions are fairly simple: they create the data structures that represent headers or questions and then delegate to the XDig.Protocol module for the actual encoding and decoding. Here's encode_dns_message/3:

xdig/lib/xdig.ex
```
defp encode_dns_message(message_id, record_type, hostname) do
  header = %XDig.Protocol.Header{
    message_id: message_id,
    qr: 0,
    opcode: 0,
    rcode: 0,
    aa: 0, tc: 0, rd: 1, ra: 0,
    an_count: 0,
    ns_count: 0,
    ar_count: 0,
    qd_count: 1
  }

  question = %XDig.Protocol.Question{
    qname: hostname,
    qtype: record_type,
    qclass: 1
  }

  [
    XDig.Protocol.encode_header(header),
    XDig.Protocol.encode_question(question)
  ]
end
```

decode_dns_message/2 does the opposite:

```
xdig/lib/xdig.ex
defp decode_dns_message(
       message_id,
       <<header::12-binary, rest::binary>> = whole_response
     ) do
  %XDig.Protocol.Header{
    qr: 1,
    message_id: ^message_id,
    opcode: 0,
    rcode: 0,
    qd_count: 1,
    an_count: answer_count
  } = XDig.Protocol.decode_header(header)

  {_question, rest} = XDig.Protocol.decode_question(rest)

  {answers, rest} =
    Enum.map_reduce(1..answer_count, rest, fn _index, rest ->
      XDig.Protocol.decode_answer(whole_response, rest)
    end)

  if rest != "" do
    raise "unexpected trailing data in DSN message"
  end

  answers
end
```

The only noteworthy part is on line 18. There, we pass the whole_response to XDig.Protocol.decode_answer/2 because the DNS binary protocol uses a trick to save bytes in answers: instead of always embedding the same NAME in each answer—which is usually the QNAME from the question—the protocol uses a system of offsets and indexes to point to the QNAME in the questions section of the message.

Once the binary protocol is out of the way (meaning code to encode and decode is provided), writing a DNS client turns out to be simple. It's just a matter of opening a UDP socket and exchanging a single request and response through it. This is one of the beauties of UDP: it forces you to design small and simple protocols that allow for these simple interactions. Granted, in DNS's case, all the limitations of UDP described in Chapter 8, Same Layer, Different Protocol:, on page 127, are not an issue. If the response gets dropped or the request never makes it to the DNS server, the :gen_udp.recv/3 call we make in XDig.lookup/3 will just time out. There's no ordering across responses, thanks to the message ID baked into the protocol.

> ### DNS over Other Network Protocols
>
> DNS as a protocol is not tied to UDP. In fact, DNS sits one layer above UDP in the OSI model (Appendix 1, The OSI Model, on page 223). While UDP sits at layer 4 (the transport layer), DNS sits at layer 5 (the application layer). This means that DNS is not technically tied to UDP. As a matter of fact, over the years, DNS has been implemented on top of other transport protocols: you have DNS over HTTPS,[a] DNS over TLS,[b] and even DNS over more niche protocols like Tor[c] and upcoming protocols like QUIC.[d] But most DNS servers still work over UDP.
>
> _____
>
> a.   https://www.rfc-editor.org/rfc/rfc8484
> b.   https://datatracker.ietf.org/doc/html/rfc7858
> c.   https://en.wikipedia.org/wiki/Tor_(network)
> d.   https://www.rfc-editor.org/rfc/rfc9250.html

You saw how simple creating a small DNS client can be, but our client is still missing a lot of functionality—for example, it has no caching and it doesn't handle all the possible record types. Luckily, Erlang's standard library includes functionality to resolve domain names through DNS, so let's explore that next.

inet_res

inet_res[8] is a simple DNS client included in the Erlang standard library. It provides more extended functionality than what we built in the previous section. At its simplest, it has a lookup/4 function that works pretty much like XDig.lookup/3. You can try it out in an IEx session:

```
iex> nameserver = {{1, 1, 1, 1}, _port = 53}
iex> :inet_res.lookup(~c"elixir-lang.org", :in, :a, nameservers: [nameserver])
[
  {185, 199, 110, 153},
  {185, 199, 108, 153},
  {185, 199, 111, 153},
  {185, 199, 109, 153}
]
```

:in is for the *class* of the requested record (:in stands for Internet addresses), while :a is the record type. We have to pass the preferred DNS server as an option—otherwise, :inet_res will fall back on the system's DNS server. The return value here is a list of the four IPv4 addresses we're starting to be familiar with.

_____

8.   https://www.erlang.org/doc/apps/kernel/inet_res.html

:inet_res also provides lower-level functions to work with the DNS protocol. For example, replace :inet_res.lookup/4 with :inet_res.resolve/4 and you'll see that the return value becomes a series of Erlang records representing the various parts of the reply DNS message.

```
iex> nameserver = {{1, 1, 1, 1}, _port = 53}
iex> domain = ~c"elixir-lang.org"
iex> :inet_res.resolve(domain, :in, :a, nameservers: [nameserver])
{:ok,
 {:dns_rec,
  {:dns_header, 5, true, :query, false, false, true, true, false, 0},
  [{:dns_query, ~c"elixir-lang.org", :a, :in, false}],
  [
    {:dns_rr, ~c"elixir-lang.org", :a, :in, 0, 137, {185, 199, 109, 153},
     :undefined, [], false},
    {:dns_rr, ~c"elixir-lang.org", :a, :in, 0, 137, {185, 199, 110, 153},
     :undefined, [], false},
    {:dns_rr, ~c"elixir-lang.org", :a, :in, 0, 137, {185, 199, 108, 153},
     :undefined, [], false},
    {:dns_rr, ~c"elixir-lang.org", :a, :in, 0, 137, {185, 199, 111, 153},
     :undefined, [], false}
  ], [], []}}
```

If you want to explore these records a bit more, you can extract their definitions from the inet.hrl Erlang header file. In Elixir, you'd use Record.extract_all/1. You can see an example of this in our XDig module:

xdig/lib/xdig.ex
```
require Record

for {record, fields} <-
      Record.extract_all(from_lib: "kernel/src/inet_dns.hrl") do
  Record.defrecord(record, fields)
end
```

If you want to play around with these records, take the :dns_rr tuples in the result of :inet_res.resolve/4 and use XDig.dns_rr to see what their elements mean. The documentation for Record.defrecord/3[9] should provide the necessary guidance.

:inet_res is great to have if you're working with DNS at a low level and you need control over different aspects of it. But if your application only needs to resolve a domain name to an IPv4 or IPv6 address, you can also use :inet.gethostbyname/1,[10] which returns a hostent Erlang record that in turn contains IP addresses:

```
iex> :inet.gethostbyname(~c"elixir-lang.org")
```

---

9. https://hexdocs.pm/elixir/Record.html#defrecord/3
10. https://www.erlang.org/doc/apps/kernel/inet.html#gethostbyname/1

```
{:ok,
 {:hostent, ~c"elixir-lang.org", [], :inet, 4,
  [
    {185, 199, 111, 153},
    {185, 199, 110, 153},
    {185, 199, 109, 153},
    {185, 199, 108, 153}
  ]}}
```

With :inet_res, you're not limited to resolving A records. For example, we can resolve elixir-lang.org's AAAA records just as easily:

```
iex> import XDig
iex> {:ok, record} = :inet_res.resolve(~c"elixir-lang.org", :in, :aaaa)
iex> answers = dns_rec(record, :anlist)
iex> for rr <- answers, do: rr |> dns_rr(:data) |> :inet.ntoa()
[
  ~c"2606:50c0:8000::153",
  ~c"2606:50c0:8001::153",
  ~c"2606:50c0:8003::153",
  ~c"2606:50c0:8002::153"
]
```

We used :aaaa as the question type and got back a dns_rec Erlang record. We extracted the :anlist field, which is the collection of resource records in the answers section. For each resource record, we extracted the :data field from the Erlang record and converted it to an IPv6 string with :inet.ntoa/1. If you're not familiar with Erlang records in Elixir, the documentation for the Record module[11] is a great resource.

If you want to explore the DNS protocol a bit more, we suggest patching up XDig and XDig.Protocol to support other record types, such as AAAA or TXT. Appendix 4, DNS Protocol Details, on page 231, has all the details you need when it comes to the DNS protocol, and you can always consult section 4 of RFC 1035.[12]

Next up, we'll quickly glance at the other side: we'll write a silly DNS server that stores records in an ETS table.

Writing a DNS Server Is So Easy

Now that we have code for working with the DNS protocol, and we know how to work with UDP and DNS servers, we might as well write a DNS server. Our server will be nothing new: a GenServer that opens a UDP socket when

---

11. https://hexdocs.pm/elixir/Record.html
12. https://www.ietf.org/rfc/rfc1035.txt

starting up and serves requests. You can find the code for the server in code/xdig/lib/xdig/server.ex, but let's take a second to break it down.

This server uses an ETS table to store mappings from record types and names to record data. Rows in the table look like this:

```
{{record_type, record_name}, record_data}
```

For example, an A record for elixir-lang.org could look like this:

```
{{:a, ["elixir-lang", "org"]}, <<185, 199, 109, 153>>}
```

When initializing, the server needs to create the ETS table and open a UDP socket. Here's the code for the init/1 callback, where we do exactly that:

xdig/lib/xdig/server.ex
```
Line 1  def init(options) do
     2    table = :ets.new(__MODULE__, [:bag, :named_table])
     3    port = Keyword.get(options, :port, 0)
     4    {:ok, socket} = :gen_udp.open(port, [:binary, active: true])
     5
     6    {:ok, actual_port} = :inet.port(socket)
     7    Logger.info("DNS server started on port: #{actual_port}")
     8
     9    {:ok, %{socket: socket, table: table}}
    10  end
```

See how on line 2 we used the :bag ETS table type? That's so we can store multiple entries under the same key—for us, that translates to storing multiple IPs for the same domain name.

For our convenience, we also have a function that we can use to store records in the ETS table: store/3. The code for store/3 and its handle_call/3 counterpart is shown next.

xdig/lib/xdig/server.ex
```
def store(qname, qtype, rdata) do
  GenServer.call(__MODULE__, {:store, qname, qtype, rdata})
end
def handle_call(
      {:store, qname, qtype, rdata},
      _from,
      %{table: table} = state
    ) do
  :ets.insert(table, {{qname, qtype}, rdata})
  {:reply, :ok, state}
end
```

The only thing left to look at is how the server handles data coming out of the UDP socket:

xdig/lib/xdig/server.ex

```elixir
def handle_info(
      {:udp, socket, ip, port, <<header::12-binary, body::binary>>},
      %{socket: socket} = state
    ) do
  Logger.info("Received DNS request from #{:inet.ntoa(ip)}:#{port}")

  header = XDig.Protocol.decode_header(header)
  {questions, _rest} = decode_questions(header, body)
  answers = Enum.flat_map(questions, &fetch_answers(state.table, &1))

  reply_header = %XDig.Protocol.Header{
    message_id: header.message_id,
    qr: 1,
    opcode: 0,
    rcode: 0,
    an_count: length(answers)
  }

  reply = [
    XDig.Protocol.encode_header(reply_header),
    Enum.map(answers, &XDig.Protocol.encode_answer/1)
  ]

  :ok = :gen_udp.send(socket, ip, port, reply)
  {:noreply, state}
end
```

We already break down the packet into a DNS header (12 bytes long) and the body on line 2.

Then, we decode the header with XDig.Protocol.decode_header/1 and the questions in the DNS query with a helper function, decode_questions/2 (line 8). Now that we know what the client is asking, we can fetch records from our ETS table (line 9), construct an answer, and send it over UDP. The helper function fetch_answers/2 is as follows:

xdig/lib/xdig/server.ex

```elixir
defp fetch_answers(table, %XDig.Protocol.Question{} = question) do
  table
  |> :ets.lookup({question.qname, question.qtype})
  |> Enum.map(fn {_key, rdata} ->
    %XDig.Protocol.Answer{
      name: question.qname,
      type: question.qtype,
      class: question.qclass,
      ttl: 300,
      rdata: rdata
    }
  end)
end
```

Let's give our server a spin. Start a new IEx session in code/xdig with iex -S mix, start up the server, and add some records to it.

```
iex> XDig.Server.start_link(port: 9392)
17:22:57.260 [info] DNS server started on port: 9392
{:ok, #PID<0.210.0>}
iex> XDig.Server.store(["elixir-lang", "org"], :a, <<12, 233, 2, 1>>)
:ok
iex> XDig.Server.store(["elixir-lang", "org"], :a, <<12, 233, 2, 2>>)
:ok
iex> XDig.Server.store(["elixir-lang", "org"], :a, <<12, 233, 2, 3>>)
:ok
```

Now, open another terminal window. To test out our server, we can use our beloved dig:

```
$ dig elixir-lang.org @localhost -p 9392 +short
12.233.2.1
12.233.2.2
12.233.2.3
```

You've got a small but working DNS server on your hands. And coding it up wasn't a lot of work, which is nice. You now know about DNS and how to work with it in Elixir and Erlang, so we're ready to move on.

Homework

 A nifty change to this server would be to turn it into a recursive DNS server (Resolving a DNS Record, on page 157). Instead of storing records, it would only cache records. When a client asks for a record, the server would first have to reach out to the root nameserver for the TLD, then follow the trail of DNS servers until arriving at the desired record. If you want inspiration, DNSimple[13] maintains a production-ready DNS server written in Erlang.[14]

Wrapping Up

You learned a lot about DNS here. We started out with a detailed overview of the protocol: DNS is a reasonably simple real-world protocol, so this deep dive also served as a way to familiarize yourself even more with network protocols and specifications. We then wrote a simple DNS client in Elixir from scratch, using our UDP knowledge from the previous two chapters. Finally, we took a peek at inet_res, Erlang's built-in DNS client.

---

13. https://dnsimple.com/
14. https://github.com/dnsimple/erldns

If you want to explore some wacky use cases for DNS, here's a short list of things that people built that are pretty fun to look at:

- Wikipedia over DNS[15]
- Wordle over DNS[16]
- DNS Toys[17]

In the next chapters, we'll dive into a protocol that sits at the same layer as DNS, but which you've likely had to deal with a lot more often: HTTP.

---

15. https://dgl.cx/wikipedia-dns
16. https://dgl.cx/2022/02/wordle-over-dns
17. https://www.dns.toys/

Part III

HTTP

HTTP sits one layer above TCP and UDP in the
network stack. It powers the web and is used in
many other applications, from the Internet of Things
to APIs that can be used to control pretty much
everything.

## CHAPTER 11

Talking the Internet Protocol: HTTP/1.1

We've journeyed through the fundamentals of network programming in Elixir, exploring sockets, TCP, and UDP to build robust and concurrent applications. Understanding these protocols is essential, but a lot of the Internet traffic today rides on the back of a different beast: HTTP.

Enter the *HyperText Transfer Protocol*, the backbone of the World Wide Web. Whether you're fetching data from a third-party API, serving up a dynamic website, or building a scalable backend service, understanding HTTP is crucial for modern network programming. At this point, your fridge is likely to talk to some server via HTTP.

In this chapter, you'll learn how to use Plug and Bandit to create lightweight and performant HTTP servers, setting the stage for building your own web applications and APIs. We'll also explore Mint, Finch, and Req for crafting HTTP clients that are both efficient and easy to use. The chapters you've read so far were quite low-level in nature. This chapter's subject, while still a network protocol, is more high-level than the protocols we've used so far. We won't implement much from scratch, but we will explore tools to build HTTP servers and clients on the BEAM.

The principles of working with HTTP that we'll talk about in this chapter are the same for Elixir and Erlang. But Elixir tools have somewhat more modern and ergonomic APIs, which makes it easier to showcase them. This is why we'll focus on the Elixir libraries we mentioned. Even though it's somewhat possible to use Elixir libraries in Erlang projects, Erlang users tend to reach for Erlang-specific HTTP clients and servers such as Hackney[1] and Cowboy.[2]

---

1. https://github.com/benoitc/hackney
2. https://github.com/ninenines/cowboy

We won't cover those here, but they work in similar ways to the Elixir tools we will cover.

Let's kick things off by giving you some information about the protocol itself.

HTTP/1.1 Protocol Basics

HTTP has a long and complicated history.[3] Suffice to say, HTTP/1 was released as a textual protocol in 1996, followed by some improvements in HTTP/1.1. HTTP/2 and HTTP/3, however, are binary protocols and take a *wildly* different approach. There's also HTTP/0.9, the pre-1.0, early-1990s version of the protocol. HTTP has evolved significantly since its inception, and the HTTP landscape has gotten wider and more complex.

At the time of writing, there are two versions of HTTP that dominate the web: HTTP/1.1 and HTTP/2. HTTP/1.1 represents the "modern" variant of the first version of HTTP/1, while HTTP/2 is a whole revision of the protocol. You're likely familiar with HTTP/1.1 since it's the most well-known and most frequently taught version of HTTP. HTTP/1.1 is an easy-to-read textual protocol.

HTTP and HTTPS

 HTTPS is *secure* HTTP. It's HTTP plus TLS. All the material you'll see in this chapter about HTTP applies to HTTPS as well, so we will use examples interchangeably.

In this section, we'll break down the HTTP protocol and look at how it works. We'll examine the request/response interaction at the heart of the protocol and look at those in detail.

But before doing that, let's take a quick detour to look at HTTP in the context of network protocols.

HTTP and the OSI Model

HTTP sits on the application layer of the OSI model (see Appendix 1, The OSI Model, on page 223). Protocols at this layer are closest to users—and often to developers working with networks.

Since the application layer is the topmost layer in the OSI model, when you work with HTTP(S) you're in fact working with all the protocols below HTTP at the same time. HTTP deals with URLs and serialization, but data flows and is routed through the TCP/IP stack. If you use HTTPS, TLS is the one doing the

---

3.   https://developer.mozilla.org/en-US/docs/Web/HTTP/Basics_of_HTTP/Evolution_of_HTTP

encryption—we've got a whole chapter on that: Chapter 7, Securing Protocols: TLS, on page 113.

The following figure is a visual representation of HTTPS in relation to some other protocols.

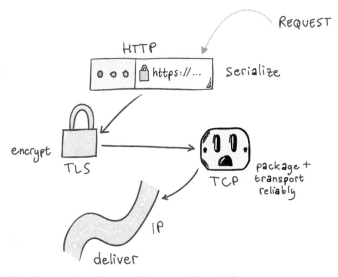

HTTP would look similar, but without TLS in the mix.

Request and Response Life Cycle

Let's make an HTTP request to a website to get a sense of how this works. We'll use curl,[4] the most common command-line HTTP client around. You should have it included in your OS—it's in all major OSes these days—but there are installation instructions on its website in case you don't.

Either way, with curl installed, hop onto a terminal and run the following:

```
> curl -i http://httpbin.org/uuid
HTTP/1.1 200 OK
Date: Sun, 29 Sep 2024 16:55:01 GMT
Content-Type: application/json
Content-Length: 53
Connection: keep-alive
Server: gunicorn/19.9.0
Access-Control-Allow-Origin: *
Access-Control-Allow-Credentials: true

{
  "uuid": "626f26f3-13f2-47ff-920a-3dc15a4626aa"
}
```

---

4. https://curl.se/

You just made an HTTP request to httpbin.org, a website built for playing around with HTTP. /uuid is the path (more on that soon), which generates and returns a UUID[5] inside a JSON object. Let's break this flow down.

In HTTP/1.1, clients make *requests* to a server. Each request from a client gets a *response* from the server.

You can inspect the request we made earlier with curl by running the same command with the -v flag (for *verbose*):

```
> curl http://httpbin.org/uuid -v
≪Connection info≫
GET /uuid HTTP/1.1
Host: httpbin.org
User-Agent: curl/8.5.0
Accept: */*

HTTP/1.1 200 OK
≪Same response as before≫
```

You might notice that neither requests nor responses have IDs of any kind. Too bad, since it means that requests and responses cannot happen in parallel on the same connection. They can only happen sequentially. The client might be able to send a few requests on the same TCP connection, but the responses to those requests will come in the same order the requests were sent in. (Sending multiple requests in a row is a thing and it's called *request pipelining*,[6] by the way.)

Let's dig into the shape of requests and responses.

HTTP/1.1 Requests

Requests are made of three components:

- A request line, consisting of a method, a path, and the HTTP version in use
- A list of headers
- An (optional) request body

A visual representation of an example HTTP/1.1 request is shown on page 179.

The *method*, also called the verb, lets the client express the kind of request it wants to perform. There are some standard methods that you probably know. For example, GET (as in the previous curl request) lets you retrieve resources, POST is for creating new resources, and DELETE is for deleting resources. These and a few others are standard HTTP methods, but you can

---

5. https://en.wikipedia.org/wiki/Universally_unique_identifier
6. https://en.wikipedia.org/wiki/HTTP_pipelining

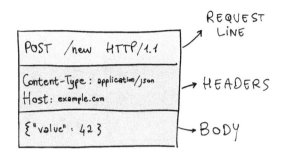

technically use any verb: as far as HTTP cares, if your server supports it then GIMME would be a nice alternative to GET.

The *path* identifies a resource on the server.

Headers are name-value pairs used as metadata for the request. They're the meat and potatoes of HTTP. They can be used for specifying the encoding of the body, its length, how long the body might be cached for, who made the request, and a myriad of other things. Some header names and their values are standardized, but any name-value pair is allowed. The following is from our curl example:

```
User-Agent: curl/8.5.0
```

That's the User-Agent header, which curl sets to curl/<installed-curl-version>.

The body is optional. For example, GET requests are not supposed to have one, which is why you didn't see one in our curl request. In general, the body's job is to provide content for the request. For POST requests, for example, the body contains the details of the resource to create.

Once the server receives a request, it can process it as it wants and then spit out a response. Let's look at responses next.

HTTP/1.1 Responses

Here's some good news: responses look awfully similar to requests. They include the following:

- A status line, made of the HTTP version and a *status code*
- A list of response headers
- An (optional) response body

An HTTP/1.1 example response could look like the figure shown on page 180.

Headers and body in responses play the same role as they do for requests.

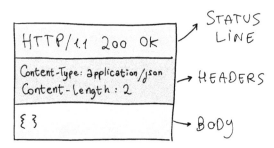

Status codes are three-digit integers ranging from 100 to 599. They tell the client the result of the request and the meaning of the responses. They're divided into five classes, identified by the first digit:

- 1xx: informational responses
- 2xx: successful requests
- 3xx: redirections
- 4xx: error in the request
- 5xx: server-side error

Servers can use any HTTP status code in the valid range, but many status codes are standardized. The 200 OK you saw in our curl request, for example, is the status indicating that the request succeeded.

RFC to the Rescue

I'd recommend that everyone—everyone!—take the barely ten minutes needed to read through the Status Codes section[7] of RFC 9110. It's short and to the point, and you'll know when to use 200 versus 204, or 401 versus 403!

While you're at it, go through the Methods section[8] of that same RFC. It's another one full of gems.

This was a brief but essential overview of HTTP. Chances are you've worked with HTTP enough in the past that you knew all this, but a quick recap can't hurt.

There are also some elements of HTTP that are somewhat less common: range requests, trailing headers, and more. We won't go deep into those here as they don't really help in learning how to work with HTTP on the BEAM, but RFC 9110[9] is a fantastic read to dig *really* deep.

---

7. https://www.rfc-editor.org/rfc/rfc9110.html#section-15
8. https://www.rfc-editor.org/rfc/rfc9110.html#name-methods
9. https://www.rfc-editor.org/rfc/rfc9110.html

Let's now jump into some action and write a little HTTP server in Elixir.

Serving JSON with Plug and Bandit

HTTP/1.1 is readable and not that complicated, but writing a serialization layer for it is a pretty crazy idea. The protocol's simplicity means that there are many corner cases—think of escaping characters when encoding headers, or encoding binary data. Plus, you want encoding requests and decoding responses to be *fast*. Using a battle-tested, optimized HTTP/1.1 serialization library is almost always the best choice.

We'll look at Plug,[10] Elixir's abstraction for HTTP server applications. Plug is an interface for implementing web servers, but it doesn't implement connection pooling or transport-layer concerns. Instead, it needs a compatible HTTP server under the hood, so we'll briefly touch on Bandit,[11] a native Elixir HTTP server that we can use with Plug.

We'll build a simple HTTP API that will respond to requests with JSON. It will support a single endpoint, /myip, which will respond with the external IP of the client making the request. This is similar to services like IfConfig[12] and Amazon AWS's IP checker.[13]

Here's what a request to our server will look like:

```
> curl http://localhost:4040/myip
{"ip": "19.59.114.192"}
```

Before diving into code, let's go over the basics of the Plug model and the abstraction it provides.

Plug: The HTTP Pipeline

Plug is the most widely used HTTP abstraction layer in the Elixir ecosystem. Its purpose is to give its users a common interface for building HTTP applications, without having to commit to a specific underlying HTTP server.

Plug takes a functional approach—as in *functional programming*—to the HTTP request-response cycle. It's all centered around a data structure, the Plug.Conn struct. We'll refer to it as *conn*. The conn contains all sorts of information about the inbound HTTP request and the outbound response to that request.

---

10. https://github.com/elixir-plug/plug
11. https://github.com/mtrudel/bandit
12. https://ifconfig.me/
13. https://checkip.amazonaws.com/

> ### Does Erlang Have Anything Built-In for Serving HTTP?
>
> Erlang (and thus Elixir) has a somewhat hidden function that you could use to parse HTTP responses: erlang:decode_packet/3.[a] This is a generic function that can decode many protocols, including HTTP. The standard library even provides its own HTTP server, httpd.[b]
>
> These tools, however, were built with simplicity in mind. They don't perform as well as modern Elixir and Erlang libraries. httpd has a limited feature set—it doesn't support HTTP/2, for example.
>
> Nowadays, you'll see most Elixir/Erlang projects reach out for libraries when it comes to HTTP servers. These libraries are actively maintained, battle-tested, optimized for performance, and often more feature-rich than the built-in tools.
>
> ---
>
> a.   https://www.erlang.org/doc/apps/erts/erlang.html#decode_packet/3
> b.   https://www.erlang.org/docs/26/man/httpd

Take a peek at just a few of the request fields in this made-up example conn:

```
%Plug.Conn{
  scheme: :https,
  host: "example.com",
  method: "GET",
  req_headers: [{"accept", "text/plain"}, {"user-agent", "curl/8.0.0"}],
  # «Many more fields»
}
```

The thing that makes the Plug approach *functional* is this: the whole request-response cycle is a series of functions that take a conn and return a potentially updated version of that conn. These functions are called *plugs*, and they're represented as modules that implement the Plug behavior.[14] This behavior only defines two callbacks:

- init/1, which can be used to configure the plug—this is mostly a performance optimization

- call/2, the function that receives the conn alongside some options and returns the updated conn

A *plug pipeline* is a sequence of calls to plugs, as shown in the figure on page 183.

The adapter mentioned in the figure is an implementation layer that wires Plug and an underlying HTTP server together. For example, Bandit[15] itself is an adapter.

---

14. https://hexdocs.pm/plug/Plug.html
15. https://github.com/mtrudel/bandit

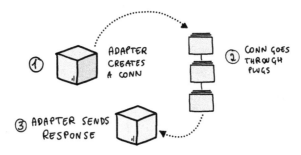

Let's quickly put together a simple plug that generates a random request ID and adds it as a response header:

```
request_id_plug.ex
defmodule RequestIDPlug do
  @behaviour Plug

  @impl true
  def init(options) do
    %{header_name: Keyword.get(options, :header_name, "request-id")}
  end

  @impl true
  def call(conn, %{header_name: header_name}) do
    request_id = Base.url_encode64(:crypto.strong_rand_bytes(5))
    conn = Plug.Conn.put_resp_header(conn, header_name, request_id)
    conn
  end
end
```

On line 6, you can see how we configure the plug through options. We could do the same for call/2, but we'd face the inefficiency of doing it for each request rather than only once at start time.

The options returned by init/1 are passed down to call/2 on line 10. In call/2, we generate a random ID, add it in a response header through Plug.Conn.put_resp_header/3, and return the updated conn.

Now, we said that the request-response cycle is a *series* of these plugs. One way to get that is to combine a sequence of plugs using Plug.Builder.[16] For example:

```
defmodule MyApp.PlugPipeline do
  use Plug.Builder

  plug RequestIDPlug, header_name: "my-request-id"
  plug Plug.Logger # Included in the Plug library
end
```

---

16. https://hexdocs.pm/plug/Plug.Builder.html

The conn goes through RequestIDPlug, and the returned (updated) conn goes through Plug.Logger. This is a powerful idea and a powerful abstraction. You can build complex pipelines of plugs, and plugs in those pipelines can themselves be nested pipelines of plugs… you get the idea.

Plug is the lingua franca of HTTP in Elixir-land. You'll find gazillions of pre-baked plugs on Hex (just search for "plug")[17]. Web frameworks such as Phoenix[18] are also built on top of Plug.

We won't go any deeper into how Plug works. The Plug documentation does a fantastic job of guiding you through building plugs or using existing plugs.

Now, a word about Bandit. Bandit is a lightweight HTTP server written in Elixir. In most cases, you won't interact directly with it, because it provides an interface to work with plugs. Essentially, Bandit takes care of the network side of the HTTP server stack, accepting connections, spawning processes, and all that jazz. But it delegates the business logic—what to do with the HTTP request and how to put together a response—to a plug passed in by the user. That's great news, because it means it hides almost all the complexity from the user.

Let's move on to actually *using* this stuff.

Writing the Server

To set things up and follow along, create a new Mix project anywhere on your system:

```
> mix new whats_my_ip --sup --module WhatsMyIP
```

All the code for this project is also available in the code/whats_my_ip directory in the book's resources.

To use Plug and Bandit, we need to add them to the project's dependencies in code/whats_my_ip/mix.exs:

```
whats_my_ip/mix.exs
defp deps do
  [
    {:bandit, "~> 1.5"},
    {:plug, "~> 1.16"}
  ]
end
```

Now, run the usual mix deps.get and we're good to go.

---

17. https://hex.pm/packages?search=plug
18. https://www.phoenixframework.org/

Are These Standard Tools?

Bandit is relatively new to the Elixir/Erlang world at the time of writing, and it might eventually be replaced by something else—albeit the chances are low.

Plug, on the other hand, was born almost at the same time as Elixir and has been the standard interface for HTTP servers this whole time. Plug won't go away anytime soon, and that's also because Plug is an *interface*: we might swap the server parts underneath eventually, but your code will only need the tiniest changes.

The first thing that you will want to do is start the supervision tree for the Bandit/Plug server we're working on. You'll do that in WhatsMyIP.Application:

whats_my_ip/lib/whats_my_ip/application.ex
```
children = [
  {Bandit, plug: WhatsMyIP.Router, port: 8080}
]
```

The options we're passing to the Bandit child specification here should be self-explanatory. :port will decide what port the server runs on, and :plug tells Bandit which plug to run requests through. Now for an interesting tidbit. Remember in Rewriting the Server with Thousand Island, on page 66, when we used Thousand Island to build our own pool of TCP handlers? Well, Bandit also runs on top of Thousand Island. It starts a supervision tree just like the ones we saw in Chapter 4, Scaling TCP on the Server Side, on page 59, where each TCP connection handler maps to an HTTP request handler.

If you try to run this application now, it'll yell at you—we didn't define any WhatsMyIP.Router module. Makes sense, so let's fix that.

Creating a Plug Router

We'll want our main entry-point plug to be a router. Plug.Router[19] gives you a flexible Domain-Specific Language (DSL) for mapping functionality to specific paths—also called *routes*. Creating a router is a matter of calling use Plug.Router and then calling the :match and :dispatch plugs (which are explicit so that you can inject functionality between them). Here's the skeleton of the router:

whats_my_ip/lib/whats_my_ip/router.ex
```
defmodule WhatsMyIP.Router do
  use Plug.Router
```

---

19. https://hexdocs.pm/plug/Plug.Router.html

```
  plug :match
  plug :dispatch
end
```

We're ready to define routes. In our case, we care about the GET /myip route. To match on that, we can use Plug.Router's get/2 macro:

whats_my_ip/lib/whats_my_ip/router.ex
```
get "/myip" do
  # «response with IP inside a JSON object»
end
```

Plug.Router macros make a special conn variable (a Plug.Conn struct) available inside the do/end block.

Now it's a matter of responding with the client's IP encoded inside a JSON object. We'll need a few things:

1. The client IP is a field of the conn struct (:remote_ip), so we don't need to call out to any external module.

2. To respond with JSON, you'll want to set the Content-Type response header to application/json—many clients look at that header to determine how a response is encoded.

3. Since Elixir 1.18 and newer, we can use the JSON module[20] to encode a JSON object. On Erlang, as long as you're running version 27 or later, that would be the :json module.[21] If you want to run this on older OTP or Elixir versions, you can use Jason[22] and replace :json.encode/1 or JSON.encode!/1 with Jason.encode!/1.

The code for this whole thing is pretty concise (it probably took more words to explain it):

whats_my_ip/lib/whats_my_ip/router.ex
```
get "/myip" do
  ip = conn.remote_ip |> :inet.ntoa() |> to_string()
  response_body = JSON.encode!(%{ip: ip})

  conn
  |> Plug.Conn.put_resp_content_type("application/json")
  |> send_resp(200, response_body)
end
```

---

20. https://hexdocs.pm/elixir/JSON.html
21. https://erlang.org/documentation/doc-15.0-rc3/lib/stdlib-6.0/doc/html/json.html
22. https://github.com/michalmuskala/jason

Let's try this out. First, you'll want the server running. You can do that by starting the :whats_my_ip application with the --no-halt flag:

```
> mix run --no-halt
18:40:44.957 [info] Running WhatsMyIP.Router with Bandit 1.5.7
                    at 0.0.0.0:8080 (http)
```

In another terminal window, use curl to send a request (the flags in the command let you also print the status line and response headers):

```
> curl -s -D - http://localhost:8080/myip
HTTP/1.1 200 OK
date: Sat, 19 Oct 2024 16:55:56 GMT
content-length: 18
vary: accept-encoding
cache-control: max-age=0, private, must-revalidate
content-type: application/json; charset=utf-8

{"ip":"127.0.0.1"}
```

127.0.0.1 makes sense because we're sending the request from the same host. In a request coming from another host, you'd see a different IP address.

If you attempt to send a request to any other route, our server will behave correctly, returning a 404 response. Try that out:

```
> curl -s -D - http://localhost:8080/whatever
HTTP/1.1 404 Not Found
date: Sat, 19 Oct 2024 16:48:31 GMT
vary: accept-encoding
cache-control: max-age=0, private, must-revalidate
```

Our small HTTP API is doing what we said it would do, so we're pretty much done.

Homework

 The 404 Not Found response from our server is semantically correct, but it's not JSON. The body is empty, after all. Use the Plug.Router.match/2 macro[23] to match on any route that is not GET /myip and return the following JSON object (with the correct Content-Type header):

```
{"error": "route not found"}
```

Before exploring HTTP clients, let's finish this section with some more thoughts about HTTP servers.

---

23. https://hexdocs.pm/plug/Plug.Router.html#match/2

HTTP Servers: Where to Go Next

One topic we haven't covered here, and haven't dedicated much attention to throughout the book in all honesty, is testing. Luckily, Plug comes with easy-to-use test helpers and convenience functions, all neatly tucked away in Plug.Test.[24]

We won't dive deep into testing here, but let's just peek at one test for our JSON API. Plug.Test allows you to build isolated Plug conns, modify the session, and assert on responses. Here's an example test for our API:

whats_my_ip/test/whats_my_ip_test.exs
```
Line 1  defmodule WhatsMyIPTest do
          use ExUnit.Case, async: true
          use Plug.Test

     5    describe "GET /myip" do
            test "returns the client's IP address" do
              assert {200, _headers, resp_body} =
                       conn(:get, "/myip")
                       |> Plug.run([{WhatsMyIP.Router, []}])
    10                 |> sent_resp()

              assert JSON.decode!(resp_body) == %{"ip" => "127.0.0.1"}
            end
          end
    15  end
```

The conn/2 and sent_resp/1 helpers make the test quite concise. There's a neat detail to notice here: that sneaky Plug.run/2 call on line 9. Plug conns are just data structures, and a plug pipeline is a list of functions that the conn goes through. Plug.run/2 lets you do exactly that: run the conn through a list of plugs. It's all tied together by the fact that modules that use Plug.Router are plugs themselves, so running a conn through our application means running it through the router plug.

Plug (and Bandit) take care of most things you need when building HTTP servers. Plug ships with many helpful plugs, such as one for requiring HTTP Basic Auth, one for logging requests, one for serving static files from the filesystem, and many others. But if you're building a larger HTTP API or website (essentially an HTTP server serving HTML), you might benefit from an HTTP framework. In Elixir, the undisputed queen of frameworks is Phoenix.[25] If you want to learn more about Phoenix, check out *Programming Phoenix 1.4 [MTV19]*.

---

24. https://hexdocs.pm/plug/1.16.1/Plug.Test.html
25. https://www.phoenixframework.org/

Let's move on to HTTP clients.

Connecting to Servers with Mint

The world of HTTP clients in BEAM-land is diverse and somewhat complicated. Before diving deeper, let's take a second to survey the landscape of clients and their use cases.

So Many HTTP Clients

Erlang ships with an HTTP client called httpc,[26] but that's not widely used. It was introduced in Erlang with the idea that it would be used mostly internally, so it has a few limitations:

- It was not designed for high-performance scenarios

- Its interface is somewhat cumbersome and not quite in line with modern Elixir/Erlang

- It does not support HTTP/2 (or anything other than HTTP/1.1)

It does support connection pooling, but that is tied to the inets application and not easily configurable for different use cases within the same application.

Mind you, httpc *works*. Its main advantage is that it comes with Erlang's standard library and requires no dependencies. Sometimes, that's such an important requirement that using it is almost mandatory. The best example of this is Hex,[27] Elixir's package manager. Hex needs to fetch dependencies via HTTP, so it needs an HTTP client, but it's itself a dependency manager, so not having dependencies is important! After all, the logic for version resolution, safe dependency downloads, verification, and more resides in Hex itself. Hex, because of this, uses httpc.[28]

For most cases, however, you'll want to use a third-party library. Easier said than done. As in many other ecosystems, there's a wide array of possible choices. Just to mention a few, there's Hackney, Mint, Finch, Req, Gun, Tesla, and HTTPoison. Head-spinning stuff. Each client has its own features, advantages, and compromises, and we're not going into every one of them. If you want some more context, the author of this book wrote a blog post[29] dedicated to this very topic.

---

26. https://www.erlang.org/docs/26/man/httpc
27. https://hex.pm/
28. https://github.com/hexpm/hex/blob/eec7a266f6e1b1c754798ee9a9c17b4b6201fff2/src/mix_hex_http_httpc.erl
29. https://andrealeopardi.com/posts/breakdown-of-http-clients-in-elixir/

What generally matters the most when picking a client is how low-level you want (or need) it to be. For example, Mint is a *very* low-level client. Req, on the other hand, prides itself on being a batteries-included type of client, providing everything you might need for all sorts of use cases.

In this book, we are definitely looking at things from the bottom up—we started with just TCP, after all. So, it makes sense for us to explore Mint first.

TCP Sockets That Understand HTTP: Mint

When Mint[30] was created, the idea was to build a low-level HTTP client that could be included in Elixir's standard library. Things evolved, and the Elixir team decided to keep it separate so that it could be iterated on quickly, but the design of the client stayed the same.

The breakthrough idea with Mint was to build a *processless* HTTP client. You see, all other Elixir and Erlang HTTP clients before Mint were architected around processes. HTTP connections would be represented as a process holding a TCP (or TLS) socket and exchanging messages with the socket and the other processes making HTTP requests. This worked, but it imposed a process architecture that could be suboptimal in some scenarios, especially when high performance was required.

The idea with Mint was this: what if the HTTP client is a smart TCP socket that understands HTTP? Think about it: a TCP socket already understands the TCP protocol and hides the implementation details from its users. You don't manually perform handshakes, you can decode packets with the :packet option, and so on. Well, that can be extended to HTTP!

That's what Mint is. A Mint connection is a data structure that wraps a TCP or TLS socket and understands HTTP.

Introducing Mint

 If you're curious about Mint and its history, the Elixir blog has a blog post[31] that introduced Mint back in 2019.

The figure shown on page 191 is a representation of the abstraction provided by a Mint connection.

---

30. https://github.com/elixir-mint/mint
31. https://elixir-lang.org/blog/2019/02/25/mint-a-new-http-library-for-elixir/

Let's play around with Mint a bit. With our JSON HTTP API running on port 8080, open up an IEx shell, install Mint, and open up a connection:

```
iex> Mix.install([:mint])
iex> {:ok, conn} = Mint.HTTP.connect(:http, "localhost", 8080)
iex> conn
%Mint.HTTP1{«fields»}
```

Mint.HTTP.connect/3 returns a Mint connection. Mint performed protocol negotiation right there and ended up opening an HTTP/1.1 connection (the returned struct would have been Mint.HTTP2 otherwise). The conn struct holds many fields, but its fields are mostly private and not meant to be accessed directly. All these fields make sense though: HTTP is a more complex protocol than TCP, so a bunch of state and information is needed for things to work. One of the fields in the conn is the TCP socket, which you can inspect with get_socket/1:

```
iex> socket = Mint.HTTP.get_socket(conn)
iex> :inet.port(socket)
{:ok, 64146}
```

Since Mint connections are just data structures, all the state is contained in the connection. This is somewhat different from TCP sockets, which hide some of the state behind the OS-level data structure that we access via the Erlang port. This is why you always need to keep updating the conn struct when making HTTP operations—it's immutable, after all. We'll see this in practice in a second.

Let's make some requests now.

Making HTTP Requests with Mint

Issuing requests with Mint mirrors TCP operations nicely:

1. First, you send a request with Mint.HTTP.request/5. This returns a *request reference* that you can use to identify responses to the request.

2. Then, you await TCP (or TLS) messages coming to the process that controls the Mint connection, just as you would do with a TCP/TLS socket. The difference here is that you need to feed these TCP/TLS messages to Mint.HTTP.stream/2 to parse and extract responses from them.

Why Not Just HTTP Messages?

It would be awesome if you could get already-parsed HTTP messages to the controlling process of a Mint connection. Sadly, the Erlang VM completely prevents you from doing that: there's no way to intercept messages in a process mailbox before the process gets to see and act on them.

Let's see this flow in practice.

```
iex> {:ok, conn, ref} =
...>    Mint.HTTP.request(
...>      conn,
...>      "GET",
...>      "/myip",
...>      [{"Accept", "application/json"}],
...>      _body = nil
...>    )
```

We're passing in the connection, the HTTP method, path, headers, and body (nil in this case since it's a GET request). request/5 returns the updated connection and a request ref. You *must* get that updated connection back. If you don't (and just run request/5 without storing the updated connection), you'll get all sorts of errors later on—the request will be sent but the old conn won't keep track of it.

Now, where's our response? The underlying TCP socket sent it to the shell process as a message. To parse that with Mint, we need to receive it first and then hand it to Mint.HTTP.stream/2:

```
iex> next_message = receive do message -> message end
iex> {:ok, conn, responses} = Mint.HTTP.stream(conn, next_message)
```

We always get back an updated conn. That's immutable data structures for you: when functions "modify" the conn, they just create an updated copy. Now, responses is a list of tuples representing interesting parts of an HTTP response (status, headers, body). Each tuple is tagged with the request ref from request/5:

```
iex> responses
[
  {:status, #Reference<0.23.10.2>, 200},
  {:headers, #Reference<0.23.10.2>,
```

```
[
  {"date", "Fri, 08 Nov 2024 11:04:48 GMT"},
  {"content-length", "18"},
  {"vary", "accept-encoding"},
  {"cache-control", "max-age=0, private, must-revalidate"},
  {"content-type", "application/json; charset=utf-8"}
]},
{:data, #Reference<0.23.10.2>, "{\"ip\":\"127.0.0.1\"}"},
{:done, #Reference<0.23.10.2>}
]
```

These responses should all look familiar. The last :done response signals that the response is over.

Responses are broken up in this way because, as you learned earlier, TCP packets can get split at any point. You might get a status line and headers in a single packet but no response body. In that case, stream/2 would return [{:status, ...}, {:headers, ...}] when the first packet comes. When another packet with the response body arrives and gets fed to stream/2, that would return {:data, ...}.

Passive Mode

 A Mint connection is a wrapper around a TCP socket, as we've said a few times. Well, remember Active and Passive Modes for Sockets, on page 14? You can choose between active and passive modes for Mint connections as well. Use Mint.HTTP.set_mode/2 to set the connection to passive mode, and Mint.HTTP.recv/3 to manually receive data from the socket. Just like TCP.

Mint itself is processless, so you can embed it in your existing processes in a way that fits your exact use case, without performance penalties. When you wrap a Mint connection in a process, you'll usually have a structure for requests and responses that looks more or less like this:

- Your process keeps a map of request refs to responses in its state

- When a TCP message comes to the process, you feed it to Mint.HTTP.stream/2 and then *reduce* over the responses

- For each response, you update the connection with the connection returned by stream/2 and put the response in the request/response map, based on the response ref key

- Whenever you get a :done response, you can remove the corresponding fully formed response from the request/response map

Here's a visual representation of this process:

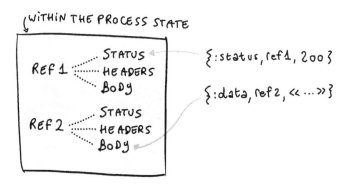

You're not limited in the type of process you can stick this architecture in. The process that holds the Mint connection could be a GenServer dedicated to the connection, or it could be any other process doing something else. For example, you could embed Mint in a GenStage pipeline. Mint's documentation has some examples.[32]

Mint is only right for a few use cases where fine-grained control or extreme performance (or both) are required. In most cases, Mint acts better as a building block that other libraries can use to create higher-level abstractions. We'll look at two of those now—Finch and Req.

Higher-Level Client Libraries: Finch and Req

Making an HTTP/1.1 request with Mint can be somewhat cumbersome. It's optimized for precise control over every aspect of the request/response flow. Usually, you'll want an HTTP client that lets you make HTTP requests but takes care of features such as pooling and streaming.

In the pyramid of abstractions of HTTP clients, Mint sits the lowest. While you have many options for what sits *on top* of Mint, these are two of the most common:

- Finch,[33] if you want connection pooling but still minimal dependencies and tight control

- Req,[34] if you want a batteries-included HTTP client (built on Finch) that covers encoding, compression, retries, and a host of other features

---

32. https://hexdocs.pm/mint/architecture.html#usage-examples
33. https://github.com/sneako/finch
34. https://github.com/wojtekmach/req

Finch is a thin layer on top of Mint that uses NimblePool to pool Mint connections. It does exactly what we did in Pooling Resources Directly with NimblePool, on page 96, when pooling TCP connections. Let's take Finch for a quick spin:

```
iex> Mix.install([:finch])
iex> Finch.start_link(name: :my_pool)
iex> request =
...>    Finch.build(
...>      :get,
...>      "http://localhost:8080/myip",
...>      [{"Accept", "application/json"}]
...>    )
iex> Finch.request(request, :my_pool)
{:ok,
 %Finch.Response{
   status: 200,
   body: "{\"ip\":\"127.0.0.1\"}",
   headers: [
     {"content-length", "18"},
     {"content-type", "application/json; charset=utf-8"},
     «More response headers»
   ],
   trailers: []
}}
```

Neat! See how the response body is still undecoded JSON? That's because Finch is not doing much other than implementing the connection pooling.

If you want an HTTP client that can do most things out of the box, Req is a great choice. Restart the IEx shell (so we can reuse Mix.install/1) and take Req for a drive:

```
iex> Mix.install([:req])
iex> Req.get("http://localhost:8080/myip")
{:ok,
 %Req.Response{
   status: 200,
   headers: %{
     "cache-control" => ["max-age=0, private, must-revalidate"],
     "content-type" => ["application/json; charset=utf-8"],
     «More response headers»
   },
   body: %{"ip" => "127.0.0.1"},
   trailers: %{},
   private: %{}
}}
```

Oof, that's a lot for a single function call. Req spins up a default connection pool and decodes the JSON response body after looking at the Content-Type response header, but it can also do much more. For many use cases—from one-off scripts to full applications—Req is a fantastic client: it stays lightweight while handling many common HTTP tasks for you.

When working with HTTP clients, think about the pyramid of abstractions we mentioned at the start of this section, as visualized here:

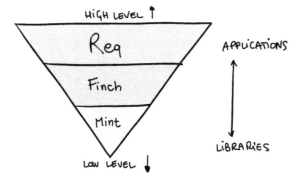

If you're working on a lower-level use case that requires precise control, performance, or both—say, writing a library that needs an HTTP client—lean toward the bottom of the pyramid. Otherwise, go toward the top. Easy peasy.

Wrapping Up

That was quite the whirlwind tour of HTTP/1.1, clients, and servers. While we didn't dive too deep into anything in particular, we got a good overview of many things. We started by exploring HTTP at the protocol level, covering requests and responses. You then learned about Plug and writing HTTP servers—and we wrote a simple HTTP API for retrieving your IP. Finally, you learned about the low-level HTTP client Mint, as well as some higher-level options.

The next chapter is going to give you a taste of the present and future of HTTP: HTTP/2 and HTTP/3.

## CHAPTER 12

HTTP/2 and the Future

Learning about HTTP/1.1 gave you a foundational understanding of HTTP—how it works and why it powers so much of the web. But as the Internet has evolved, the limitations of HTTP/1.1 have become more apparent. Internet traffic, predominantly reliant on HTTP, has surged dramatically, and the volume of data exchanged has grown in tandem. Websites are now more powerful, interactive, and media-rich than ever before.

In 2015, the initial specification for a new version of HTTP/1.1 was published, and HTTP/2 was born. HTTP/2, presented in RFC 7540,[1] is a complete over-haul of HTTP/1.1 and the first major revision since HTTP/1.1's debut in 1997. Shortly after HTTP/2, HTTP/3 made its first appearance (circa 2018) and was standardized in 2022. At the time of writing, HTTP/2 and HTTP/3 account for between 60 and 80 percent of website traffic (Web Almanac).[2]

Compatibility

HTTP/1.1 and HTTP/2 are not compatible at the protocol level. The HTTP/2 spec mandates how servers and clients negotiate which protocol to use, but that doesn't mean they can simply swap one for the other, and the same goes for HTTP/3.

But the designers of HTTP/2 and HTTP/3 did a fantastic job of ensuring they *feel* like HTTP/1. As mentioned, HTTP/1.1 accounts for less than half of Internet traffic at the time of writing, but it's unlikely you'd notice unless you started inspecting requests and responses. The semantics of requests, responses, URIs, methods, headers, and so on remain the same, even though the underlying architecture changed completely.

---

1. https://datatracker.ietf.org/doc/html/rfc7540
2. https://almanac.httparchive.org/en/2020/http#http2-adoption

This chapter focuses primarily on HTTP/2. You'll learn about its unique features and how it differs from and is similar to HTTP/1.1. You'll learn to utilize HTTP/2's capabilities using Plug on the server side and Mint on the client side. We'll also touch briefly on HTTP/3, but support for this newer protocol in BEAM-land is not quite there yet, so we won't dive too deep.

HTTP/2: Why It Was Needed and What Changed

HTTP/2 was created to address the limitations of HTTP/1.1. Consider the usual use case for HTTP/1.1: browsers make requests to servers to load websites. To work, most websites need resources such as HTML, CSS, and JavaScript files, fonts, images, and more. HTTP/1.1's request model requires one request per resource, which can be slow and inefficient. Browsers evolved by starting to open multiple TCP/TLS connections (usually up to six) when loading a website to parallelize HTTP/1.1 requests, queuing multiple requests on each connection, as shown in the following figure:

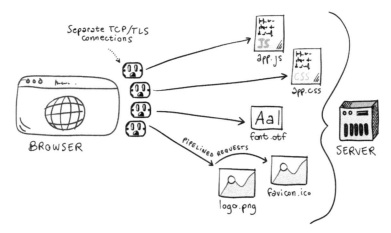

This is resource-intensive—especially for the server, since it may need to serve many clients at the same time. But there's no other way to make parallel requests with HTTP/1.1. Another problem, known as *head-of-line (HoL) blocking*, meant that if one request stalled, all requests on that same connection would be held up. Moreover, HTTP/1.1 lacks a way to identify requests uniquely, so requests and responses must be sent and received in strict order.

HTTP/1.1 has other limitations, too. Being a textual protocol means that data is not efficiently and compactly encoded. Header information is often redundant and has to be re-encoded over and over. And backpressure—limiting request numbers to avoid overwhelming servers—is impossible to manage.

HTTP/2 fixes all these things. Let's take a closer look at how.

Persistent Connections and Streams

HTTP/2 is significantly different at the protocol level. First and foremost, it's a binary protocol, not a textual protocol like HTTP/1.1. It might be harder for humans to read, but there's efficiency to be gained in serializing and transmitting data this way.

HTTP/2 connections are also *persistent*. The implications of this are transformative for HTTP. Now, server and client establish a connection through which they can exchange data at will and for longer periods of time, without being limited to ordered request-response cycles. This also reduces the overhead of opening and closing connections repeatedly.

To fully take advantage of a persistent connection, HTTP/2 allows clients to send multiple requests on that connection—and concurrently too! In fact, a single connection can have multiple open *streams*. Streams are lightweight channels for concurrent—but separate—data streams. Each new request is sent over a new or existing stream. Streams also have IDs. Let's say you open streams A and B and send a request on each in that order. You might get back the response to the request on stream B first, but this is totally fine—you can identify which request (stream) the response belongs to and process it correctly based on the stream ID. Say goodbye to head-of-line blocking.

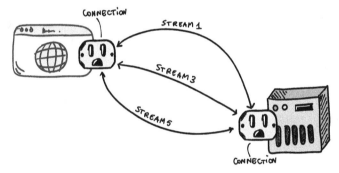

There's also a major protocol change in HTTP/2: the introduction of *frames*. These are self-contained pieces of information defined at the protocol level. HTTP/1.1 requests and responses consist of multiple parts—request/response line, headers, and body—and you can't determine when a message is complete until you've received the whole thing. The parts have to be in a specific order, and there are no meta-messages about the protocol itself. But HTTP/2 peers exchange frames on streams. Frames can contain headers, a piece of a request/response body, error information, and more. Generally speaking, you might not need to know everything about frames in deep detail, but it's nice to know how data is packed up and shipped around.

Frames in Binary Protocols

Packing data into frames and the like is a common practice when designing binary protocols. For example, Apache Cassandra's native protocol[3] also uses frames—and calls them that. MySQL calls them *packets*,[4] but the idea is the same.

These few changes enable a more efficient and streamlined communication between client and server. For example, browsers no longer need to open multiple network connections, since they can request resources concurrently on a single connection. And resources that take longer to fetch won't block other resources either.

Backpressure and Flow Control

HTTP/2 introduces crucial mechanisms for managing the flow of data over a connection. In HTTP/1.1, there aren't inherent limits on the volume of data exchanged or the rate of data transfer between client and server. As a result, servers can struggle to control the resources a client consumes, leading to potential inefficiencies and overloads.

To address this, HTTP/2 introduces specific frame types dedicated to *flow control*. Flow control is a network feature that ensures data flows at a manageable rate. Both connections and streams maintain a *flow control window* that limits how much data can be in transit at any given time. Clients and servers have to actively manage these windows, essentially adjusting them to receive more data once they're ready for it.

This approach directly incorporates *backpressure* as a fundamental aspect of communication, ensuring peers only send data when the receiving end signals that it's ready to handle it.

While this might seem complex, flow control fundamentally enhances the stability and performance of HTTP/2 connections, ensuring balanced data exchange and protecting both clients and servers from potential overloads. This all occurs seamlessly, without requiring HTTP/2 users to be aware of these underlying processes.

---

3. https://github.com/apache/cassandra/blob/63d3538ba7352635b7b61a205b40e035e62b8d5d/doc/native_protocol_v5.spec#L71

4. https://dev.mysql.com/doc/dev/mysql-server/9.2.0/page_protocol_basic_packets.html

Push Promises

HTTP/2 connections are persistent, and they can stay open even if there are no in-flight requests (or open streams). The protocol originally took advantage of this to introduce another groundbreaking feature (at the time): *push promises*, also known as *Server Push.*[5]

Push promises allow servers to initiate the transmission of resources before the client explicitly requests them. Essentially, the server predicts likely client requests and "promises" those responses preemptively. By doing so, it reduces the latency associated with web page loading. The following figure shows the server preemptively sending JavaScript and CSS resources to the browser:

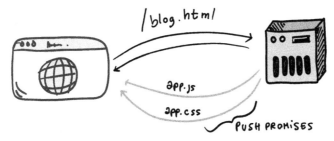

Push promises are on their way out. While great on paper, major browsers stopped supporting them,[6] citing lack of usage and better alternatives.

Push Promise No More

The web opted for other solutions to the use case of server-initiated data transmission for HTTP. Here are some resources to check out:

- Preload links:[7] <link> HTML elements that suggest resources for the browser to fetch

- Early hints:[8] HTTP status code (103) allowing you to send preliminary responses before the final response

- A fantastic blog post[9] on the complexities of server push

---

We went through a short feature tour. Now, let's look at how to *use* these features in Elixir.

---

5.   https://en.wikipedia.org/wiki/HTTP/2_Server_Push
6.   https://developer.chrome.com/blog/removing-push
7.   https://web.dev/articles/preload-critical-assets
8.   https://developer.chrome.com/docs/web-platform/early-hints
9.   https://jakearchibald.com/2017/h2-push-tougher-than-i-thought/

Using HTTP/2 with Plug and Mint

Most HTTP tooling nowadays supports HTTP/2. Plug and Mint are no exception, so let's look at examples of using HTTP/2 with these tools.

Here's the kicker: most of the time, you can (and will) use HTTP/2 without
having to do anything explicitly. Try it for yourself. Fire up an IEx session,
install Mint, and connect to elixir-lang.org:

```
iex> Mix.install([:mint])
iex> {:ok, conn} = Mint.HTTP.connect(:https, "elixir-lang.org", 443)
iex> conn.__struct__
Mint.HTTP2
```

The same goes for the server side: Bandit supports HTTP/2 out of the box,
for example.

Plug and Mint also support HTTP/2-specific features, such as push promises
and flow control. Let's use the conn from the previous IEx section to get the
size of the flow control window, which is a feature that only exists in HTTP/2
and not in HTTP/1.1:

```
iex> Mint.HTTP2.get_window_size(conn, :connection)
65535
```

Even though push promises are getting phased out, both Plug and Mint
support them out of the box. With Plug, you can use Plug.Conn.push/3. Here's a
simplified example:

```
get "/index.html" do
  conn
  |> push!("/assets/app.css", [{"content-type", "text/css"}])
  |> push!("/assets/app.js", [{"content-type", "text/javascript"}])
  |> send_resp(200, "<html>...</html>")
end
```

The responses you'd get by making a GET /index.html with Mint would include
:push_promise responses alongside additional :status/:headers/:data/:done responses
for the promised resources.

That was a short whirlwind tour of HTTP/2 and how it differs from HTTP/1,
but the HTTP saga is not over: there's one more version of HTTP to learn
about.

Evolving in Parallel with QUIC and HTTP/3

The development of HTTP/2 was almost immediately followed by that of
HTTP/3. That's because HTTP/2 and HTTP/3 solve essentially the same

problems but are meant for different underlying protocol stacks. HTTP/2 is meant to work with TCP/TLS, while HTTP/3 is designed for *QUIC*, a new transport layer based on UDP. In this section, we'll elaborate on the differences between the protocols and the need for HTTP/3.

The Limits of TCP and the Role of QUIC

HTTP/2 solves many of the issues caused by limitations in HTTP/1.1, but some problems with HTTP/1.1 are in fact problems with the underlying transport protocol, TCP.

First, establishing a TCP connection requires a handshake. This takes a full network round trip before any data can be transmitted.

One of the main issues with TCP is its performance in lossy networks—networks where connections are unstable and packets frequently get lost. Imagine you're sending three HTTP/2 responses—A, B, and C—each made of multiple TCP packets (three packets in the following figure), and imagine that these packets can intersperse. If a packet for response B gets lost, the client needs to resend all the packets after it. It doesn't matter if those packets have already been sent and possibly delivered to the receiver. TCP won't allow the receiver to access other packets—even for responses A and C, which are completely independent. You can see this in the following figure.

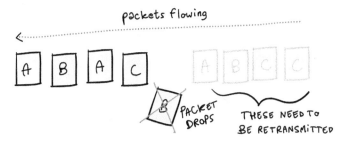

You heard about this already earlier in the chapter: it's head-of-line blocking all over again, but independent of HTTP. All TCP traffic suffers from it in one way or another. Subsequent packets are blocked until all previous packets are delivered. This behavior comes from the fact that TCP doesn't distinguish what the contents of the data being exchanged are. It only knows about a single byte stream. So, even though HTTP/2 is a multiplexed protocol capable of multiple concurrent in-flight requests, it still suffers from head-of-line blocking on a single TCP connection.

The solution to these problems doesn't lie in a new version of HTTP but rather in an alternative to TCP itself. Enter $QUIC^{10}$ (it's not an acronym). QUIC is *semantically* a transport protocol—an alternative to TCP or UDP. It implements features that resemble HTTP/2 in some ways and features that can make QUIC more scalable than TCP. One of these is not needing a handshake. Another important feature is that QUIC is aware of multiple byte streams on a single QUIC connection. This solves head-of-line blocking: if our packet B gets lost but packets A and C are on different streams within the same connection, they can still be delivered to the receiver. Only the packets on the stream that dropped need to be retransmitted. The following figure should help to visualize this.

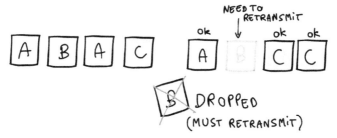

Now for the twist: QUIC is built on top of UDP! That's why it's not *technically* a layer-4 transport protocol—it's already built on another transport protocol. So, QUIC is sort of a TCP on steroids, reimplemented on top of UDP. It provides the guarantees that make TCP so useful (guaranteed delivery and ordering) but solves some of the performance issues.

With QUIC under our belt, we can now talk about HTTP/3.

HTTP/3: HTTP/2 for QUIC

We've finally come to *HTTP/3.*[11] HTTP/3 is essentially HTTP/2 but on top of QUIC rather than TCP. That's pretty much it.

At this point, you might be wondering why all this mess. The main reason for all these protocols is that the Internet is used by a lot (a *lot*) of people *and infrastructures*. Compatibility is a primary concern for protocol designers: not breaking existing software is paramount. Upgrading or modifying infrastructure is costly and hard.

This is what's behind the choices made for these protocols. HTTP/2 might not solve all of HTTP/1.1's problems, but it solves a bunch of them while still

---

10. https://en.wikipedia.org/wiki/QUIC
11. https://en.wikipedia.org/wiki/HTTP/3

running on top of TCP. That means that all sorts of applications, such as TCP proxies, traffic scanners, analysis tools, and firewalls, still work out of the box with HTTP/2. So, you get an improved protocol that doesn't require infrastructure-level changes—and often not even *application* changes.

The same reasoning applies to QUIC: building QUIC on top of UDP rather than as a new layer-4 protocol means that the Internet infrastructure, such as routers and switches, doesn't need to be adapted or updated to understand a new protocol. HTTP/3 is only justified as a "QUIC version" of HTTP/2. HTTP/2 could have been designed to work on TCP *and* QUIC, but because QUIC implements several HTTP/2 features, there would have been significant feature duplication between QUIC and HTTP/2, which justified introducing a new, trimmed-down protocol (HTTP/3).

When it comes to choosing between these protocols, there are no clear guidelines that apply to all use cases. HTTP/2 is more than sufficient for most real-world scenarios today. It's a proven protocol, well-supported in web servers, clients, and frameworks. If you want a smoother path and a stable setup, HTTP/2 is your best bet. HTTP/3 might give you some advantage when it comes to latency or poorly performing networks, but configuration and troubleshooting are still a bit more complex, so it might not be worth the switch.

The future is looking great for HTTP. While HTTP/2 continues to be the primary workhorse of the web, HTTP/3 is steadily growing. By familiarizing yourself with both, you'll be prepared to work with whichever one you need to use.

Additional Resources

QUIC and HTTP/3 are not well-supported in the Elixir/Erlang ecosystem quite yet. They're fairly recent protocols and not widely adopted. That's why there's no dedicated chapter about them in this book.

If you want to learn more about the protocols in general, here's a handy list of resources. First, QUIC:

- Chromium's introduction to QUIC[12]
- RFC 9000[13]
- CloudFlare's series about the history of QUIC[14]

---

12. https://www.chromium.org/quic/
13. https://datatracker.ietf.org/doc/rfc9000/
14. https://blog.cloudflare.com/the-road-to-quic/

For HTTP/3:

- RFC 9114[15]
- *HTTP/3 from A to Z*, by Smashing Magazine[16]

There's also a young but promising project, Quicer,[17] which provides QUIC support for Elixir and Erlang. It's probably a lot of fun to experiment with.

Wrapping Up

This was a short chapter. You learned about HTTP/2, why it was created, the main differences from HTTP/1.1, and how to use HTTP/2-specific features with Plug and Mint. You also went through a quick introduction to QUIC (no pun intended) and HTTP/3.

You're almost at the end of this book. The last chapter will teach you about how a lot of the real-time traffic on the web happens: via WebSockets.

---

15. https://datatracker.ietf.org/doc/html/rfc9114
16. https://www.smashingmagazine.com/2021/08/http3-core-concepts-part1/
17. https://github.com/emqx/quic

## CHAPTER 13

Communicating in Real Time with WebSockets

In the previous chapter, you learned about HTTP/2 and HTTP/3, both of which can technically support real-time, two-way communication between client and server. But these protocols were not specifically designed with real-time interactions as their primary focus. Instead, their real-time capabilities are more about enhancing the efficiency of traditional HTTP browser-based workflows. That's where *WebSocket* comes in. WebSocket is the go-to protocol for implementing real-time communication on the web.

Today, WebSockets are ubiquitous in many products you use daily. Chat apps such as Slack, for example, use WebSockets to instantly deliver messages. This protocol is a staple for live updates of all sorts, such as live sports scores and financial dashboards. It's also the backbone of online multiplayer games and collaborative tools such as Figma. With such a rich repertoire, understanding WebSockets is essential for any network programming expert.

In this chapter, we'll dive into the core concepts of the protocol and explore the Elixir and Erlang tools you can use to work with it. We'll build on our previous project—a JSON API from Chapter 11, Talking the Internet Protocol: HTTP/1.1, on page 175—and create a simple CLI that updates in real time.

The WebSocket Protocol

Let's start with a good look at the WebSocket protocol. WebSocket is a binary protocol (Binary Protocols and Textual Protocols, on page 34) that allows for full-duplex communication between a client and a server—client and server can exchange messages at any time. But WebSocket connections start out as HTTP connections. Let's break this part down.

> ## Phoenix Channels and Phoenix LiveView
>
> Many folks gravitate toward Elixir because of tools such as Phoenix channels[a] and Phoenix LiveView.[b] These frameworks provide users with real-time functionality. Phoenix channels are a generic abstraction for server-client communication in real-time, with support for topics, broadcasting, and more. Phoenix LiveView is a framework for rendering HTML on the server and sending small diff payloads to clients in response to real-time events.
>
> Both these technologies rely heavily on the WebSocket protocol to achieve their efficiency and real-time features.
>
> ---
>
> a.   https://hexdocs.pm/phoenix/channels.html
> b.   https://hexdocs.pm/phoenix_live_view/welcome.html

Secure Communication

 WebSocket itself doesn't provide an encryption layer. If you want to communicate securely over WebSocket, all you have to do is start from an HTTPS connection rather than an HTTP connection.

The WebSocket Handshake

To start a WebSocket connection to a server, a client sends an HTTP GET request with some specific headers:

```
GET /{path} HTTP/1.1
Connection: Upgrade
Upgrade: websocket
Sec-WebSocket-Key: {key}
Sec-WebSocket-Version: 13
```

Connection: Upgrade indicates that the client wishes to upgrade the connection, and the Upgrade header specifies the desired protocol. {path} is the path at which the server listens for WebSockets connections—this should be known to the client. The Sec-WebSocket-Key and Sec-WebSocket-Version headers are used to negotiate the WebSocket connection. The version is self-explanatory, while the key is a random 16-byte value encoded in base 64.

If the server accepts the upgrade request, it responds with an HTTP 101 Switching Protocols status code:

```
HTTP/1.1 101 Switching Protocols
Connection: Upgrade
Upgrade: websocket
Sec-WebSocket-Accept: {hash}
```

The Sec-WebSocket-Accept header is a hash of the client's key concatenated with a predefined GUID, encoded in base 64. This hash is used to verify the client's key and ensure that the server is a WebSocket server.

Here's a visual representation of the WebSocket handshake:

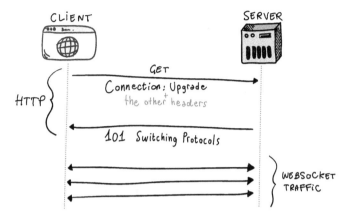

After this handshake, the underlying TCP or TLS connection is not an HTTP connection anymore. Instead, it's just binary messages encoded through the WebSocket serialization protocol.

Homework

Run through the handshake from the perspective of a client using Mint. Pick a public WebSocket server, such as the WebSocket Echo Server,[1] then start an :https Mint connection, send the upgrade request to /, and read the response—it should be the 101 Switching Protocols status code.

If you want to peek at a simple but working solution, check out code/websockets/websocket_handshake_example.exs in the book's code repository. You can run the example with the following command:

```
> elixir websocket_handshake_example.exs
```

Let's take a short look at the WebSocket protocol format itself.

The Binary Protocol

The WebSocket protocol is a binary protocol made of frames exchanged by client and server—in both directions. We're going to spend a little more time on the format of this protocol than we did on the previous protocols. This is the last chapter of the book, so let's take this chance to look at how these

---

1.   https://echo.websocket.org/

specifications often define binary formats. WebSocket is a good protocol to get your feet wet with this, since it has a relatively simple serialization format.

A WebSocket frame—a complete, self-contained protocol message—is made of an arbitrary number of bytes. RFC 6455 § 5.2[2] details a frame using this notation:

```
 0 1 2 3 4 5 6 7 8 9 0 1 2 3 4 5 6 7 8 9 0 1 2 3 4 5 6 7 8 9 0 1
+-+-+-+-+-------+-+-------------+-------------------------------+
|F|R|R|R| opcode|M| Payload len |    Extended payload length    |
|I|S|S|S|  (4)  |A|     (7)     |             (16/64)           |
|N|V|V|V|       |S|             |   (if payload len==126/127)   |
| |1|2|3|       |K|             |                               |
+-+-+-+-+-------+-+-------------+ - - - - - - - - - - - - - - - +
|     Extended payload length continued, if payload len == 127  |
+ - - - - - - - - - - - - - - - +-------------------------------+
|                               |Masking-key, if MASK set to 1  |
+-------------------------------+-------------------------------+
| Masking-key (continued)       |          Payload Data         |
+-------------------------------- - - - - - - - - - - - - - - - +
:                     Payload Data continued ...                :
+ - - - - - - - - - - - - - - - - - - - - - - - - - - - - - - - +
|                     Payload Data continued ...                |
+---------------------------------------------------------------+
```

This is fantastic news for you, since variations of this formatting are the norm for binary protocols. The exact ASCII-based table format might vary, but representing a protocol's frame encoding with this kind of table is common.

The numbers on the first row of this table represent bit positions. Actually, each number represents the last digit of the bit position as it loops from 0 to 9. After bit position 9, we go to bit 10, 11, and so on, but we still show only the last digit of the bit position to keep the table compact. Vertical size in this table doesn't matter other than for readability purposes.

Let's go into a little more detail:

- Bit 0 is the FIN flag. It's a flag because it can only be 0 (false) or 1 (true), being a single bit. It signals whether this frame is the last fragment of a series of split-up frames.

- The next three RSV bits are reserved bits, unused for the time being.

- Then, you have a four-bit field, opcode. This represents the frame type. For example, the value 0 0 0 1 represents a text frame, while 1 0 0 1 (or 9, in base ten) represents a *connection close* frame.

---

2. https://datatracker.ietf.org/doc/html/rfc6455#section-5.2

- MASK is next, another flag representing whether the payload is masked—without diving too deep, this is used to identify the WebSocket protocol, mostly in proxies. This prevents attacks such as *cache poisoning*. RFC 6455 § 10.3[3] has more information.

- Then, you have a series of bits and bytes representing the payload length.

- The masking key comes after, but only if MASK is set to 1.

- Last but not least is the actual frame payload.

That was possibly Too Much Information (TMI), but it's a helpful exercise in deciphering (that is an appropriate verb here) the protocol.

Homework

Craft a WebSocket frame of type text and with the contents Hello world!. Then, send it over to the WebSocket Echo Server[4] using the code you wrote for the handshake exercise. Receive the response and decode it.

This is not trivial but also not out-of-reach. You will need to consult RFC 6455 to learn about how masking works in practice. If you're stuck, there's a working example in code/websockets/websocket_echo-ing_frames.exs (in the book's code repository).

Now, let's move on to a practical example of using WebSockets, from both the server and client perspectives.

Making a Silly Real-Time Game

In this section, we'll build a silly example of real-time server-to-client communication over WebSocket. It's silly because it's not realistic, but we want to keep it concise and simple so that we can focus on the details of working with WebSockets.

We'll build a game where

1. Clients open a WebSocket connection to the server.

2. The server sends a WebSocket message (a ping) to clients at random intervals.

3. If the client replies with a message (a pong) within one second, it wins.

---

3. https://www.rfc-editor.org/rfc/rfc6455#section-10.3

4. https://echo.websocket.org/

This game is not going to win any awards, but it'll get the job done for us. Before diving in, you can follow along by creating a new Mix project:

```
> mix new silly_game --sup
```

Then, add the following dependencies to mix.exs:

silly_game/mix.exs
```
[
  {:mint_web_socket, "~> 1.0"},
  {:bandit, "~> 1.6"},
  {:websock_adapter, "~> 0.5.8"}
]
```

Fetch the dependencies with mix deps.get and we're ready to roll.

Handling Clients on the Server Side

We're using Bandit as the HTTP server. For handling WebSocket connections, we're using the websock_adapter[5] developed by the team behind the Phoenix[6] web framework.

websock_adapter gives us a familiar way of working with WebSockets: a behavior that you can implement to build handlers. This is similar to how GenServers work. The WebSock behavior exposes several callbacks, such as the following:

- init/1 to initialize the state of the handler when the WebSocket connection is established

- handle_in/2 for handling messages coming from the client side of the connection

- handle_info/2 to handle Erlang messages coming to the handler process

Let's take a peek at our server implementation. First things first, you'll need the HTTP server running and serving WebSocket connections at some path. To start the server, add it to the children of the top-level supervisor:

silly_game/lib/silly_game/application.ex
```
children = [
  {Bandit,
   plug: SillyGame.Router,
   scheme: :http,
   port: String.to_integer(System.get_env("SILLY_GAME_PORT", "9393"))}
]
```

---

5. https://github.com/phoenixframework/websock_adapter
6. https://www.phoenixframework.org

That SillyGame.Router is a Plug router (Creating a Plug Router, on page 185). We want it so that we can have a path where HTTP requests can get upgraded to WebSocket requests, which is a matter of calling WebSockAdapter.upgrade/4:

```
silly_game/lib/silly_game/router.ex
get "/websocket" do
  conn
  |> WebSockAdapter.upgrade(SillyGame.Server, [], timeout: 600_000)
  |> halt()
end
```

SillyGame.Server is the implementation of our WebSockets handler, so let's move on to that.

The init/1 callback just schedules a *tick* and returns an empty state:

```
silly_game/lib/silly_game/server.ex
@behaviour WebSock
# State
defstruct [:phase, :timer_ref]

@impl WebSock
def init(_options) do
  Logger.info("Started WebSocket connection handler")
  state = schedule_next_tick(%__MODULE__{})
  {:ok, state}
end

defp schedule_next_tick(state) do
  timeout = Enum.random(5_000..10_000)
  Process.send_after(self(), :tick, timeout)
  Logger.info("Scheduled next tick in #{timeout}ms")
  %{state | phase: :idle}
end
```

The tick is just a message that the handler sends to itself and that it handles in its handle_info/2 callback implementation. Let's look at that next:

```
silly_game/lib/silly_game/server.ex
Line 1  def handle_info(:tick, %__MODULE__{phase: :idle} = state) do
     2    Logger.info("Ticked! Client has 1 second to respond")
     3
     4    timer_ref = Process.send_after(self(), :tick_expired, 1000)
     5    state = %{state | phase: :ticked, timer_ref: timer_ref}
     6
     7    {:push, {:text, "ping"}, state}
     8  end
```

This code does two important things:

1. It schedules another message, :tick_expired, whose job is to make sure that the client playing responds within one second (line 4).

2. It pushes a ping message to the client (line 7). This is where the magic of WebSockets happens! The WebSockets library we're using understands the {:push, message, state} value and takes care of encoding and sending the message to the client.

Now it's up to the client to reply in time. Two things can happen at this point: either the :tick_expired message gets to the server before the client can reply, or the client replies in time. To handle the first case, we have to add another clause to the handle_info/2 callback:

silly_game/lib/silly_game/server.ex
```
def handle_info(:tick_expired, %__MODULE__{phase: :ticked} = state) do
  Logger.info("Tick expired! Client didn't respond in time")

  state = schedule_next_tick(%{state | timer_ref: nil})
  {:push, {:text, "expired"}, state}
end
```

Just some logging and scheduling of a new tick message there. If the client replies in time, the handle_in/2 callback fires, with the first argument being the inbound WebSockets message. The implementation handles the pong message both in the idle state (erroring to the client) and in the ticket state (meaning the client replied in time):

silly_game/lib/silly_game/server.ex
```
def handle_in(
      {"pong", [opcode: :text]},
      %__MODULE__{phase: :ticked} = state
    ) do
  Logger.info("Client responded in time! You won!")

  state =
    state
    |> cancel_expiration_timer()
    |> schedule_next_tick()

  {:push, {:text, "won"}, state}
end

def handle_in(
      {"pong", [opcode: :text]},
      %__MODULE__{phase: :idle} = state
    ) do
  Logger.info("Client responded without being asked")
  {:push, {:text, "early"}, state}
end
```

That's a wrap for the server. The WebSockets adapter library does a good job of abstracting away details of the protocol itself: you only had to interact with messages coming in (already decoded) and send messages by returning simple {:text, "..."} tuples. Nice! Let's move on to the client.

Sending and Receiving Messages as Clients

We'll write our client—the part that plays the game—as a Mix task called mix play. We did the same back in Chatting with Clients, on page 55. Our client will do the following:

- Start a WebSocket connection to the server
- Spawn a process to read user input from standard input
- Listen to both user input and WebSocket messages from the server and act accordingly

We can establish the WebSocket connection in the run/1 function of the task. Start by creating a Mix.Tasks.Play module:

```
silly_game/lib/mix/tasks/play.ex
defmodule Mix.Tasks.Play do
  use Mix.Task

  def run([] = _args) do
    port = String.to_integer(System.get_env("SILLY_GAME_PORT", "9393"))
❶  {:ok, conn} = Mint.HTTP.connect(:http, "localhost", port)

❷  {:ok, conn, ref} = Mint.WebSocket.upgrade(:ws, conn, "/websocket", [])

❸  http_reply =
      receive do
        message -> message
      after
        1000 -> Mix.raise("No response from the server within 1s")
      end

    {:ok, conn,
     [
       {:status, ^ref, status},
       {:headers, ^ref, headers},
       {:done, ^ref}
     ]} =
❹      Mint.WebSocket.stream(conn, http_reply)

❺  {:ok, conn, websocket} = Mint.WebSocket.new(conn, ref, status, headers)

❻  receive_loop(conn, websocket, ref, spawn_prompt_task())
  end
end
```

That's a lot of code. Let's look at it step by step.

❶ We establish a normal HTTP connection with Mint. This connection is not specific to WebSockets. It's just an HTTP connection that could be used for normal HTTP traffic or upgraded to a WebSocket connection.

❷ This is the upgrade to the WebSocket protocol we just discussed. Mint.WebSocket.upgrade/4 specifies the path where the server is accepting WebSocket upgrade requests—/websocket in our case.

❸ Time to wait for a message arriving at this process, which should be the HTTP response from the server.

❹ Instead of Mint.HTTP.stream/2, we use Mint.WebSocket.stream/2 here. This function confirms the upgrade to the WebSocket protocol and returns the response's status and headers.

❺ Mint.WebSocket.new/4 returns a new %Mint.WebSocket{} struct. We'll use this struct for encoding and decoding frames.

❻ Finally, time to start a recursive loop where we'll listen for server messages or user input.

spawn_prompt_task/0, in the last line of our run/1 function, just spawns a task that listens for user input:

silly_game/lib/mix/tasks/play.ex
```
defp spawn_prompt_task do
  Task.async(fn -> Mix.shell().prompt("Ready> ") end)
end
```

Now, we have two main events to handle in receive_loop/4: the user prompt returning text and a server message.

When the user finishes typing, our process receives a {ref, text} message with the reference of the %Task{} struct:

silly_game/lib/mix/tasks/play.ex
```
defp receive_loop(
      conn,
      websocket,
      ws_ref,
      %Task{ref: ref} = prompt_task
    ) do
  receive do
    # Task result, which is the contents of the message typed by the user.
    {^ref, _message} ->
      {:ok, websocket, data} =
        Mint.WebSocket.encode(websocket, {:text, "pong"})

      {:ok, conn} =
        Mint.WebSocket.stream_request_body(conn, ws_ref, data)
```

```
        Process.demonitor(ref, [:flush])
        receive_loop(conn, websocket, ws_ref, spawn_prompt_task())
    end
end
```

Regardless of what the user typed, we do the following:

1. Encode a pong WebSocket message of type text
2. Send this message through our conn using Mint.WebSocket.stream_request_body/3
3. Clean up the task monitor with Process.demonitor/2—otherwise, we'd get the :DOWN message even on successful tasks

Nice, you've already learned how to send WebSocket messages to the server. As for receiving them, we need to do it the Mint way: receive any message and feed it to Mint.WebSocket.stream/2, which is what we're doing in the next receive clause:

silly_game/lib/mix/tasks/play.ex
```
message ->
  case Mint.WebSocket.stream(conn, message) do
    {:ok, conn, [{:data, ^ws_ref, data}]} ->
      {:ok, websocket, [{:text, text}]} =
        Mint.WebSocket.decode(websocket, data)

      handle_text(text)
      receive_loop(conn, websocket, ws_ref, prompt_task)

    {:error, _conn, reason, _responses} ->
      Mix.raise("WebSocket error: #{inspect(reason)}")

    :unknown ->
      Mix.raise("Unknown message")
  end
```

If message is a valid WebSocket message from the server, we decode its contents with Mint.WebSocket.decode/2 and feed the results to a handle_text/1 helper function that either prints something on standard output or raises an error. In any other case, this receive clause errors out.

That's all there is to our client. You can see the complete code in code/silly_game/lib/mix/tasks/play.ex.

Testing Out Our Game

To see our creation in action, start the server in a terminal:

```
> mix run --no-halt
[info] Running SillyGame.Router with Bandit 1.6.1 at 0.0.0.0:9393 (http)
```

Now, open another terminal and start the client:

```
> mix play
Ready>
```

You should see logs on the server side that tell you how long is left before a server tick. The client will see a ping message after that time has elapsed.

You can see a session in action in the following screenshot:

```
~/Writing/alnpee/book/code/silly_game        ~/Writing/alnpee/Book/code/silly_game
→ mix run --no-halt                           → mix play
                                              Ready>  PING! Press enter within 1s!
12:46:14.179 [info] Running SillyGame.Rou
ter with Bandit 1.6.1 at 0.0.0.0:9393 (ht    Ready>  You won!
tp)                                           ~/Writing/alnpee/Book/code/silly_game
                                              →
12:46:21.344 [info] GET /websocket

12:46:21.354 [info] Started WebSocket con
nection handler

12:46:21.354 [info] Scheduled next tick i
n 8757ms

12:46:30.112 [info] Ticked! Client has 1
second to respond
```

This game has hopefully given you an idea of how WebSockets work in practice and how to use low-level tools to work with them in Elixir with maximum control.

Phoenix Channels and Phoenix LiveView

You'll find that most folks in Elixir-land prefer to use Phoenix channels[7] over raw WebSockets. Phoenix channels are a server- and client-side abstraction for real-time communication that ship with the Phoenix web framework. In most scenarios, channels use WebSockets under the hood, but they provide powerful abstractions for communicating on different topics, broadcasting data to many channels (with a pub/sub mechanism), and more.

If you're an Elixir user, there's a good chance you're already somewhat familiar with Phoenix channels. But knowing a language-agnostic protocol for real-time communication on the web will give you a better understanding of how all this works.

---

7. https://hexdocs.pm/phoenix/channels.html

Phoenix Channels and Phoenix LiveView

Phoenix LiveView,[8] a real-time server-rendered HTML framework for Phoenix, is built on top of Phoenix channels, which means it also takes advantage of WebSockets whenever possible.

Wrapping Up

At last, we've reached the end of the book. WebSocket was the last prominent network protocol to explore. In this chapter, you learned about the WebSocket protocol itself, diving a bit deeper than usual into the binary protocol and the upgrade process. Then, we built a silly game to play around with the real-time functionality that the protocol enables.

WebSocket is going to stick around. While HTTP/2 technically provides some overlapping features—server-initiated pushes and persistent connections—WebSocket is the de facto standard for real-time communication, and that is not expected to change anytime soon.

Well, how do you feel? Like the network expert you now are? We hope so! Go into the world and make computers talk to each other. There's a good chance you were doing that already if you read this book, but now you'll hopefully have a deeper understanding of *how* computers talk to each other.

---

8. https://hexdocs.pm/phoenix_live_view/welcome.html

Part IV

Appendixes

---

*The appendixes include details about the protocols
we explored that are not truly necessary to work
with them but are essential for a deeper understanding of the protocols themselves.*

The OSI Model

In the late 1970s, the ISO (International Organization for Standardization) developed the *Open Systems Interconnection model* (OSI). It's a way to identify *layers* of protocols and infrastructure that make up the current global networking infrastructure. While the OSI model is mostly a logical representation of the layers, it's useful to have a mental image of it whenever we talk about network programming. We refer to the OSI model here and there throughout the book to put things in context. The following image is a standard way to represent the OSI model.

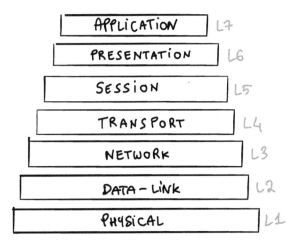

Layer 1, the *physical layer*, defines how the data is physically transported on the network. Working at this layer tends to be closer to physics and electrical engineering than to software engineering. Layer 2 (the *data link layer*) and 3 (the *network layer*) are responsible for formatting and routing the data on the same network (layer 2) or across networks (layer 3). These two layers are essentially what allow data to be routed across routers and switches around the world to reach computers in networks.

The lowest layer we'll explore is layer 4, the *transport layer*. This layer is responsible for carrying bytes of information around the network. Protocols that operate at this layer use the lower layers to route data to the right machines on the network. The goal of protocols at layer 4 is to serve data to the layers above, particularly the *application layer*, in such a way that applications don't have to care about the details of routing and packing data.

Layer 5, the *session layer*, is responsible for opening, closing, and managing sessions between two connected devices. This layer is usually implemented either in protocols that operate also at layer 4, such as TCP, or directly in application code.

Layer 6, the *presentation layer*, is responsible for formatting and translating raw data to be used by the *application layer* (layer 7). Encryption and compression, for example, are at this layer.

Finally, layer 7 (the *application layer*) is the business logic of layers. It's the layer closest to the end user, and it's the one you're most likely to be working in. Examples of protocols at the application layer are HTTP, FTP, and SMTP.

Knowing what the OSI model is and roughly what the layers we use the most are responsible for is enough to build effective network applications. Thinking about such a representation of our network stack can also help to frame the relationship between layers: each layer takes complexity and details away from higher layers.

If you're using Elixir or Erlang and reading this book, chances are you're mostly working at layers 4 and above, which are the focus of this book.

TCP Protocol Details

For most network protocols, you don't have to worry too much about the intricate details. The protocol—often multiple layers of protocols—abstracts away significant complexity for you. But if you start digging, it's rabbit hole after rabbit hole.

Still, it can be helpful to have a basic understanding of how widely used protocols such as TCP work under the hood.

That's what this appendix is for.

TCP Binary Format

TCP takes a stream of data (sent by a client or server), splits it up into chunks, and packs up those chunks by adding a header. These *data chunks plus header* are usually called *segments*.

A TCP segment is structured as follows (RFC 793 § 3.1):[1]

```
 0                   1                   2                   3
 0 1 2 3 4 5 6 7 8 9 0 1 2 3 4 5 6 7 8 9 0 1 2 3 4 5 6 7 8 9 0 1
+-+-+-+-+-+-+-+-+-+-+-+-+-+-+-+-+-+-+-+-+-+-+-+-+-+-+-+-+-+-+-+-+
|          Source Port          |       Destination Port        |
+-+-+-+-+-+-+-+-+-+-+-+-+-+-+-+-+-+-+-+-+-+-+-+-+-+-+-+-+-+-+-+-+
|                        Sequence Number                        |
+-+-+-+-+-+-+-+-+-+-+-+-+-+-+-+-+-+-+-+-+-+-+-+-+-+-+-+-+-+-+-+-+
|                    Acknowledgment Number                      |
+-+-+-+-+-+-+-+-+-+-+-+-+-+-+-+-+-+-+-+-+-+-+-+-+-+-+-+-+-+-+-+-+
| Data |           |U|A|P|R|S|F|                                |
| Offset| Reserved |R|C|S|S|Y|I|            Window              |
|       |           |G|K|H|T|N|N|                                |
+-+-+-+-+-+-+-+-+-+-+-+-+-+-+-+-+-+-+-+-+-+-+-+-+-+-+-+-+-+-+-+-+
|           Checksum            |         Urgent Pointer        |
```

---

1.   https://datatracker.ietf.org/doc/html/rfc793#section-3.1

```
+-+-+-+-+-+-+-+-+-+-+-+-+-+-+-+-+-+-+-+-+-+-+-+-+-+-+-+-+-+-+-+-+
|                      Options                  |    Padding    |
+-+-+-+-+-+-+-+-+-+-+-+-+-+-+-+-+-+-+-+-+-+-+-+-+-+-+-+-+-+-+-+-+
|                           data                                |
+-+-+-+-+-+-+-+-+-+-+-+-+-+-+-+-+-+-+-+-+-+-+-+-+-+-+-+-+-+-+-+-+
```

We won't go into too much detail on each individual part of the header, but here are some highlights:

- *Source port* and *destination port* specify the sending and receiving ports

- *Sequence number* and *acknowledgment number* are used during the initial handshake (Connection Establishment, on page 227) and then to keep track of what has been transmitted and received

- The data offset specifies how long the header is in terms of *words* (one word is four bytes). It ranges from a minimum of five words (20 bytes), for headers with no trailing options, up to a maximum of fifteen words (60 bytes)

- The *window* field is used to implement *flow control*

- The *checksum* is used to perform error checking on the TCP segment

- *Options* carry standardized parameters for various additional functionality

---

Where's the Payload Length?

Eagle-eyed readers will notice there's nothing in the TCP header indicating how large the payload is.

That's because TCP segments ride inside *IP datagrams*. The IP datagram signals the total length of the data it carries. Since the size of the TCP header is known, the length of the payload can be obtained by subtracting the header size from the datagram's total length. If you're having a particularly boring day, have fun digging in deeper.[2]

Connection States

TCP connections can be in one of three general phases: establishing the connection, transferring data, or terminating the connection. Let's take a look at these.

---

2. https://en.wikipedia.org/wiki/IPv4#Header

Connection Establishment

TCP connections are established through a three-step handshake. Establishing a connection requires a server listening on a bound port. Once that passive listener is in place, the handshake goes as follows:

1. The client sends a SYN (for *synchronize*) to the server, asking to establish a connection. The SYN contains a *sequence number* that the client sets to a random number A.

2. To accept the connection, the server responds with a SYN-ACK. It sets the acknowledgment number to A + 1 and the sequence number of the SYN-ACK packet to a different random number B.

3. To finalize the handshake, the client sends back an ACK packet with the sequence number set to A + 1 and the acknowledgment number set to B + 1.

Connection's on!

Data Transfer

Once the three-way handshake completes, the connection is ready to carry data in both directions. TCP is a stream-based protocol, which means it doesn't preserve any message boundaries—just a continuous flow of bytes. Under the hood, each side tracks how much data has been sent and received:

- The *sequence number* keeps track of where in the byte stream the current segment of data belongs

- The *acknowledgment number* indicates which bytes have already arrived successfully on the other side

- The *window* (flow control) mechanism ensures that a fast sender won't overwhelm a slower receiver—essentially, each side tells the other how many more bytes it's prepared to receive before buffer space runs out

TCP also handles retransmissions automatically if segments get lost or corrupted in transit.

Connection Termination

Terminating a connection is symmetrical, meaning both sides of the connection perform similar steps to close down independently.

Each side sends a FIN packet, and the other side replies with an ACK. That's a four-step handshake overall. Some systems optimize this process by replying to a FIN with a packet that has both ACK set for the received FIN and FIN set to close the connection in one go, making it effectively a three-step handshake.

Closing connections is generally easier than opening them. The multi-step handshake helps ensure that all data has been processed properly before shutting down. But in practice, you'll also see abrupt disconnections (power losses, network outages, and so on). Your applications should always be prepared for sudden drops no matter what.

UDP Broadcast and Multicast

In Chapter 8, Same Layer, Different Protocol:, on page 127, we focused on *unicast* communication—that is, one-to-one communication.

UDP also supports *broadcast* communication and *multicast* communication.

Broadcast

UDP broadcasting is a form of one-to-many communication where a peer can send packets to all devices on a subnet.

Erlang's gen_udp supports broadcasting out of the box. Let's say you have a UDP socket open:

```
{:ok, socket} =
  :gen_udp.open(5000, [:binary, ip: {0, 0, 0, 0}, reuseaddr: true])
```

You can start a *broadcast socket* by setting the :broadcast option to true:

```
{:ok, socket} = :gen_udp.open(0, [:binary, broadcast: true])
```

Now, sending packets on your network's broadcast address will route them correctly:

```
:ok = :gen_udp.send(socket, {192, 168, 68, 255}, 5000, "Hello, broadcast!")
```

See code/udp_broadcast.ex for a full example you can run.

Multicast

With UDP multicasting, one peer sends data to a specific multicast IP range. That range is fixed[1] and goes from 224.0.0.0 to 239.255.255.255. Only devices that

---

1. https://en.wikipedia.org/wiki/Multicast_address

explicitly join the multicast group receive the data. This communication is still one-to-many, but it's more selective than broadcasting.

Erlang's gen_udp has full-fledged support for UDP multicasting. For example, you can start a UDP listener socket that binds to a multicast group:

```
{:ok, socket} =
  :gen_udp.open(5000, [
    :binary,
    reuseaddr: true,
    # Bind to all interfaces:
    ip: {0, 0, 0, 0},
    # Join multicast group:
    add_membership: {{239, 0, 0, 1}, {0, 0, 0, 0}}
  ])
```

To send messages, you can create a UDP socket and use the normal :gen_udp.send/4, specifying the desired multicast address:

```
{:ok, sender} = :gen_udp.open(0, [:binary])
:gen_udp.send(sender, {239, 0, 0, 1}, 5000, "Hello, multicast!")
```

You can play around with this by running code/udp_multicast.ex in your shell:

```
> elixir code/udp_multicast.ex
Started listening on port 5000 (#Port<0.4>)
Opened sender socket (#Port<0.3>)
Received message from 192.168.68.104:54103: "Hello, multicast!"
```

Multicasting is used in various scenarios where there's a need for efficient data distribution to multiple recipients, such as the following:

- Audio/video streams such as IPTV and broadcasts
- Service discovery, where devices can discover each other dynamically on a network
- Real-time collaboration and real-time games

DNS Protocol Details

The textual protocol in use for DNS is worth peeking at. It's simple enough, and it tells you a lot about the protocol itself. The protocol is *symmetrical*, meaning that the message format is the same for messages from server to client and the other way around. Let's look at the breakdown of a message, which is made of a header and a body.

DNS Message Header

The header of a DNS message is packed with information. Here's a visual breakdown of what each bit represents:

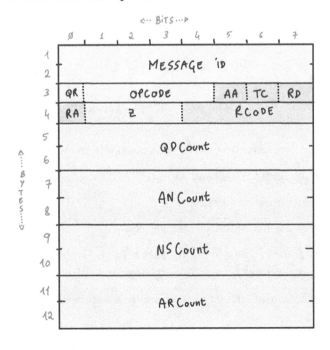

The following table contains a concise description of what each part of the header does.

Name	Bits	Description
ID	16	An ID for the request
QR	1	Whether this is a *query* (0) or a *reply* (1)
OPCODE	4	Code to identify the operation
AA	1	Whether the answer was from an authoritative server
TC	1	Whether the answer was truncated
RD	1	Whether recursion is desired
RA	1	Whether recursion is available
Z	3	Reserved for the future
RCODE	4	Response code, or 0 for no errors
QDCount	16	Number of questions in the message
ANCount	16	Number of resource records in the *answers* section
NSCount	16	Number of resource records in the *authority* section
ARCount	16	Number of resource records in the *additional* section

Let's construct a DNS header that we will use to ask a DNS server to resolve elixir-lang.org for us. We'll set the following values:

- ID to an auto-generated ID

- QR to 0, since ours is a *query*

- OPCODE to 0, which represents a standard QUERY (we can ignore other possible values for now)

- AA and TC to 0, since these are ignored in queries and are only valid in *replies*

- RD to 1, since we want to enable recursion when resolving

- RA to 0 for the same reason as AA and TC

- Z to 0, since it must always be 0

- RCODE to 0, since it's only valid for replies

- QDCOUNT to 1, since there's one *question* in the questions section, which we'll see in a second

- ANCount, NSCount, and ARCount to 0, since those sections of our message will all be empty

With Elixir, this pretty much translates directly to binary construction syntax:

```
iex> id = :crypto.strong_rand_bytes(2)
<<236, 241>>
iex> <<
...>    id::2-binary,  # ID
...>    0::1,          # QR
...>    0::4,          # OPCODE
...>    0::1,          # AA flag
...>    0::1,          # TC flag
...>    1::1,          # RD flag
...>    0::1,          # RA flag
...>    0::3,          # Z
...>    0::4,          # RCODE
...>    1::8,          # QDCount
...>    0::8,          # ANCount
...>    0::8,          # NSCount
...>    0::8           # ARCount
...> >>
<<236, 241, 1, 0, 1, 0, 0, 0>>
```

The first two bytes (the message id) will be different for you, but the rest should be the same. Cool, we got a header on our hands. Let's move on to the body of DNS messages.

DNS Message Body

A DNS message body can contain *questions*, *answers*, or both. For our example, let's start with questions. A question has this shape:

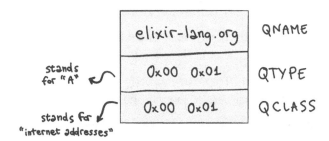

The QNAME is a sequence of strings representing each component of the domain name. *Components* are just the parts between dots: elixir-lang and org in our example. QTYPE specifies what record type we're interested in, such as A or AAAA. A is encoded as <<00, 01>>. QCLASS is for the class of the query. We don't have to pay attention to this, since we can just use <<00, 01>>, which stands for *Internet addresses*.

We have to take a short detour to look into how strings are encoded. Each string in a sequence of strings is encoded as follows:

- One byte for the length of the string
- Followed by the bytes of the string itself

The sequence terminates with a single *null byte*, 0. Encoding strings in Elixir can be a one-line function. Here, we take a list of strings and return some iodata:

xdig/lib/xdig/protocol.ex
```
def encode_strings(strings) when is_list(strings) do
  [Enum.map(strings, &[byte_size(&1), &1]) | [0x00]]
end
```

We'll ask the DNS server about elixir-lang.org, so let's see how we'd encode that.

```
def encode_strings(strings) when is_list(strings) do
  [Enum.map(strings, &[byte_size(&1), &1]) | [0x00]]
end
```

That looks like just a bunch of bytes, but we can easily break it down. ?e is Elixir syntactic sugar for the byte value of the e ASCII character, 101. The preceding binary is the same as this:

```
<<_length = 11,
  ?e, ?l, ?i, ?x, ?i, ?r, ?-, ?l, ?a, ?n, g,
  _length = 3,
  ?o, ?r, g,
  0>>
```

Self-explanatory enough. Looks like we're ready to send our first query! Ah, but that involves the network. Let's put a pin in that and finish off our protocol exploration by looking at DNS answers. Don't worry, it'll be pretty short.

A DNS answer is similar to a question, but it has a few more fields. Its shape is this:

- A NAME, TYPE, and CLASS. These are exactly the same as their QNAME, QTYPE, and QCLASS counterparts. NAME is encoded just like QNAME, too.

- TTL is an integer that represents the Time To Live of the record, expressed in seconds.

- RDLENGTH is the length, in bytes, of the next field (RDATA).

- RDATA is for additional record data.

Controlling Other Machines with SSH

Secure Shell (SSH) is a protocol used to securely access and operate computers across a network.

It's based on asymmetrical cryptography. During the handshake, remote machines sign some session data—shared with the client—with their private key. This lets the client verify the signature using the remote machine's public key, which is a known key. This process is similar to TLS certificate verification (Chapter 7, Securing Protocols: TLS, on page 113). Optionally, the server can then require the client to provide a password to authenticate itself, or it can perform an inverse public/private key verification with the private key of the client. In the latter case, administrators or other trusted parties store the public key of allowed clients somewhere on the remote machine, which can then verify something signed by the client's private key to confirm its identity.

Okay, we've covered authentication. But secure communication definitely requires encrypting in-flight data as well. SSH doesn't rely on TLS for that. Instead, it generally uses plain old TCP as a transport and implements its own encryption layer.

The good news here is that Erlang has built-in support for SSH through the ssh application[1] and its main ssh module.[2]

Wow, This Erlang Documentation

 The Erlang documentation we just linked to is *a treasure trove* of useful and interesting information about SSH. It contains an overview of the protocol,[3] practical examples,[4] and more.

---

1. https://www.erlang.org/doc/apps/ssh/api-reference.html
2. https://www.erlang.org/doc/apps/ssh/ssh.html
3. https://www.erlang.org/doc/apps/ssh/introduction.html
4. https://www.erlang.org/doc/apps/ssh/using_ssh.html

Let's take a quick look at how to use it.

Using SSH as Clients

To try things out here, you'll want to have a remote machine somewhere running SSH on a port that is exposed to the Internet—the standard SSH port is 22. You could test this out with a local Docker container[5] if you don't have a machine to SSH to.

Use :ssh.connect/3[6] to establish an SSH connection. The user you specify needs to be able to SSH into the machine. ssh looks up keys for the user based on filename. The API is somewhat quirky if you want arbitrary key names, so for simplicity you might want to name your user's key one of id_dsa, id_rsa, id_ecdsa, id_ecdsa, or id_ed448—depending on the key algorithm.

```
iex> Application.ensure_all_started(:ssh)
iex> connect_options = [user: ~c"andrea", user_dir: ~c"/ssh_dir"]
iex> {:ok, conn} = :ssh.connect({158, 0, 0, 1}, 22, connect_options)
```

You've got yourself an SSH connection, but to issue commands you'll want to open a *channel*—use :ssh_connection.session_channel/2.[7]

```
iex> {:ok, channel} = :ssh_connection.session_channel(conn, _timeout = 5000)
```

We're ready to issue a command:

```
iex(4)> :ssh_connection.exec(conn, channel, ~c"pwd", _timeout = 5000)
:success
```

The return value is just :success, because the actual command result and output are asynchronous and come back as messages. You can verify this by flushing messages from IEx's mailbox:

```
iex(5)> flush()
{:ssh_cm, #PID<0.116.0>, {:data, 0, 0, "/home/ubuntu\n"}}
{:ssh_cm, #PID<0.116.0>, {:eof, 0}}
{:ssh_cm, #PID<0.116.0>, {:exit_status, 0, 0}}
{:ssh_cm, #PID<0.116.0>, {:closed, 0}}
```

The second element of those :ssh_cm tuples is the conn PID, so it will be different for you if you try this out, just as the /home/ubuntu output string will be. But hey, we have a working SSH client!

You can even use Erlang's ssh to run a full-blown SSH interactive shell with :ssh.shell/3:

---

5.   https://hub.docker.com/r/linuxserver/openssh-server
6.   https://www.erlang.org/doc/apps/ssh/ssh.html#connect/3
7.   https://www.erlang.org/doc/apps/ssh/ssh_connection.html#session_channel/2

```
iex> Application.ensure_all_started(:ssh)
iex> connect_options = [user: ~c"andrea", user_dir: ~c"/ssh_dir"]
iex> :ssh.shell({158, 0, 0, 1}, 22, connect_options)
```

If you run this, you'll be dropped into a shell on the remote system, similarly to what would happen when running an ssh command.

SSH Server

ssh is not limited to its use as a client. In fact, you can also use it for the other side: listening for remote connections on a server. This is called an SSH *daemon*. You can use :ssh.daemon/2[8] to start a daemon:

```
iex> Application.ensure_all_started(:ssh)
iex> port = 10222
iex :ssh.daemon(port, auth_methods: ~c"publickey", system_dir: ~c"tmp/system")
```

You'll need to generate a host key in the system directory specified in the previous snippet. And that's pretty much it.

Running an SSH daemon from Erlang can be useful for when your system is a minimal Erlang distribution or when you want to expose only some SSH functionality. These are definitely infrequent use cases, but it's awesome to have all these tools in the standard library.

---

8.   https://www.erlang.org/doc/apps/ssh/ssh.html#daemon/2

Bibliography

[CV16]   Francesco Cesarini and Steve Vinoski. *Designing for Scalability with Erlang/OTP*. O'Reilly Media, Inc., Sebastopol, CA, 2016.

[MTV19] Chris McCord, Bruce Tate, and José Valim. *Programming Phoenix 1.4*. The Pragmatic Bookshelf, Dallas, TX, 2019.

Index

SYMBOLS

"" (double quotes)
  Elixir binaries, 13
  Erlang strings, 13
'' (single quotes), Erlang strings, 13
<<>> syntax
  binaries, 13, 22
  bitstring syntax, 41

DIGITS

1.1.1.1 server, 162
8.8.8.8 server, 162

A

:a (inet_res), 166
A DNS record type, 159, 161, 168
AA DNS message headers, 232
AAAA DNS record type, 159, 161, 168
accept, TCP connections, 17–22, 59
accepting
  chat system example, 59–66
  TCP connections, 17–22
acceptor pools, chat system example, 59–66
accessors, 25
acknowledgment number, TCP, 226–227
acknowledgments, 151–153, 226
actions (gen_statem), 104

active mode
  Mint connections, 193
  TCP sockets, 14–15, 21, 28–30, 81, 98–99
  UDP sockets, 131, 137
adapters, Plug, 182
additional section, DNS message headers, 232
Agent, 52
ALIAS DNS record type, 159
Amazon AWS, 181
ANCount DNS message headers, 232
answers, DNS, 162–163, 170, 232–233
Apache Cassandra, 34, 200
application layer
  DNS, 166
  HTTP, 176
  OSI model, 224
ARCount DNS message headers, 232
ASCII, 34, 234
authentication
  HTTP apps with Plug, 188
  pillars of security, 114
  SSH, 235
authoritative nameservers, 158
authority, DNS message headers, 232
await_many (Task), 28

B

:backlog, 19, 48
backlogs
  chat system example, 48
  TCP connections, 19, 48
backoffs
  connection storms, 106
  exponential, 106
  TCP clients as state machines, 102
  TCP reconnections, 81
backpressure
  HTTP/1 limitations, 198
  HTTP/2, 200
:bag ETS table type, 169
Bagdi, Harry, 12
Bandit
  about, 181, 184
  HTTP/2 and, 202
  ping pong game example, 212
  as Plug adapter, 182
  serving JSON example, 181–189
  serving JSON example with Mint, 191–194
  Thousand Island and, 67, 185
base::hex, 37
BEAM
  advantages, xi, 2
  binary storage, 44, 90
  controlling processes, 21
  distributed systems, 2
  Erlang processes, 3
  network comparison, 3
big endianness, 35

binaries
    <<>> syntax, 13, 22
    byte size, obtaining, 37
    converting iodata to, 44,
      46, 76
    defined, 13
    double quotes ("") for, 13
    empty, 22
    heap binaries, 90
    hex representation, ob-
      taining, 37
    as iodata, 44
    memory, 44, 90
    performance, 44
    refc binaries, 90
    resources on, 90
    size, 90
    sub binaries, 90
    syntax options, 43
    UDP metrics daemon,
      137
binary option
    TCP connections, 12
    UDP metrics daemon,
      137
binary protocols
    about, 155
    binary protocols, 35
    chat system example,
      specifying, 36–38
    defined, 34
    DNS as, 161, 165
    endianness, 35
    formatting, 210
    frames, 200
    HTTP/2 as, 34, 176, 199
    HTTP/3 as, 176
    leftover data and, 40, 42
    messages, broadcast, 38
    messages, register, 37
    messages, types, 36
    messages, unidirection-
      al/multidirectional, 37
    :packet options, 31
    size, 35
    vs. textual protocols, 34–
      36
    WebSockets as, 207, 209
binding, 16
bit positions, WebSocket
    frames, 210
bitstring syntax (<<>>), 41
blocking
    head-of-line blocking,
      198, 203
    HTTP/2, 203
    socket checkout, 82
    TCP limitations, 203

body
    DNS messages, 161, 233
    HTTP requests, 178
    HTTP responses, 179
:broadcast, 51, 229
broadcast messages
    binary protocols, 38
    chat system example, 51–
      55
    UDP, 229
broadcast sockets, 229
buffers
    advantages, 25
    splitting, 24
    structs, 22
    TCP, 24–27, 227
Builder (Plug), 183
bulk strings, RESP data type,
    74
byte_size, 37
bytes
    byte value of ASCII char-
      acters, 234
    number of bytes read
      from TCP sockets, 15
    representing, 36–37
    size, obtaining, 37

C

CA Certificate List, 119
CAA DNS record type, 159
cache poisoning, 210
call, HTTP apps with Plug, 182
:caller_monitor, 80, 84
Cassandra, 34, 200
cast, UDP metrics daemon ex-
    ample, 140
CAStore, 117
Certificate Authorities, 117,
    119
certificates
    CAA DNS record type, 160
    Certificate Authorities,
      117, 119
    certificate chains, 117,
      119
    chat system example,
      119–120, 122
    operating system, obtain-
      ing, 116
    resources on, 117
    root certificates, 116
    self-signed, 119–120, 122
Cesarini, Francesco, 2

channels
    Phoenix, 208, 218
    SSH, 236
    WebSockets, 218
charlists, TCP connections,
    12
chat system example
    about, 33
    broadcasting, 51–55
    chat protocol code, 39–46
    chat system example,
      Thousand Island, 66–
      70
    chatting with clients, 55–
      58
    clients, registering, 49–51
    decoding, 39–43
    encoding, 39, 43–46
    exercises, 123
    protocol design, 34–46
    server setup, 46–55
    server with multiple ac-
      ceptors, 59–66
    specifying binary proto-
      col, 36–38
    supervision tree, 60, 65–
      66
    testing, 42, 46, 50, 54,
      65–66, 70
    TLS, 118–123
checkin (Poolboy), 95
checkout (Poolboy), 95
checkout clients
    building, 78–85
    pooling sockets, 93–100
    pros and cons, 89–91
    Redis example, 82–89
checksum, TCP binary for-
    mat, 226
child_spec, 64
CLASS, DNS answers, 234
cleanup, registries, 51
clients, DNS, 155
clients, HTTP
    with Finch, 194–196
    flow control, 200–201
    HTTP request/response
      cycle, 178–181
    HTTP request/response
      cycle with Plug, 182–
      184
    with Mint, 189–194
    with Req, 194–196
    tools for, 189
clients, SSH, 236

clients, TCP
  building with gen_tcp, 12–15
  chat system example, broadcasting, 51–55
  chat system example, chatting, 55–58
  chat system example, registering, 49–51
  defined, 9
  diagram, 10
  handling, 22–25
  pooling challenges, 73
  Redis client example, about, 73
  Redis client example, building, 78–85
  Redis client example, pooling sockets, 93–100
  Redis client example, queuing requests, 85–91
  Redis client example, state machine version, 100–110
  Redis, understanding RESP, 74–78
  simulating multiple, 28
  testing, 26
  uses, 111
clients, UDP, 131
clients, WebSockets
  basics, 207–211
  handshakes, 208–209
  ping pong game example, 215–218
clock drift, 150
CNAME DNS record type, 159
code, keeping protocol and networking code separate, 39
code for this book
  book website, xiii
  DNS protocol, 161
  DNS server example, 168
  DNS simple client example, 162
  Elixir vs. Erlang, xiii, 5
  HTTP serving JSON example, 184
  metrics daemon example, 135
  ping pong game example, 217
  RESP encoding/decoding, 76
  testing, 142

TLS, 120
WebSockets exercises, 209, 211
collectors
  UDP metrics daemon, building, 136–139
  UDP metrics daemon, testing, 141–143
command (Redis), 74
concurrency, see also pooling
  BEAM advantages, xi
  Redis client example, state machine version, 100–110
conn (Plug), 186, 188, 191
connect (Mint), 191
connect (SSH), 236
connect_fun, pooling, 98
connection storms, 106
connections, HTTP
  with Mint, 191
  persistence, 199, 201
  pooling, 189, 194
connections, Mint, 191, 193
connections, SSH, 236–237
connections, TCP
  accepting, 17–22
  accepting, chat system example, 46–49, 59–66
  closing and Redis client example, 81
  closing with Thousand Island, 69
  connection states, 226–228
  connection storms, 106
  defined, 10
  handshakes, 36, 79, 115, 203, 226
  multiplexing, 89
  reconnections and back offs, 81
  supervisors, 47–49, 51, 60–66, 70
  TCP clients, handling, 22–25
  terminating, 227
  upgrading to TLS, 118
connections, TLS
  listeners, 120
  with ssl application, 116–118
  upgrading TCP connections to, 118

conns (Plug)
  building HTTP apps, 181–184
  routes, 186
  serving JSON example, with Mint, 191
  testing, 188
  updating, 191
continuations
  decoding with RESP, 77
  socket checkout, 84
:continue, 63, 69
controlling processes, sockets, 20–22, 28
controlling_process (gen_tcp), 22
counters
  defined, 134
  metrics daemon example, ignoring order of, 148
  metrics daemon protocol, 134–136, 138–139
  missing packets, detecting, 150, 152
  missing packets, order, 151
  resetting, 139, 142
  values, 138
Cowboy, 175
crashes, isolation from, 3
CRLF sequence, 75
cryptography
  public-key cryptography and TLS, 114
  SSH, 235
curl
  HTTP request/response cycle, understanding, 177–181
  serving JSON example, 181–189
  verbose flag, 178

D

daemon (SSH), 237
DaemonServer, 142
data, see also parsing
  DNS records property, 159
  incomplete data and RESP, 76
  incomplete data and split packets, 77
  leftover data handling, 40, 42, 76
  receiving with UDP sockets, 131

RESP data types, 74
TCP data transfer, 227
as term, 103
databases
    DNS as key-value
        database, 156
    pooling, 96
datagrams, IP, 226
db_connection, 96
decimal base, 36
decode (WebSockets), 217
decode_packet, 182
decoding
    binary protocols, 34
    chat system example, 39–43
    DNS server example, 170
    HTTP serialization tools, 181
    HTTP/1 limitations, 198
    JSON, 186
    RESP, 76
    simple DNS client, 163–165
    symmetrical protocols, 75
    WebSockets ping pong
        game example, 216
defstruct, 22
DELETE (HTTP), 178
demonitor (Process), 84
demonitor (WebSockets), 217
denial-of-service attacks, 28
deserialization, see decoding
Designing for Scalability with
    Erlang/OTP, 2
destination ports, TCP, 226
dig, 158
:dispatch (Plug), 185
dispatch (Registry), 53
distributed systems, 2
DNS
    answers, 162–163, 170,
        232–233
    as binary protocol, 161,
        165
    client example, about,
        155
    client example, writing
        simple, 162–166
    HTTPS and, 166
    inet_res example, 166–168
    as key-value database,
        156
    OSI layer, 155, 166
    protocol details, 231–234

questions, 162–163, 170,
    232–233
resolution, 156–159,
    166–168
resource records, defined,
    156
resource records, extract-
    ing definitions, 167
resource records, inet_res
    and, 166–168
resource records, types,
    159, 168, 233
resource records, under-
    standing, 159–161
resources on, 167
server example, exercises,
    171
server example, writing,
    168–171
as symmetrical protocol,
    161, 231
TCP and, 155
TLS and, 166
transport protocol op-
    tions, 166
understanding, 156–162
use cases, 172
DNS messages
    body, 161, 233
    DNS protocol, 161
    headers, 161, 231–233
    IDs, 162
    order, 162, 165
    structure, 161, 231–234
DNS Toys, 172
DNSimple, 171
domain names
    DNS routing, 156–159
    parent domain, 157
    registering, 157
    registrable domains, 157
    resolution with inet_res ex-
        ample, 166–168
    structure of, 156
    subdomains, 157
    TLD, 156
Domain Names System,
    see DNS
double quotes ("")
    Elixir binaries, 13
    Erlang strings, 13
:DOWN
    chat system example, 57
    socket checkout errors,
        84

DTLS, 113
DynamicSupervisor, chat system
    example, 47–49, 51, 61

E
echo server
    defined, 129
    TCP, active once sockets,
        30
    TCP, building, 15–25
    TCP, exercises, 27
    TCP, packet options, 31
    TCP, testing, 25–28
    UDP, simple, 129
Elixir
    accessors, 25
    advantages, 2–4
    code for this book and,
        xiii, 5
    development of, 2
    ecosystem, xi, 4
    Erlang similarities, xiii, 4
    HTTP tools, 175, 182,
        189
    opening interactive shell,
        12
    resources on, 5
    use and level of applica-
        tions, 4
encode (RESP), 76, 79
encode! (Jason), 186
encode_metrics, 136, 140
encoding
    binary protocols, 34, 36
    chat system example,
        39, 43–46
    DNS message body, 233
    HTTP serialization tools,
        181
    HTTP/1 limitations, 198
    JSON, 186
    metrics, 136, 140
    protocol selection and, 35
    RESP, 76, 79
    simple DNS client, 163–
        165
    symmetrical protocols, 75
    textual protocols, 34
    WebSockets ping pong
        game example, 214,
        216
encryption
    chat system example,
        118–123
    pillars of security, 114
    SSH, 235
    WebSockets and, 208

endianness, 35

ent_resp (Plug), 188

environment variables and running tests, 65

Erlang
  advantages, 2–4
  development of, xi, 2
  distributed Erlang, 2
  ecosystem, xi, 4
  Elixir similarities, xiii, 4
  Erlang strings and TCP connections, 13
  HTTP parsing, 182
  HTTP tools, 175, 182, 189
  Observer, 66
  records, 23, 168
  resources on, 168, 235
  use and level of applications, 4

errors
  chat system example, 57
  :error vs. :incomplete, 40
  HTTP requests with Mint, 192
  HTTP status codes, 180, 187
  metrics daemon example, 138, 147
  pooling with NimblePool, 98
  pooling with registries, 110
  POSIX error codes, 13
  Redis client example, 81
  RESP, 74, 76
  socket checkout, 83–86
  structs, 23
  TCP clients as state machines, 102, 105
  TCP sockets, 14
  TLS, 117

ETS tables
  DNS server example, 169
  uniqueness, checking for, 52

:exit_on_close, 19

exponential backoffs, 106

F

Figma, 207

FIN, 210, 227

Finch, 111, 189, 194–196

finite state machines
  about, 101

diagram, 102
Redis client example, 100–110

flow control
  HTTP/2, 200–201
  TCP, 226–227

flush (IEx), 14, 131

flush (String), 142

:flush_io_device, 137

flush_queue, 88

frames
  binary protocols, 200
  HTTP/2, 199
  WebSockets, 209, 216

frameworks, see also Phoenix LiveView
  HTML, 208
  HTTP, 188

from_username, 38

from tuples, queues and, 86

full-duplex protocols
  TCP as, 100
  WebSockets as, 207

functional programming, Plug and, 181

G

garbage collection, 3, 90

gauges
  defined, 134
  duplicate packets, handling, 153
  metrics daemon, ignoring order of, 148
  metrics daemon, protocol, 134–136, 138–139
  values, overriding, 138

gen_statem
  building TCP clients as state machines, 102–107
  handle event mode, 103
  state functions mode, 103

gen_tcp
  active socket options, 28–30
  chat system example, multiple acceptors, 59–66
  controlling process, changing, 22
  iodata and, 45
  :packet option, 28, 30
  similarities to ssl application, 116

storing TCP sockets in processes example, 80–91
TCP clients, building, 12–15
TCP clients, handling, 22–25
TCP servers, building, 15–25

gen_udp
  broadcasting support, 229
  multicasting support, 230
  simple UDP server, 129–132
  UDP metrics daemon, collector, 136–139
  UDP metrics daemon, reporter, 139

GenServer
  continue, 63, 69
  DNS server example, 168–171
  initialization and, 20
  storing TCP sockets in processes, 80–91
  TCP connections, accepting, 17–21
  TCP connections, handling clients, 22–25
  Thousand Island handlers as, 69
  UDP metrics daemon, collector, 136–139
  UDP metrics daemon, reporter, 139

get (Plug), 186

GET (HTTP), 178

get_socket (Mint), 191

gethostbyname (inet_res), 167

Google Public DNS, 157

Gun, 189

H

Hackney, 175, 189

handle event mode (gen_statem), 103

handle_cast, metrics daemon example, 147

handle_in (WebSock), 212, 214

handle_info (WebSock), 212

handle_new_data (gen_tcp), 24

:handler_module (Thousand Island), 70

handshake (ssl), 121

handshakes
    lack of in QUIC, 204
    lack of in UDP, 128
    SSH, 235
    TCP, 36, 79, 115, 203,
        226
    TLS, 115, 121
    WebSockets, 208–209
head-of-line blocking, 198,
    203
headers
    DNS messages, 161, 231–
        233
    HTTP requests, 178
    HTTP responses, 179
    HTTP serving JSON exam-
        ple with Plug and Ban-
        dit, 186
    WebSockets, 208
heap binaries, 90
Hex, 189
hex notation, 36
hex representation of bina-
    ries, 37
hexadecimal base, 36
hints, HTTP status codes, 201
HPACK header serialization
    protocol, 34
HTTP, see also clients, HTTP;
    connections, HTTP; servers,
    HTTP
    about, 173
    development of, 176
    Elixir tools, 175, 182,
        189
    Erlang tools, 175, 182,
        189
    with Finch, 194–196
    frameworks, 188
    hints, 201
    OSI layer, 176
    preloading links, 201
    with Req, 194–196
    request components, 178
    request pipelining, 178
    request/response cycle,
        177–184
    resources on, 180
    response components,
        179
    serialization tools, 181
    serving JSON example,
        with Mint, 191–194
    serving JSON example,
        with Plug and Bandit,
        181–189

status codes, 179, 187,
    201, 208
TCP and, 9, 113, 176
TLS and, 176
uses, 175
WebSockets and, 207
HTTP/0.9, 176
HTTP/1
    basics, 176–181
    development of, 176
    with Finch, 194–196
    incompatibility with
        HTTP/2 and HTTP/2,
        197
    limitations, 197–198
    with Req, 194–196
    request components, 178
    request pipelining, 178
    request/response cycle,
        177–184
    response components,
        179
    serialization tools, 181
    serving JSON example,
        with Mint, 191–194
    serving JSON example,
        with Plug and Bandit,
        181–189
    as textual protocol, 35,
        176, 198
HTTP/2
    backpressure, 200
    with Bandit, 202
    as binary protocol, 34,
        176, 199
    connections as persis-
        tent, 199, 201
    development of, 176
    flow control, 200–201
    frames, 199
    head-of-line blocking,
        203
    history, 197–198
    HPACK header serializa-
        tion protocol, 34
    incompatibility with
        HTTP/1, 197
    with Plug and Mint, 202
    push promises, 201–202
    streams, 199
    when to use, 205
HTTP/3
    as binary protocol, 176
    development of, 176, 197
    incompatibility with
        HTTP/1, 197
    QUIC, 204–206

resources on, 205
    when to use, 205
HTTP/3 from A to Z, 206
httpc, 189
httpd, 182
HTTPoison, 189
HTTPS
    DNS and, 166
    OSI layer, 177
    TLS and, 113, 116, 118,
        176
    WebSockets and, 208
HyperText Transfer Protocol,
    see HTTP

I
IANA (Internet Assigned
    Numbers Authority), 158
ID DNS message headers, 232
idempotence, 153
IDs, DNS messages, 162, 232
IETF (Internet Engineering
    Task Force), 114
IEx
    inspecting messages, 14
    opening interactive shell,
        12
    printing messages, 14,
        131
IfConfig, 181
:in (inet_res), 166
:incomplete, 40
INCR (Redis), 74
index offsets, 165
:inet, 29–30
inet_res, 155, 166–168
info (IEx), 14
initialization
    GenServer and, 20
    HTTP apps with Plug, 182
    WebSockets ping pong
        game example, 212
inspect, hex representation,
    obtaining, 37
integers, RESP data type, 74
integrity, 114–115
Internet Assigned Numbers
    Authority (IANA), 158
Internet Engineering Task
    Force (IETF), 114
iodata
    binaries as, 44

converting to binaries,
44, 46, 76
defined, 44
DNS message body, 234
encoding chat system ex-
ample, 43–46
encoding in RESP, 76, 79
length, obtaining, 46
lists as, 44
memory, 44
performance, 44
writing directly to socket,
45, 79
iodata_length, 46
iodata_to_binary, 44, 46
iolist_size, 46
iolist_to_binary, 44
IP addresses
binding, 16
DNS routing, 156–159
format, 11
HTTP serving JSON exam-
ple with Plug and Ban-
dit, 186
IPv4 vs. IPv6, 160
notation, 156
TCP clients, building, 12
TCP servers, understand-
ing, 16
UDP sockets, 128–131
IP checker, 181
IP datagrams, 226
IPv4
A DNS record type, 159,
161
defined, 160
resources on, 160
IPv6
AAAA DNS record type,
159, 161
defined, 160
resources on, 160
isolation
crashes and, 3
supervisors, 47

J

Jason, 186
jitter, 106
JSON
encoding/decoding, 186
serving JSON example of
HTTP/1 with Mint,
191–194

serving JSON example of
HTTP/1 with Plug and
Bandit, 181–189
as textual protocol, 34
json module (Erlang), 186
JSON module (Elixir), 186

K

:keep_state_and_data (gen_statem),
105
keys
DNS as key-value
database, 156
pooling with registries,
108
public-key cryptography,
114
registries, 51
self-signed certificates,
119
SSH, 235
storing multiple ETS ta-
ble entries, 169
WebSockets, 208, 210

L

-l flag (netcat), 129
LALR parsers, 77
:line (:packet), 30
line-based protocols, 134
linked lists, 45
links, preloading, 201
listen, TCP connections, 17, 19
listen sockets, 17, 20
listeners, TLS connections,
120
lists
converting to strings, 76
as iodata, 44
linked, 45
little endianness, 35
Logger (Plug), 184
logs, WebSockets ping pong
game example, 218
look_up (inet_res), 166

M

maps, pattern matching, 23
MASK (WebSockets), 210
masking, WebSockets, 210
match (Plug), 185, 187
Maximum Transmission Unit
(MTU), 147

memory
binaries, 44, 90
controlling processes,
21, 28
iodata, 44
isolation advantages, 3
queues, 90
socket checkout, 83, 89–
90
messages, see also DNS messages
printing from IEx, 14,
131
sending to self(), 20
TCP sockets in active
mode, 14, 28
messages, binary protocols
broadcast messages, 38
register messages, 37
types, 36
unidirectional/multidirec-
tional, 37
metadata, HTTP requests,
179
methods, HTTP requests,
178, 180
metrics
names, 134
pattern matching, 138
performance, 133
reliability, 133
resource efficiency, 133
metrics daemon example
building, 132–143
collector, 136–139
diagram, 136
duplicate packets, 153
errors, 138
exercises, 142
missing packets, 148,
150–153
order of packet, 148–151
printing output, 137
protocol, 134–136
reporter, 136, 139, 147
split packages, avoiding,
147
as textual protocol, 134
timestamps, 149
Mint
development of, 190
Finch and, 195
HTTP clients, 189–194
HTTP/2 and, 202
performance, 194
as processless, 190, 193
push promises, 202

resources on, 194
TCP client use, 111
WebSockets exercise, 209
WebSockets ping pong
game example, 215
minutes, 12
Mix
chat system example,
chatting, 55–58
creating projects, 16, 39
supervision trees, scaffolding, 16, 39
WebSocket connections,
starting, 215
--module (Mix), 16
monitor (Process), 80, 84
monitoring, checking sockets
in/out of processes, 80, 84
Mozilla CA Certificate List,
119
MTU (Maximum Transmission
Unit), 147
multi-metric packets, 146
multicasting
UDP, 229
uses, 230
multiplexing, TCP, 89
MX DNS record type, 159
MySQL, 200
MyXQL, 96

N
:n (active socket option), 28–
29
NAME, DNS answers, 234
names, see also DNS; domain
names
DNS answers, 234
DNS records, 159
field names and structs,
23
metrics, 134
registries, 52
SSH keys, 236
usernames and broadcast
messages, 38
usernames and register
messages, 37
nameservers
authoritative, 158
root, 158, 171
nc and line-based protocols,
134

netcat
simple server example,
129, 131
testing TCP echo server,
25–28
network programming
BEAM comparison, 3
defined, 1
types of, 1
new (WebSocket), 215
newlines, line-based protocols, 134
:next_event (gen_statem), 104
:next_state (gen_statem), 105
NimblePool, 96–100, 194
:nn modifier, bitstring syntax,
41
NSCount DNS message headers,
232
null byte termination, 234

O
Observer, 66
offsets
data offsets and TCP binary format, 226
index, 165
:once (active socket option),
28–30, 81, 137
:one_for_all strategy, 62
:one_for_one strategy, 64
opcode (WebSockets), 210
OPCODE DNS message headers,
232
open (gen_udp), 129–132
Open Systems Interconnec-
tion model, see OSI model
OpenSSL, 119
OptionParser, 56
options, TCP binary format,
226
order
DNS messages, 162, 165
HTTP/1 requests, 178,
198–199
ordering with times-
tamps, 149
packets, missing, 151
packets, recombining,
146
restarts, 62
supervision and child or-
der, 61

TCP, 10, 128
UDP, 128, 135, 145, 147–
151
OSI model
DNS, 155, 166
HTTP, 176
HTTPS, 177
TCP, 128
UDP, 128, 166
understanding, 223–224

P
:packet option, 28, 30
packets
DNS messages, 161
length, specifying, 31
MySQL, 200
resources on, 30
packets, TCP
duplicate, 10
order, 10, 128
splitting, 193
packets, UDP
acknowledgments, 151–
153
duplicate, 153
missing, 145, 148, 150–
153
missing, resending, 151–
153
multi-metric, 146
order, 128, 135, 145,
147–151
ordering with times-
tamps, 149
size, 147
splitting, 145–148
parent domains, 157
parse_metrics, 135, 138
parser combinators, 77
parsetools, 77
parsing
HTTP, 182, 191
metrics, 135, 138
socket checkout errors
and, 84
TCP, 28, 30
tools for, 77
passive mode
Mint connections, 193
TCP sockets, 14–15, 21,
84
paths
HTTP requests, 178
Plug routers, 185
WebSockets, 208

pattern matching
  maps, 23
  metrics, 138
  structs, 23
payloads
  payload length and TCP
    binary format, 226
  WebSockets, 210
performance
  binaries, 35, 44
  HTTP/2, 200
  iodata, 44
  metrics daemon, 133
  Mint, 194
  pooling, 90
  protocols, 35
  TCP, 203
  textual protocols, 35
  UDP, 127–128, 133
Phoenix, 184, 188, 208, 218
Phoenix Channels, 208, 218
Phoenix LiveView, 208, 218
physical layer, OSI model,
  223
ping pong game example,
  211–218
pipelines
  HTTP requests, 178
  plugs, 182, 188
Plug
  about, 181
  building HTTP apps, 181–
    184
  functional programming
    approach, 181
  HTTP/2 and, 202
  ping pong game example,
    213
  push promises, 202
  reliability of, 185
  resources on, 184
  routers, 185, 213
  serving JSON example,
    181–189
  serving JSON example
    with Mint, 191–194
  testing support, 188
:plug option, 185
plugs
  HTTP request/response
    cycle, 182–184
  pipelines, 182, 188
  routers, 185
Poolboy, 94–96, 107
pooling
  acceptor pools, 59–66

databases with db_connec-
    tion, 96
  HTTP connections, 189,
    194
  with NimblePool, 96–
    100, 194
  performance, 90
  with Poolboy, 94–96, 107
  random client strategy,
    110
  with registries, 100, 107–
    110
  with schedulers, 100
  TCP clients, challenges,
    73
  TCP sockets, Redis client
    example, 93–100
  TLS connections, 121
ports
  address-port formats, 11
  binding, 16
  destination ports, TCP,
    226
  Erlang ports vs. network
    ports, 11
  HTTP serving JSON exam-
    ple with Plug and Ban-
    dit, 185
  processes, similarities to,
    11
  resources on, 11
  socket basics, 11
  source ports, 226
  SSH, 236
  TCP clients, building, 12
  TCP servers, understand-
    ing, 16
  Thousand Island, 70
  UDP sockets, 128–131
POSIX error codes, 13
POST (HTTP), 178
Postgrex, 96, 111
preloading links, 201
presentation layer, OSI model, 224
printing
  from IEx, 14, 131
  UDP metrics daemon
    output, 137
processes
  controlling processes, 20–
    22, 28
  Erlang process diagram,
    3
  HTTP clients with Mint,
    190, 193
  isolation from crashes, 3

pooling with Poolboy, 94–
    96, 107
  ports, similarities to, 11
  process-oriented design
    and BEAM, xi
  Redis client example,
    state machine version,
    100–110
  registries, 51
  sharing UDP sockets, 139
  spawning, 17
  spawning in WebSockets,
    215–216
  starting under supervi-
    sors, 62
  storing TCP sockets in,
    79–91
  TCP connections, accept-
    ing in, 17–21
  unregistering, 110
Programming Phoenix 1.4, 188
promises, HTTP/2 push, 201–
  202
Protobuf, 34
protocols, *see also* binary
  protocols; chat service example; DNS; HTTP; RESP;
  SSH; TCP; textual protocols; UDP; WebSockets
  chat system example, de-
    sign, 34–46
  choosing, 35
  full-duplex, 100, 207
  importance of defining,
    34
  leftover data and, 40, 42,
    76
  line-based protocols, 134
  performance, 35
  resources on, 34
  separating from network-
    ing code, 39
  specifications, 34
  stateful protocols, 10,
    128
  stateless protocols, 128,
    132
  symmetrical, 75, 231
public-key cryptography, TLS,
  114
push promises, HTTP/2, 201–
  202

Q
QCLASS, 233
QDCount DNS message head-
  ers, 232

QNAME, 165, 233
QR DNS message headers, 232
QR flag, 161
QTYPE, 233
queries, DNS message headers, 232
questions, DNS, 162–163, 170, 232–233
queue module, 86
queues
    chat system example, 48
    memory, 90
    pooling with registries, 110
    Redis client example, queuing requests, 85–91
    simple queue without reconnections, 86–89
    size, bounds on, 90
    TCP connections, 19
QUIC, 166, 202–206
Quicer, 206
quotes
    Elixir binaries, 13
    Erlang strings, 13

R
\r\n sequence, 75
RA DNS message headers, 232
race conditions, socket checkout, 84, 86
:raw (:packet), 30
RCODE DNS message headers, 232
RD DNS message headers, 232
RDATA, DNS answers, 234
RDLENGTH, DNS answers, 234
receive_loop (WebSockets), 216
receive_response, 84
reconnections
    canceling, 106
    connection storms, 106
    TCP, automatic, 227
    TCP, back offs, 81
    TCP, clients as state machines, 105
records, Erlang, 23, 168
records, DNS, see resource records, DNS

recursion
    DNS message headers, 232
    iodata as recursive data structures, 44
recv (Mint), 193
recv (gen_tcp), 15, 21
redirections, HTTP status codes, 180
Redis
    client example, about, 73
    client example, building, 78–85
    client example, pooling TCP sockets, 93–100
    client example, queuing requests, 85–91
    client example, state machine version, 100–110
    resources on, 78
    RESP, 34, 74–78
Redis Serialization Protocol, see RESP
Redix, 76, 111
refc (reference-counted) binaries, 90
register, 52
register messages
    binary protocols, 37
    chat system example, 49–51
registering domain names, 157
registrable domains, 157
registries
    chat system example, broadcasting, 51–55
    cleanup, 51
    keys, 51
    names, 52
    pooling with, 100, 107–110
    processes, 51
    random client strategy, 110
    resources on, 110
    uniqueness, checking for, 52
    values, 52
Registry
    chat system example, broadcasting, 51–55
    pooling with, 100, 107–110
    resources on, 110
:remove (NimblePool), 98

replies, DNS message headers, 232
reporters, UDP metrics daemon
    location, 136, 139
    packet size and, 147
    testing, 141–143
Req, 189, 194–196
request (Mint), 191–194
request references, 191–194
RequestIDPlug, 184
requests, HTTP
    components, 178
    HTTP request/response cycle, 177–184
    with Mint, 191–194
    order, 178, 198–199
    queuing multiple, 198
    request pipelining, 178
    upgrading to WebSocket requests, 208, 213, 215
resiliency
    metrics daemon example, 138, 148
    UDP errors, 138, 148
resolution, DNS, 156–159, 166–168
resolve (inet_res), 167
resource records, DNS
    defined, 156
    extracting definitions, 167
    inet_res and, 166–168
    resources on, 167
    types, 159, 168, 233
    understanding, 159–161
resources
    metrics daemon and resource efficiency, 133
    path in HTTP requests, 179
    pooling with NimblePool, 96–100
resources for this book
    binaries, 90
    bitstring syntax, 41
    book website, xiii
    certificates, 117
    distributed systems, 2
    DNS, 167
    Elixir, 5
    Erlang, 235
    Erlang records, 168
    HTTP methods, 180
    HTTP status codes, 180
    HTTP/3, 205

IPv4 and IPv6, 160
Mint, 194
:packet options, 30
Phoenix, 188
Plug, 184
ports, 11
POSIX error codes, 13
protocols, 34
QUIC, 205
Redis, 78
registries, 110
socket programming, 11
SSH, 235
ssl application, 118
state machines, 101
TLS, 118
RESP
    data types, 74
    encoding/decoding, 76,
        79
    incomplete data and, 76
    spec example, 34
    as symmetrical protocol,
        75
    as textual protocol, 74
    understanding, 74–78
responses, HTTP
    components, 179
    HTTP request/response
        cycle, 177–184
    with Mint, 191–194
rest value, 40
:rest_for_one strategy, 62, 109
restarts
    child order, 62
    supervisors, 47–48, 62
    :temporary option, 47–48
:reuseaddr option, 19
RFC 147, 10
RFC 2246, 114
RFC 6455, 210
RFC 7540, 197
RFC 9000, 205
RFC 9110, 180
RFC 9114, 206
root certificates, 116
root nameservers, 158, 171
Router (Plug), 185
routers, Plug, 185, 213
RSV (WebSockets), 210
run (Mix), 55, 215

S
schedulers, pooling with, 100
Sec-WebSocket-Accept, 209

Sec-WebSocket-Key, 208
Sec-WebSocket-Version, 208
secrets, TCP handshake, 115
Secure Shell, see SSH
Secure Socket Layer, see SSL;
    TLS
security, see also HTTPS
    active sockets, 28
    authentication, 114
    cache poisoning, 210
    denial-of-service attacks,
        28
    DTLS, 113
    encryption, 114
    integrity, 114
    pillars of, 114
    SSH, 235–237
    SSL, 114
    supervisors, 48
    TLS, 113–123
    WebSockets, 208, 210
self(), sending message to, 20
self-signed certificates, TLS,
    119–120, 122
send
    iodata, 45
    TCP clients, 13
    Thousand Island, 69
    UDP data, 130
    UDP metrics daemon,
        140
send_metric, 140
sequence number, TCP, 226–
    227
serialization, see encoding
Server Push, see push
    promises
servers, DNS, 168–171
servers, HTTP
    flow control, 200–201
    HTTP request/response
        cycle, 178–181
    HTTP request/response
        cycle with Plug, 184
    JSON example with Ban-
        dit and Plug, 181–189
    push promises, 201–202
    testing, 188
servers, SSH, 237
servers, TCP
    binding IP address and
        port, 16
    building with gen_tcp, 15–
        25
    chat system example,
        broadcasting, 51–55

chat system example,
    chatting with clients,
    55–58
chat system example,
    multiple acceptors, 59–
    66
chat system example,
    registering clients, 49–
    51
chat system example,
    setup, 46–55
chat system example,
    Thousand Island, 66–
    70
connections, accepting,
    17–22
defined, 9
diagram, 10
listener options, 19
shutdown options, 19
testing, 25–28
vs. UDP servers, 130
understanding, 16
servers, TLS, chat system ex-
    ample, 118–123
servers, UDP, 129–131
servers, WebSockets
    basics, 207–211
    handshakes, 208–209
    ping pong game example,
        211–218
session layer, OSI model, 224
session_channel (SSH), 236
SET (Redis), 74
set_mode (Mint), 193
setopts (:inet), 29–30
shell, opening interactive, 12
+short option (dig), 159
shutdowns, supervisors, 47
signatures, integrity checks,
    115
simple strings, RESP data
    type, 74
single quotes ("), Erlang
    strings, 13
:size (Poolboy), 95
Slack, 207
sockets, see also WebSockets
    active mode, TCP, 14–15,
        21, 28–30, 81, 98–99
    active mode, UDP, 131,
        137
    active once sockets, 28–
        30, 81, 137
    broadcast, 229

controlling processes, 20–22, 28
as data structures, 11
defined, 10
as independent of protocols, 132
listen sockets, 17, 20
mode, changing, 29, 84
passive mode, 14–15, 21, 84
resources on, 11
term, 10
writing iodata directly to, 45, 79
sockets, SSL, 29
sockets, TCP
active mode, 14–15, 21, 28–30, 81, 98–99
active once sockets, 28–30, 81
checking in, 80, 88
checking out, 80
checking out, Redis example, 82–89
checking out, pros and cons, 89–91
client shutdowns and, 19
closing, 14, 19, 21
controlling processes, 20–22, 28
errors, 14
HTTP clients with Mint, 190–194
inspecting, 191
mode, changing, 29, 84
multiplexing, 89
parsing with :packet option, 28, 30
passive mode, 14–15, 21, 84
pooling, 93–100
queuing requests, 85–91
Redis client example, building, 78
Redis client example, state machine version, 100–110
state, 191
storing in processes, 79–91
TCP clients, building, 12–15
vs. UDP sockets, 129–132
understanding, 10–12
sockets, TLS, 116, 190
sockets, UDP
active mode, 131, 137
active once sockets, 137

address and port combinations, 128–131
changing socket mode, 29
DNS client example, 165
opening, 129–132
sharing across processes, 139
statelessness and, 128, 132
vs. TCP sockets, 129–132
source ports, TCP, 226
spawn_prompt_task (WebSockets), 216
split (String), 24
splitting
buffers, 24
packets, 77, 145–148, 193
SSH, 235–237
ssh application, 235–237
ssh module, 235–237
SSL (Secure Socket Layer), 114, 219, see also TLS
ssl application
about, 29
chat system example, 118–123
resources on, 118
understanding, 116–118
state
Mint connections, 191
switching in gen_statem, 105
TCP sockets, 191
as term, 103
UDP sockets, 128, 132
state functions mode (gen_statem), 103
state machines
about, 101
diagram, 102
Redis client example, 100–110
resources on, 101
stateful protocols, TCP as, 10, 128
stateless protocols, UDP as, 128, 132
StatsD, 134, 146, 148
status codes, HTTP, 179, 187, 201, 208
:stdio, 137
stream (Mint), 191–194
stream (WebSocket), 215

stream_request_body (WebSockets), 217
streams
HTTP/2, 199
TCP, 227
WebSockets, 215
StringIO, testing with, 142
strings
converting lists to, 76
double quotes ("") for, 13
encoding length of in binary protocols, 36
RESP data types, 74
single quotes (') for, 13
TCP connections and Erlang strings, 13
structs
defining, 22
field names and, 23
sub binaries, 90
subdomains, 157
--sup (Mix), 16, 39
supervision trees
chat system example, 60, 65–66
HTTP serving JSON example, 185
pooling with registries, 108
Redis client example, 108
scaffolding with Mix, 16, 39
sketching, 65
supervisors
acceptor pools, 60–66
child IDs, 64
child order, 61
:one_for_all strategy, 62
:one_for_one strategy, 64
pooling with registries, 107–110
:rest_for_one strategy, 62, 109
restarts, 47–48, 62
security, 48
shutdowns, 47
starting processes under, 62
TCP connections, 47–49, 51, 60–66, 70
Thousand Island, 70
TLS connections, 121
Switching Protocols status code, 208
symmetrical protocols
DNS as, 161, 231
RESP as, 75

T

tasks
    chat system example with Mix tasks, 55–58
    Elixir tasks and simulating multiple TCP clients, 28
    spawning in WebSockets, 216

TC DNS message headers, 232

TCP, *see also* chat system example; clients, TCP; connections, TCP; packets, TCP; servers, TCP; sockets, TCP
    about, 7, 9
    basics, 9–15
    binary format, 225
    buffers, 24–27, 227
    data transfer, 227
    DNS and, 155
    echo server example, building TCP client, 12–15
    echo server example, building TCP server, 15–25
    echo server example, handling TCP client, 22–25
    echo server example, testing, 25–28
    exercises, 27
    flow control, 226–227
    flow diagram, 130
    as full-duplex protocol, 100
    header format as protocol spec example, 34
    HTTP and, 9, 113, 176
    multiplexing, 89
    OSI layer, 128
    packet options, 28, 30
    performance, 203
    protocol details, 225–228
    QUIC and, 203–204
    segments, 225
    serialization format as binary protocol, 34
    SSH and, 235
    as stateful protocol, 10, 128
    as stream-based protocol, 227
    TLS and, 113
    UDP comparison, 128, 145, 153
    uses, 9, 111, 127

TCP/IP, *see* TCP

Telegraf, 148

:temporary option, restarts, 47–48

Tesla, 189

Test (Plug), 188

testing
    broadcasting, 54
    chat system example, 42, 46, 50, 54, 65–66, 70
    environment variables and running tests, 65
    HTTP servers, 188
    manual vs. automated, 142
    serving JSON example with Plug and Bandit, 188
    TCP echo server example, 25–28
    TCP servers, building, 16
    UDP metrics daemon, 137, 141–143
    WebSockets ping pong game example, 217

textual protocols
    vs. binary protocols, 34–36
    defined, 34
    HTTP/1 as, 35, 176, 198
    JSON as, 34
    metrics daemon example as, 134
    performance, 35
    RESP as, 74
    size, 35

Thousand Island, 66–70, 185

Time To Live (TTL), DNS records, 159, 234

timeout, 12

timeouts
    milliseconds and, 12
    resending packages, 152
    TCP clients as state machines, 102, 105
    TCP connections, 12, 15, 17, 20

timers, UDP metrics daemon, 137

timestamps
    clock drift and, 150
    duplicate packets, handling, 153
    ordering packets with, 149

TLD (Top Level Domain), 156

TLS, *see also* connections, TLS
    chat system example, 118–123
    DNS and, 166
    HTTP and, 176
    HTTPS and, 113, 116, 118, 176
    Mint and, 190
    public-key cryptography, 114
    resources on, 118
    root certificates, 116
    self-signed certificates, 119–120, 122
    ssl application, 116–118
    TCP and, 113
    transport layer, 114
    understanding, 114–115

to_timeout, 12

Top Level Domain (TLD), 156

Tor, 166

+trace option (dig), 159

transaction (Poolboy), 94

transport layer
    OSI model, 224
    TCP, 128
    TLS, 114
    UDP, 128, 166

TTL, DNS answers, 234

TTL (Time To Live), DNS records, 159, 234

TXT DNS record type, 159

TYPE, DNS answers, 234

types
    binary protocols message types, 36
    DNS answers, 234
    DNS records, 159

U

-u flag (netcat), 129

UDP, *see also* metrics daemon example; packets, UDP; sockets, UDP
    about, 125
    basics, 128–132
    broadcasting and multicasting, 229
    DTLS and, 113
    duplicate packets, 153
    flow diagram, 130
    lack of guarantees in, 128, 145, 147–148
    lack of order in, 128, 135, 145, 147–151

level of control with, 127
missing packets, 145, 148, 150–153
missing packets, resending, 151–153
multi-metric packets, 146
OSI layer, 128, 166
performance, 127–128, 133
QUIC and, 204
splitting packets, 145–148
as stateless protocol, 128, 132
TCP comparison, 128, 145, 153
uses, 127
uniqueness, checking for, 52
update_in macro, 25
upgrade (WebSockAdapter), 213, 215
Upgrade (WebSockets), 208
User Datagram Protocol, *see* UDP

User-Agent header, 179
usernames
broadcast messages, binary protocols, 38
register messages, binary protocols, 37
UTF-8, 36

V

-v (curl), 178
validation, certificates, 116
values
counters, 138
DNS as key-value database, 156
gauges, 138
registries, 52
Verisign, 117
versions, HTTP requests, 178

W

websock_adapter, 212
WebSockets
basics, 207–211

as binary protocol, 207, 209
exercises, 209, 211
as full-duplex protocol, 207
handshakes, 208–209
ping pong game example, 211–218
uses, 207
whole_response, 165
Wikipedia over DNS, 172
window field, TCP binary format, 226–227
Wireshark, 123
Wordle over DNS, 172
:worker (NimblePool), 97
:worker_module (Poolboy), 95
workers, Poolboy, 94, 97
write (File), iodata, 45
wxWidgets, 66

Z

Z DNS message headers, 232

Thank you!

We hope you enjoyed this book and that you're already thinking about what you want to learn next. To help make that decision easier, we're offering you this gift.

Head on over to https://pragprog.com right now, and use the coupon code BUYANOTHER2025 to save 30% on your next ebook. Offer is void where prohibited or restricted. This offer does not apply to any edition of *The Pragmatic Programmer* ebook.

And if you'd like to share your own expertise with the world, why not propose a writing idea to us? After all, many of our best authors started off as our readers, just like you. With up to a 50% royalty, world-class editorial services, and a name you trust, there's nothing to lose. Visit https://pragprog.com/become-an-author/ today to learn more and to get started.

Thank you for your continued support. We hope to hear from you again soon!

The Pragmatic Bookshelf

Exploring Graphs with Elixir

Data is everywhere—it's just not very well connected, which makes it super hard to relate dataset to dataset. Using graphs as the underlying glue, you can readily join data together and create navigation paths across diverse sets of data. Add Elixir, with its awesome power of concurrency, and you'll soon be mastering data networks. Learn how different graph models can be accessed and used from within Elixir and how you can build a robust semantics overlay on top of graph data structures. We'll start from the basics and examine the main graph paradigms. Get ready to embrace the world of connected data!

Tony Hammond
(294 pages) ISBN: 9781680508406. $47.95
https://pragprog.com/book/thgraphs

Testing Elixir

Elixir offers new paradigms, and challenges you to test in unconventional ways. Start with ExUnit: almost everything you need to write tests covering all levels of detail, from unit to integration, but only if you know how to use it to the fullest—we'll show you how. Explore testing Elixir-specific challenges such as OTP-based modules, asynchronous code, Ecto-based applications, and Phoenix applications. Explore new tools like Mox for mocks and StreamData for property-based testing. Armed with this knowledge, you can create test suites that add value to your production cycle and guard you from regressions.

Andrea Leopardi and Jeffrey Matthias
(262 pages) ISBN: 9781680507829. $45.95
https://pragprog.com/book/lmelixir

Programming Ecto

Languages may come and go, but the relational database endures. Learn how to use Ecto, the premier database library for Elixir, to connect your Elixir and Phoenix apps to databases. Get a firm handle on Ecto fundamentals with a module-by-module tour of the critical parts of Ecto. Then move on to more advanced topics and advice on best practices with a series of recipes that provide clear, step-by-step instructions on scenarios commonly encountered by app developers. Co-authored by the creator of Ecto, this title provides all the essentials you need to use Ecto effectively.

Darin Wilson and Eric Meadows-Jönsson
(242 pages) ISBN: 9781680502824. $45.95
https://pragprog.com/book/wmecto

Property-Based Testing with PropEr, Erlang, and Elixir

Property-based testing helps you create better, more solid tests with little code. By using the PropEr framework in both Erlang and Elixir, this book teaches you how to automatically generate test cases, test stateful programs, and change how you design your software for more principled and reliable approaches. You will be able to better explore the problem space, validate the assumptions you make when coming up with program behavior, and expose unexpected weaknesses in your design. PropEr will even show you how to reproduce the bugs it found. With this book, you will be writing efficient property-based tests in no time.

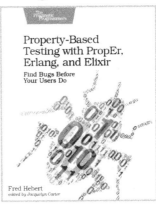

Fred Hebert
(374 pages) ISBN: 9781680506211. $45.95
https://pragprog.com/book/fhproper

The Pragmatic Bookshelf

The Pragmatic Bookshelf features books written by professional developers for professional developers. The titles continue the well-known Pragmatic Programmer style and continue to garner awards and rave reviews. As development gets more and more difficult, the Pragmatic Programmers will be there with more titles and products to help you stay on top of your game.

Visit Us Online

This Book's Home Page
https://pragprog.com/book/alnpee
Source code from this book, errata, and other resources. Come give us feedback, too!

Keep Up-to-Date
https://pragprog.com
Join our announcement mailing list (low volume) or follow us on Twitter @pragprog for new titles, sales, coupons, hot tips, and more.

New and Noteworthy
https://pragprog.com/news
Check out the latest Pragmatic developments, new titles, and other offerings.

Save on the ebook

Save on the ebook versions of this title. Owning the paper version of this book entitles you to purchase the electronic versions at a terrific discount.

PDFs are great for carrying around on your laptop—they are hyperlinked, have color, and are fully searchable. Most titles are also available for the iPhone and iPod touch, Amazon Kindle, and other popular e-book readers.

Send a copy of your receipt to support@pragprog.com and we'll provide you with a discount coupon.

Contact Us

Online Orders:	*https://pragprog.com/catalog*
Customer Service:	*support@pragprog.com*
International Rights:	*translations@pragprog.com*
Academic Use:	*academic@pragprog.com*
Write for Us:	*http://write-for-us.pragprog.com*

www.ingramcontent.com/pod-product-compliance
Lightning Source LLC
LaVergne TN
LVHW081338050326
832903LV00024B/1196